Migrating to iPhone and iPad for .NET Developers

Mark Mamone

Apress®

Migrating to iPhone and iPad for .NET Developers

ISBN-13 (pbk): 978-1-4302-3858-4

ISBN-13 (electronic): 978-1-4302-3859-1

President and Publisher: Paul Manning
Lead Editor: Mark Beckner
Development Editor: Chris Nelson
Technical Reviewer: John Allen
Editorial Board: Steve Anglin, Mark Beckner, Ewan Buckingham, Gary Cornell, Morgan Engel, Jonathan Gennick, Jonathan Hassell, Robert Hutchinson, Michelle Lowman, James Markham, Matthew Moodie, Jeff Olson, Jeffrey Pepper, Douglas Pundick, Ben Renow-Clarke, Dominic Shakeshaft, Gwenan Spearing, Matt Wade, Tom Welsh
Coordinating Editor: Jennifer L. Blackwell
Copy Editors: Marilyn Smith, Tiffany Taylor, and Kim Wimpsett
Compositor: MacPS, LLC
Indexer: BIM Indexing & Proofreading Services
Artist: SPi Global
Cover Designer: Anna Ishchenko

Distributed to the book trade worldwide by Springer Science+Business Media, LLC., 233 Spring Street, 6th Floor, New York, NY 10013. Phone 1-800-SPRINGER, fax (201) 348-4505, e-mail orders-ny@springer-sbm.com, or visit www.springeronline.com.

For information on translations, please e-mail rights@apress.com, or visit www.apress.com.

Apress and friends of ED books may be purchased in bulk for academic, corporate, or promotional use. eBook versions and licenses are also available for most titles. For more information, reference our Special Bulk Sales–eBook Licensing web page at www.apress.com/bulk-sales.

Any source code or other supplementary materials referenced by the author in this text is available to readers at www.apress.com. For detailed information about how to locate your book's source code, go to http://www.apress.com/source-code/.

*I dedicate this book to my wife, children, and friends
for always believing in me.*

Contents at a Glance

Contents

Chapter 7: Get the Data: Storing and Retrieving Data and Configuring your Applications 187

Chapter 8: Extend Your Apps: Extending Your iOS Application with Libraries 207

Chapter 9: Get Published: Testing, Deploying and Distributing Your Applications 223

About the Author

Mark Mamone is Global Head of Professional Services for Local Government & Commercial at Serco. He has 23 years of IT experience and has been involved with Microsoft .NET since its beta, Mono since its inception, and Objective-C and iPhone development since launch. A Certified Enterprise Architect and experienced chief technology officer, Mark has authored and coauthored several books on topics that include Linux, .NET, Mono, and databases.

About the Technical Reviewer

 **John Allen** is a Senior Manager and Enterprise Architect with BAE Systems Detica. He has over 15 years experience in the design and development of large-scale enterprise systems and is an expert in the field of software engineering and modern delivery methodologies. John has been involved in a number of open source projects and IT startups and continues to program for fun and profit, with his current focus being mobile applications, big data, and real-time analytics.

Acknowledgments

I would like to thank Rachel for supporting me and Oliver and Harry for reminding me on a daily basis why I work so hard. I would also like to thank John Allen for agreeing to be the technical reviewer for this book and for helping me to make this book the best it can be. Finally, I'd like to thank those at Apress who supported me in the creation of this book, especially Chris—you're a star!

Introduction

Ever since I spotted and started reading my first computer book in 1981, I knew Information Technology (IT) was going to be an important part of my life. I feel privileged to have been able to make a career out of something I enjoy, and the fact that it changes on what seems to be a monthly basis means it never gets boring. It still astounds me that mobile telephones have come so far in such a short time; and when the iPhone was launched, I knew the role of smartphones would be pivotal in all that we do—both in our private and our corporate lives. They are not only useful tools for managing your contacts or calendar, they are now a mechanism for doing all sorts of things such as buying a cinema ticket, keeping in touch with your friends through social media, and playing games,

However, why should those who don't know Objective-C or Xcode not be able to take advantage of such a wonderful world, especially if you have come to know and love Microsoft's .NET and C# but don't want to be exclusive to Microsoft Mobile–based smartphones? It doesn't have to be that way—a plethora of options exist, including using this book to understand the similarities and differences between C# and Objective-C, Visual Studio and Xcode 4, and the .NET Framework and the iOS SDK, and also how to exploit third-party options such as Mono and MonoTouch.

This book has been created to do just that. It provides you with all the information you need to make that transition, leaving you empowered and capable of using your experience to create world-class iOS-based applications. I even take you through the process of publishing your application to Apple's App Store.

I hope you enjoy this book and the opportunities it may afford you. Thank you for reading it.

Get Set Up: Tools and Development on Apple's Platforms and Technologies

In 2007, during a keynote speech at Macworld Expo, Steve Jobs (CEO of Apple) announced both a change of name to the organization (from Apple Computers, Inc., to just Apple, Inc.) and a change of product emphasis, moving from a focus on personal computers to an emphasis on mobile electronic devices. During the same announcement, Steve Jobs introduced two new devices: the iPhone and the Apple TV. The former has changed the face of the mobile landscape and consumer experience for mobile devices forever. Apple has gone on to launch its fifth generation iPhone and repeat its success with the introduction of its second-generation tablet, selling millions of devices and creating billions of dollars of revenue.

Apple's success can be attributed to the quality of the devices, the "coolness" associated with owning them, and the intuitive interface. But much more significantly than those factors is the introduction of the App Store in 2008, and the subsequent and growing availability of cheap (often free) fun and productive applications, which has skyrocketed Apple into a world leader in the mobile marketplace. Apple announced in July 2011 that the App Store now has almost half a million applications downloaded billions of times, and more important, anyone can write and submit applications for sale and distribution. So, *you* could make the next best-selling mobile application that everyone is playing, such as Angry Birds!

So, what's stopping you? Nothing, provided that you're familiar with development tool sets such as Apple's Xcode and its default programming language, Objective-C. For .NET developers and others, this has sometimes been a barrier for entry. After all, while everyone likes to learn something new, it doesn't mean you won't want to reuse that experience to get up and running more quickly.

In this book, you will learn how to transfer your skills from .NET to the Apple development framework, using both the tools provided and the comprehensive iOS SDK library. You also will learn about some of the third-party tools that leverage .NET and other non-Apple technology that might be more familiar and thus more comfortable to use. These third-party tools were introduced into the market to provide alternatives to the Apple-only tool set. Although using these tools is not the focus of this book, I'll introduce some of the key third-party tools, providing you with an overview on how to get up and running with them.

This chapter provides key information about the Apple development framework, as well as some of the alternative options. The following topics are covered:

- A description of how to register as an Apple Developer and why you would want to do that

- An overview of the Application development models

- An introduction to Apple's mobile operating system (iOS) and development tools

- A tour of third-party options, including the Mono family, DragonFire SDK, Titanium Mobile, Marmalade SDK, and Flash Professional CS5

- An introduction to the App Store and how to sell your new application

Registering As an Apple Developer

Before we discuss any of the software development kits (SDKs) or tools, you'll need to register as an Apple Developer. This is necessary not only to provide you with useful access to technical sources and information about developing applications that run on iOS-based mobile devices (the iPhone, iPad, and iPod touch), but also to download the tools you need, such as the iOS SDK and Xcode. These downloads are required for the Chapter 2 examples, so registering as an Apple Developer now is highly recommended.

To sign up, start up a browser session and navigate to `http://developer.apple.com/programs/register`, which presents you with a screen similar to the one shown in Figure 1–1.

Figure 1–1. *Apple Developer registration home page*

On this home page, you'll notice the option to Get Started, and register as an Apple Developer for free. Choose this link, and then proceed to follow the instructions to either create a new Apple ID or use an existing Apple ID (which you may already have through the use of iTunes, for example). Complete the steps required to register as an Apple Developer.

After successfully registering as an Apple Developer, you'll be able to gain access to a number of online resources that will provide you with some of the necessary tools and support. A couple of these resources are listed in Table 1–1.

Table 1–1. *Online Apple Resources*

Resource	Cost	URL	Purpose
iOS Dev Center	Free	http://developer.apple.com/devcenter/ios	Provides free technical resources and tools
iOS Developer	$99	http://developer.apple.com/program/ios	Membership permits you to distribute applications on Apple's App Store

You should now proceed to the iOS Dev Center and download the free iOS SDK, which provides the essential tools and libraries for starting to design and develop applications for your mobile Apple device. This disk image (with a .dmg extension) includes both the Xcode and the iOS SDK, so it is quite large, and you might want to make a drink while you are waiting for it to download. Alternatively, you may choose to download an older version of Xcode, which is free, although it does have limitations as to which Apple iOS versions it can target.

At this point, you may be wondering what the difference is between registering for an Apple ID and downloading the free SDK, and registering as an official iOS Developer, at a cost of $99, and gaining access to the very latest version of Xcode. Since the release of Xcode 4, Apple has mandated that you must be registered as an iOS Developer on the Apple Developer Connection (ADC) web site to gain access to it, which is covered by the annual $99 fee.

> **NOTE:** If you just want to experiment with Xcode 4 before making a commitment, you can install Xcode 4 through the Mac App Store at a cost of $4.99—much cheaper. However, the key difference between the two options is that with the App Store version, you cannot deploy your software to physical devices for testing, submit your apps to the App Store for publication, or access certain online resources. So, once you're comfortable and have plans for your "must-have" Apple application, you might want to commit to the full version.

But which version do you need? Well, that very much depends on which mechanism you're going to use to write your iPhone or iPad applications. We'll be looking at writing applications using a number of different methods, but we'll focus mainly on the Objective-C language.

My plan for this book is to target the latest Apple mobile devices, and I want to showcase the latest tooling options. So, the examples here use the latest version of Xcode available at the time of writing: Xcode 4. This version is improved significantly in usability, and so productivity. Such improvements result in it comparing more closely to Microsoft's own Visual Studio. So, while older versions of Xcode might work and be free, I recommend that you pursue more recent versions and invest the fee required to get started.

Application Development Considerations

Whether you are using Apple's own native tools or a third-party tool, there are certain principles to keep in mind as you develop. These principles will help to ensure your road to writing your award-winning application is smooth, or at least smoother. Each of the options we'll discuss is developed around some overarching principles, which both guide and constrain the way they work and how the resulting applications might execute, especially in the case of the third-party options.

Generic Development Principles

The following principles are common, irrespective of whether you are using Apple's own native resources or a third-party resource:

- *Design patterns*: Many of the frameworks use well-known design patterns for implementing your application. For example, the Model-View-Controller (MVC) design pattern is very common, and so an understanding of how this pattern works will help you enormously.

- *Licensing:* It's also worth understanding how the licensing model works for the third-party applications, and any limitations or conditions that may be enforced when you sign up to use the tools these applications provide. Also be aware of any restrictions that Apple's App Store policy might enforce.

- *Device compatibility*: Writing an application for one device doesn't mean it will automatically run or behave the same on another device. Take some time to understand the constraints and differences, and design your application for a multi-device scenario, if applicable. These differences are highlighted in upcoming chapters when relevant. For example, the iPad has more real estate that an iPhone, and we'll explore this in Chapter 6, where we look at enhancing your user interface.

Third-Party Development Principles

The following principles are generally common to all nonnative mobile application development solutions, as described later in this chapter:

- *API limits*: As with many operating system abstraction techniques, the API exposed by the tool you are using to write your mobile application is very often incomplete, and so will either implement a subset of the APIs available to the native iOS SDK or even provide different API calls. Take the time to understand the API, its constraints, and how it should be used by following the documentation and guidance provided.

- *Prerequisites*: It's important to note that not all of the third-party products work with the latest versions of Apple's native tools. Take some time to understand any prerequisites and ensure you download the components required by your tool and as indicated in the supporting documentation. The prerequisites go for hardware, too. Some of the options run only on the Mac OS X operating system. So, ensure you have the correct hardware, especially before spending money!

- *Cost*: Not all of the options are free, and some of the options have limitations. You may need to buy additional "bundles" as your application development progresses.

You need to be aware of these principles and understand not only how they work, but also the types of applications they output and the application model paradigms they use.

> **NOTE:** Third-party tools may simplify the development process, but sometimes at the cost of not supporting native applications or to the detriment of performance. In this chapter, and in the more detailed coverage in Chapter 3, I will provide information that will help you determine which options best suit your needs.

Application Approaches

Application development can be classified as one of two application paradigms: a *web application* or a *native application*. Understanding these types will better prepare you for the development of your application. You'll want to know the constraints of each and the implications they have on stages of development, such as debugging and distribution.

Web Applications

The option to develop an application using the web paradigm still remains and is always an option. In this paradigm, the app is hosted outside the mobile device and uses the implicit features of Apple's mobile browser, Safari, to execute the code and provide the required user interface and functionality. Of course, this constrains the kind of application you can build, the richness of its features, the functionality possible, and the way in which the application is accessed and made available.

For example, a browser-based application is available only when you have online connectivity, but in some cases, this might be quite appropriate. Suppose that you wanted to target many devices without being as dependent on the functionality provided by their operating system. In that case, you might consider a web-based application. Yes, it may require online connectivity, but if your application requires capabilities typically only provided by a web browser, such as HTML or JavaScript, then a web application may do just fine. However, Apple prides itself on a rich, intuitive, and interactive user experience, which is far easier to provide when exploiting the capabilities of Apple devices and their operating systems. But note that it is fair to say that, as the browser experience grows and as new technologies are introduced, the gap between web and native is definitely closing!

Native Applications

The alternative to a web-based application is a native application, and this type is the thrust of this book. We'll be looking at applications that are downloaded to and reside on the mobile device itself, and are written using Apple's own tools (Xcode and the iOS SDK) or those from a third-party provider.

Now that we've covered the basic development principles and approaches, we'll look at some core concepts surrounding application development using Apple tools, and then take a look at the third-party options available for application development. We'll be discussing these options throughout the book, and I will guide you through creating applications using the different mechanisms.

Apple Platforms and Technologies

Apple provides a variety of development resources that allow you to target a number of its devices or platforms. These include the Mac (via the Max OS X operating system), the Safari browser, and of course, Apple's mobile devices. This section introduces the underlying concepts, and then discusses the iOS and Apple tool set in more detail.

Apple Terminology and Concepts

Let's start with some of the key terms you should recognize before starting your journey, to provide some context for subsequent details provided in later sections. I want you to be able to build up a mental picture of the key concepts provided as part of Apple's core platforms and technologies before I introduce how, if at all, third-party options interface to them.

Table 1–2. *Key Apple Platform and Technology Concepts*

Term	Description
iOS	iOS is the mobile operating system that powers Apple's mobile devices. It was originally developed for the iPhone but more recently extended to power the iPod touch, iPad, and Apple TV.
iOS SDK	The iOS SDK provides the supporting tools (called a *toolchain*) and framework necessary to develop mobile applications, including: ▪ Cocoa Touch ▪ Media ▪ Core Services ▪ OS X kernel ▪ iPhone simulator
Xcode	Xcode is Apple's complete tool set for building Mac OS X and iOS applications. This package includes the integrated development environment: ▪ Compiler ▪ Tools for performance and behavior analysis ▪ iOS simulator

Term	Description
Objective-C	Objective-C is Apple's programming language, derived from the C programming language but with object-oriented and message-based extensions.
Cocoa\Cocoa Touch	Cocoa is one of Apple's native application programming interfaces. It provides a prebuilt set of libraries that support you in developing applications. In the case of Cocoa Touch, this includes extensions to support gesture recognition and animation on iPhone, iPod touch, and iPad devices.
Apple Developer	Registration as an Apple Developer is not only required to download resources such as the iOS SDK and Xcode, but it also provides you with access to key resources to support you through the iOS Dev Center.
Third-party tool	A third-party tool is a product or package specifically provided to solve a problem. In this case, the problem is mobile application development without using the traditional Apple tool set.

Figure 1–2 is a diagram that presents these concepts in a logical order (as they say, "a picture paints a thousand words"). I will build on this diagram as the chapter progresses, placing each of the concepts we encounter in relation to one another, and explaining their purpose and relationship. The diagram represents the "layers" provided, and the boundaries of the boxes shouldn't be seen as the only interfaces available to you. As I introduce each of the core layers, this will become clearer.

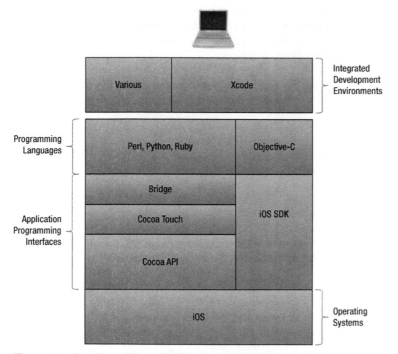

Figure 1–2. *Apple's mobile application development framework*

As you can see in Figure 1–2, on top of the iOS sits both the iOS SDK and the Cocoa API with the Touch extensions. The Bridge technology is another API, which provides the framework to link these resources to non-Apple and interpreted languages such as Perl, Python, and Ruby. Finally, the Xcode suite of tools provides graphical user interfaces (GUIs) to use the program languages, APIs, and libraries supplied through an integrated development environment (IDE)—all sitting on top of your Apple Mac computer.

You should now be comfortable with some of the high-level concepts associated with developing for Apple's mobile devices, if not the approaches or patterns of development yet, and have an understanding of some of the relationships among these core components. You should have also downloaded the iOS SDK, although we won't use it until the next chapter.

Both the iOS and the associated SDK are required to build and run mobile applications. Let's take a look at them at a high level. This will help you to understand some of the intricacies of the different mobile devices and also provide further background on how the operating system's features are accessed by the APIs and SDKs above them.

Understanding the iOS

Originally developed for the iPhone and derived from Mac OS X, iOS is the operating system at the heart of Apple's mobile devices, including the iPhone, iPod touch, and more recently, iPad devices. As with most operating systems, iOS takes a layered approach to providing the necessary functionality. Each layer builds upon another and provides clean lines of abstraction between them. The layers provided within iOS are shown in Figure 1–3.

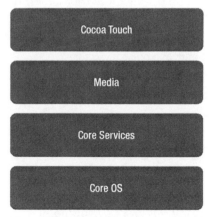

Figure 1–3. *iOS architecture*

Let's start at the bottom of the stack, dealing with the low-level services first and working our way up to those elements that we as humans will interact with directly and use for building iOS applications.

Core OS: This provides a layer of abstraction from the physical hardware and contains the low-level features used by the layers above it. Each element of the layer is provided as a series of frameworks: the Accelerate framework, External Accessory framework, Security framework, and System framework. A *framework* in this context is a collection of associated APIs that provide the framework's functionality. As we progress through the book, we'll explore these frameworks and the APIs they expose in more detail, and demonstrate examples of how to use them.

Core Services: Building on the Core OS layer, the Core Services layer contains the fundamental system services for applications. This layer is split into a set of Core Services, which combine to provide a number of essential high-level features. Some of the services provided are for programmatic support (language support, data types, and so on), data management support, and telephony.

Media: This layer, as its name suggests, provides graphic, audio, and video support. It is tasked with providing the best multimedia support available through the device being used. This layer includes frameworks that provide core audio, graphics, text, video, and MIDI support, as well as support for animation, media playing, and much more.

Cocoa Touch: This layer provides support and the key building blocks for building applications, including multitasking, touch-based input, notifications, and user-interface support. This layer also provides support for file sharing and printing, as well as peer-to-peer services for wireless connectivity.

While most of this functionality is packed into special libraries known as *frameworks*, this is not the case for all layers and all functionality. For example, some of the specialized libraries within the Core OS and Core Services layers are provided as dynamic link libraries (DLLs) with symbolic links used to point the iOS to the latest version on your device. Such techniques are common for managing code, and we'll look at them in more detail when talking about version control in Chapter 2.

> **NOTE:** Here, I will introduce the key concepts within each framework and present working examples to illustrate their use. More detail on the iOS frameworks and the versions of iOS in which they are supported can be found in the iOS Developer Library documentation.

Application Development Using Apple Components

You should now have a general appreciation for the operating system, the layers from which it is constructed, and the functionality it provides. Before we delve into the details of the iOS SDK, let's look at some of the history surrounding software development using Apple components.

When the iPhone was originally launched, you had two options: use the native tools and languages, such as Objective-C and the Mac OS X, or use web-based applications that are executed within the mobile Safari browser. The latter is naturally limited to languages such as HTML, Cascading Style Sheets (CSS), and JavaScript. Now this is still a valid development option today, but limiting in the kind of functionality and user experience possible.

The release of the second-generation iPhone introduced the iOS SDK, the Apple App Store, and the ability to use Xcode and Objective-C to write native applications. This provided virtually complete access to the iOS, and thus to the iPhone features, and also satisfied the mandated native-binaries-only option for distribution through the App Store.

Using the iOS SDK, and so Xcode and Objective-C, is still possible, and indeed favored by some individuals as the standard mechanism to use for application development. However, it is also true that developers may want to create applications that run on many mobile devices, not just Apple's. Or indeed, they may favor the Apple mobile devices but not Mac OS X, or maybe they do not like the development tools and languages mandated. For these reasons, a number of alternatives have been introduced, as we'll discuss in the book. In some cases, the options depend, at least in part, on the iOS SDK.

So, enough history. Now let's look at the options available for developing applications using the Apple-provided tools. Apple provides the following core components for developing applications:

- *Xcode*: This is a suite of tools, developed by Apple, for creating software both for the Mac OS X (as used in iMacs, MacBooks, and so on) and iOS.

- *iOS SDK*: This is the SDK released to allow developers to make applications for Apple's mobile devices and the Apple TV.

Xcode

At the time of writing, the most recent release of Xcode is Xcode 4, available from the Mac App Store for $4.99 and from the Apple Developer Connection web site for those registered as an Apple Developer, but at a cost of $99 for annual membership. Xcode version 3 is still available, free of charge (although, as you would expect, the versions of iOS supported are constrained).

Xcode comes with the following:

- **IDE**: Xcode is the standard IDE from Apple, which allows you to develop software for both the Mac OS X and iOS operating systems. It supports many programming languages, and provides many of the features you expect from a professional IDE, such as syntax highlighting, autocomplete, debugging, and source-code control. It's comparable with other industry-favored IDEs such as Eclipse and Microsoft's Visual Studio.

- **Interface Builder**: Since the introduction of Xcode 4, Interface Builder has moved from being a separate application to being completely integrated into the Xcode IDE, but its purpose remains the same: to provide a tool to aid the creation of user interfaces. It does this through a GUI supporting frameworks such as Cocoa and presents a palette of user interface objects and controls for you to drag and drop onto your canvas as required. You can even go a step further and provide the source-code implementation for events from these controls, such as a button click.

- **Compiler**: The compiler is an essential component. It takes your source code and generates the binaries required for execution of your mobile device and for App Store execution. Apple's LLVM (from the LLVM.org project) is a fast, feature-rich compiler that creates optimized applications for your mobile devices. It supports a number of languages, including C, C++, and Objective-C.

- **Debugger**: Another contribution from Apple to the LLVM.org open source project, the debugger provided as part of Xcode is fast and efficient. It supplies an integrated debugging interface that includes the usual features, such as stack tracing and step-by-step debugging, and also comprehensive multithreading support.

iOS SDK

The iOS SDK is the SDK launched by Apple in 2008 to enable you to develop native applications for the iOS operating system. The iOS SDK is broken down into *sets* that match the layers provided within the iOS framework (see Figure 1–3 earlier in the chapter). This includes the following:

- Cocoa Touch
    - Multitouch events and controls
    - Accelerometer support
    - View hierarchy
    - Localization
    - Camera support
- Media
    - OpenAL
    - Audio mixing and recording
    - Video playback
    - Image file formats

- Quartz
- Core animation
- OpenGL ES
- Core Services
  - Networking
  - Embedded SQLite database
  - Core Location
  - Concurrency
  - Core Motion
- OS X kernel
  - TCP/IP
  - Sockets
  - Power management
  - Threads
  - Filesystem
  - Security

Along with the Xcode toolchain, the SDK contains the iPhone simulator, a program used to emulate the look and feel of the iPhone on the developer's desktop. The SDK requires an Intel Mac running Mac OS X Snow Leopard or later. Other operating systems, including Microsoft Windows and older versions of Mac OS X, are not supported. More information can be found on the iOS Dev Center web site.

Third-Party Options

The reliance on Apple-only tooling for application development on Apple's mobile devices has long been a sore point for a number of people. This is not a reflection on the quality or features provided within the Apple options—quite the contrary. They are extremely powerful and productive tools that enable you to develop for both Apple's desktop and laptop devices (iMac, MacBook, and MacBook Pro) and mobile devices (the iPhone, iPod touch, and iPad) individually or as a team, using its team development features.

But, humans being humans, we get comfortable with what we know. We like familiarity. Those who have been brought up on different operating systems, different technologies, and different tools may be reluctant to change, and might not see the need to do so. For example, if you're a Java developer, you may love the Java programming language and the Eclipse (or similar) IDE you are using. Given you're a .NET developer, chances are you've been exposed to other languages. While this book focuses on bridging the gap between .NET and Apple's tool set, understanding the third-party options available to you is likely to provide relevant context. If you've been exposed to only Microsoft .NET, your familiarity with tools such as Visual Studio and the .NET Framework will stand you in good stead in making the transition.

Whether your experience is Microsoft-based or more mixed, you may also be more comfortable with the Windows or Linux operating system, and so are hesitant to learn a new operating system on which to develop your applications. "After all," I hear many people argue, "it's the mobile device and its operating system that are of most relevance, not how you get there."

So, how do you best use the experience you have and what exists to make your transition easier? My guess is you are not afraid to learn something new—after all, it's fun— but would rather reuse elements of the development environment that you are already familiar with—specifically, .NET. This hasn't gone unnoticed, and open source initiatives and commercial organizations have attempted to tackle and capitalize on the problem. There are many options available, and some scenarios may suit you more than others, such as Mono providing an open source and Apple-friendly implementation of .NET. Other options, while not .NET-focused, are relevant in helping you make the transition, even if you choose to ignore them and stick with Apple's own SDK and tools. Here, we'll take a quick look at the following third-party options:

- Mono
- Appcelerator's Titanium Mobile
- Marmalade SDK
- Flash Professional CS5

Mono Family

Mono is an open source (community-built) implementation of the .NET Framework and associated components for platforms other than Windows. The Mono environment can be classified as the Core Mono environment and additional components that offer enhanced functionality. When looking at the development of applications for Apple's mobile devices, you can think of Core Mono as the foundation with additional components, such as MonoTouch, built on top, completing the family.

The Mono family includes a number of components of significance when developing applications: the compiler, the framework, and the supporting tools. These components are called Core Mono (the compiler and runtime), MonoTouch (the .NET implementation of Cocoa Touch), and MonoDevelop (the IDE).

Core Mono

As a core part of the Mono development environment, Core Mono provides a compiler that supports a number of programming languages, including C#. It includes an implementation of the Common Language Runtime, and more important, provides a comprehensive set of APIs to implement the .NET Framework. Specifically, Core Mono includes the .NET Framework Class Library implementation, which is a set of libraries that provides the Mono implementation of the .NET Framework Class Library.

MonoTouch

MonoTouch provides a .NET-based implementation of Apple's own Cocoa Touch library. It allows developers to create C#- and .NET-based applications that run on Apple's iPhone, iPad, and iPod touch devices, while taking advantage of the iPhone APIs and reusing code and libraries built for .NET, as well as existing skills. It seems obvious now, but the introduction of MonoTouch was a touch of genius. It binds the Objective-C and C APIs from the Cocoa Touch API provided by Apple to the C#/Common Intermediate Language (CIL) APIs. In addition to the core base class libraries that are part of Mono, MonoTouch ships with bindings for various iPhone APIs to allow developers to create native iPhone applications with Mono. How does MonoTouch do this?

At the core of MonoTouch is an interoperability (interop) engine, which provides the bindings for the Cocoa Touch API, including Foundation, Core Foundation, and UIKit. This also includes graphical APIs such as Core Graphics and OpenGL ES.

Although MonoTouch provides bridges to the Cocoa Touch API, there is also an implementation of Mono targeted at allowing you to write applications for the Mac OS X operating system calling MonoMac, which uses the same principles. In fact, at the time of writing, a new version of Mono allows you to employ the same principles to write Android operating system applications using MonoDroid (although this is at a much earlier stage of its development).

MonoDevelop

While it's perfectly possible to use the command-line tools provided with Core Mono, and there are those who would argue that hard-core programmers deal only with command-line tools, I for one am grateful for a little help from enhanced tools. Nowadays, the IDE in the form of some graphical tool is ubiquitous. Those of you who have seen or used Microsoft's development tool, Visual Studio, will know how the whole experience of writing applications is made easier and faster through the use of such tools. Thankfully, Mono is no different, and the MonoDevelop tool suits our needs nicely as a great IDE.

As shown in Figure 1–4, MonoDevelop runs on the Mac OS X operating system. In fact, it runs on a number of operating systems, including various Linux distributions and Windows.

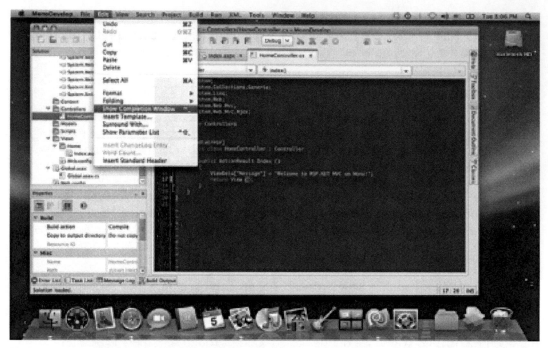

Figure 1–4. *A MonoDevelop application running on Mac OS X*

In Chapter 3, we'll look at MonoDevelop, along with the Mono framework and MonoTouch. You'll get a tutorial on how to install, use, and develop your own application for Apple's mobile devices using these components and the .NET Framework.

MonoTouch (including Core Mono) can be downloaded from http://www.monotouch.net, and MonoDevelop is available from http://www.monodevelop.com.

DragonFire SDK

We've looked at both Apple's native development environment and the support Mono provides for application development using the .NET Framework, but this may still be limiting for you. For example, what if your programming language of choice is C or C++. While Objective-C is provided as part of the Mac operating system, syntactically, it's quite different, and again, you may not want to be restricted to Mac OS X. The DragonFire SDK product was created for this very purpose.

DragonFire's target is Windows developers who wish to write native iPhone applications using Visual C++, its debugger, and the C/C++ language. It doesn't require a Mac of any description nor familiarity with Objective-C. As it says on the web site, "Bring your App idea to life in standard C/C++ and never leave your Windows platform."

Figure 1–5 illustrates how the Dragonfire SDK compares with Apple's existing mobile application development framework.

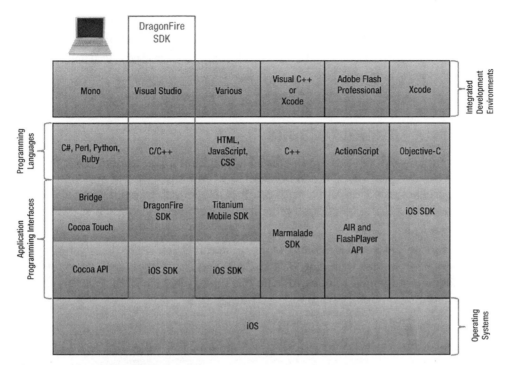

Figure 1–5. *DragonFire SDK framework*

The goal was to allow 2D games to be written and debugged in Windows, and be fully compliant for distribution via Apple's App Store. Although this is great if you're writing a game, you may find the API lacking in other areas. For example, as an API, it's not as complete as Apple's own API—for example, it lacks complete support for the Location-based API—but it is constantly being enhanced. The DragonFire SDK Enterprise Edition is being launched (at the time of writing, it is suggested that this version will launch toward the end of 2011), and this version will feature database support, as well as more drag-and-drop functionality and options for displaying text and graphics.

The unique aspect of DragonFire's SDK is that once you have written your application using its API and tested it using the on-screen simulator (all on the Windows operating system, remember), then you package up your application as instructed and upload this via the web site for compilation, and if requested, iTunes App Store bundling.

The DragonFire SDK is commercially available from its own web site at http://www.dragonfiresdk.com/. It's relatively inexpensive and aimed at "weekend projects," according to its authors. I'll let you decide if you like it, but it certainly removes some of the complexity of the other options. And it is the only option that allows full iPhone, iPod touch, and iPad development on the Windows platform.

> **NOTE:** I won't be covering the DragonFire SDK in detail in this book. Its construct is similar to some of the other third-party tools I'll introduce and demonstrate. I'll leave playing with the DragonFire SDK to you to have some fun.

Appcelerator's Titanium Mobile

Appcelerator's Titanium Mobile is an open source application development platform. In the same way as the DragonFire SDK can be used to write native iPhone applications using C/C++, Appcelerator's Titanium Mobile product allows you to write iPhone, iPad, and Android applications using languages other than Objective-C (iPhone and iPad) and Java (Android).

Titanium Mobile has an approach similar to Mono, in that it takes well-known languages (in this case, various languages including HTML, CSS, and JavaScript) and provides an API that binds these languages to native APIs (in this case, the iOS SDK). Figure 1–6 illustrates its architecture in comparison to the other options.

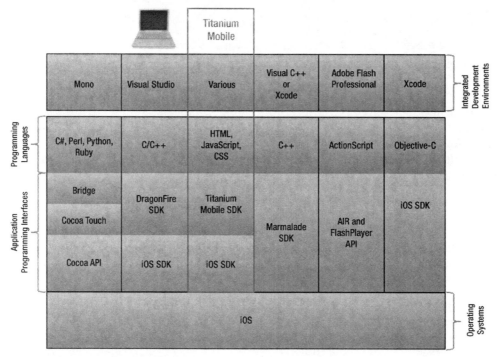

Figure 1–6. *Titanium Mobile framework*

Titanium Mobile differs from Mono in the process that it takes with your bespoke code in the language you love. Your original code is processed and eventually converted into native, executable code through a series of steps that involve preprocessing and compilation against first its own API into native code, and then native code into a native executable. These steps are illustrated in Figure 1–7, which shows the life cycle from written code to an executable ready for testing and, eventually, distribution via the App Store.

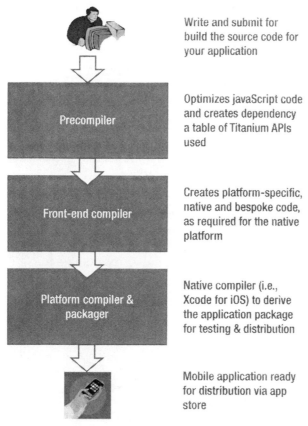

Write and submit for build the source code for your application

Optimizes javaScript code and creates dependency a table of Titanium APIs used

Creates platform-specific, native and bespoke code, as required for the native platform

Native compiler (i.e., Xcode for iOS) to derive the application package for testing & distribution

Mobile application ready for distribution via app store

Figure 1–7. *Titanium Mobile processing stages*

Appcelerator's Titanium Mobile is available from its own web site at http://www.appcelerator.com/. It's free for individuals using it personally or within small organizations (fewer than 25 employees), and has editions for corporate users of 25 and over and 100 and over. It has versions not only for mobile development, but also for desktop, commerce, analytics, and more.

Chapter 3 provides a tutorial on how to download, install, and use the product to create an iPhone application. In that chapter, we'll take a closer look at what the Titanium Mobile package can do, and discuss its advantages and disadvantages.

Marmalade SDK

As I start to introduce the Marmalade SDK, you'll see a theme emerging in the way these application development platforms—whether commercial or open source—are implemented. Marmalade is similar to the Mono and Titanium Mobile packages in many ways, except that it supports only C++. However, it does support development on both the Windows and Mac OS X operating systems, and allows you to create native mobile applications for the iOS operating system. In fact, the product lets you compile for other operating systems, such as Android, Symbian, Windows Mobile 6.*x*, and game consoles!

The Marmalade package consists of two major components:

- *Marmalade System*: The Marmalade System is an operating system abstraction API, together with the associated runtime libraries and application build system. It provides the binding between the native operating system API and the code you write, in the same way as Mono and Titanium Mobile do.

- *Marmalade Studio*: This is a suite of tools and runtime components, focused on high-performance 2D/3D graphics and animation.

The package allows you to use Visual C++ on Windows or Xcode on Mac OS X to write your application using the API provided. It then supports a two-stage deployment process. In the first stage, you compile your application for debugging. This creates a DLL (.dll file), which requires the Marmalade Simulator to execute. Then when you are happy with your application, you can compile your code into a native executable for distribution.

Figure 1–8 illustrates the Marmalade architecture in relation to the other packages we've discussed so far.

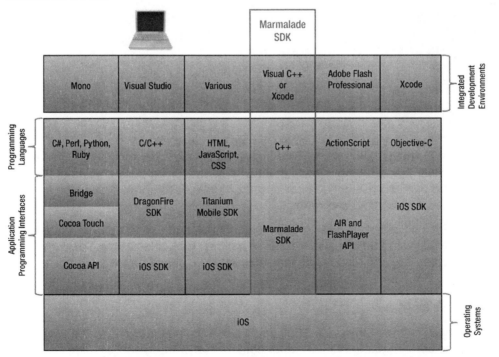

Figure 1–8. *Marmalade SDK framework*

In order to use the SDK, you must register an account on the web site, at which point you will be supplied with an evaluation license. Any registered user can then download a fully functional evaluation version of the Marmalade SDK. The evaluation version allows deployment to all platforms, but does not allow public distribution of applications. You can purchase the latest version of the Marmalade SDK from http://www.madewithmarmalade.com.

Flash Professional Creative Studio 5

Last, but definitely not least, is Adobe's Flash platform, which is arguably the most complete solution given here, in part due to its maturity in both the market and its work to support the iPhone back in 2010, when Apple lifted its restriction on its third-party developer guidelines. It allows you to build stand-alone applications for the iPhone, iPod touch, and iPad using the updated Packager for iPhone, which is included with Adobe Flash Professional Creative Studio (CS) 5 and with the AIR SDK on Adobe Labs.

Flash Professional CS5 works in a similar way to the other packages, allowing you to develop your application using the language you are familiar with (in this case, ActionScript). You compile this against the included APIs (the AIR and Flash Player APIs) into native iPhone applications, which are then ready for testing and deployment.

Figure 1–9 shows the Flash Professional CS5 architecture, again relative to the others we've discussed in this chapter.

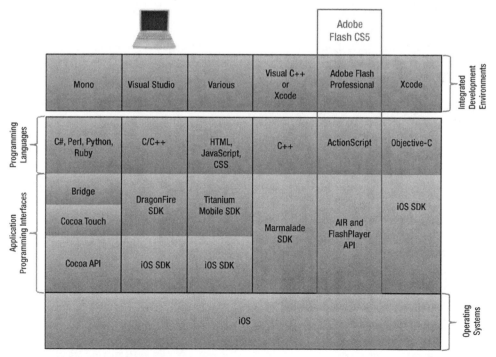

Figure 1–9. *Adobe Creative Suite 5 framework*

This option is by far the most comprehensive solution, but at a cost—both financially, as Adobe's Creative Studio is not cheap, and in complexity, as the product and its extensive API are not trivial to understand. For this reason, this option is not covered in this book. But after looking at the other options available, you should be well prepared to try out Flash Professional CS5 should you desire.

Overview of the App Store

The App Store is a digital application distribution platform for iOS devices, developed and maintained by Apple. Through the iTunes Store, accessed from either the Internet or the device itself, Apple allows service users to browse and download applications, paying for them as required. Applications can be downloaded to the device directly or to a desktop and subsequently transferred, if appropriate.

The App Store is accessible from a number of devices, including the iPhone (shown in Figure 1–10), iPod touch, and iPad. For Mac laptop and desktop users, the Mac App Store was launched more recently to cater to nonmobile applications.

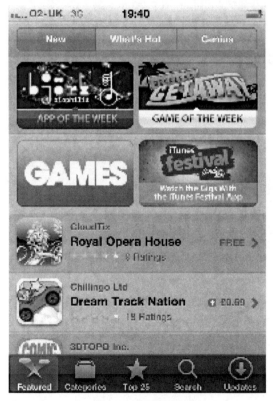

Figure 1–10. *App Store on the iPhone 4*

The App Store has been tremendously successful for both Apple and application producers, with the billionth application download boundary broken back in 2009. As mentioned, the concept has been mimicked by other organizations, most notably the other major mobile service providers. Figure 1–11 shows the global revenue share among these platforms. Apple's dominance is obvious.

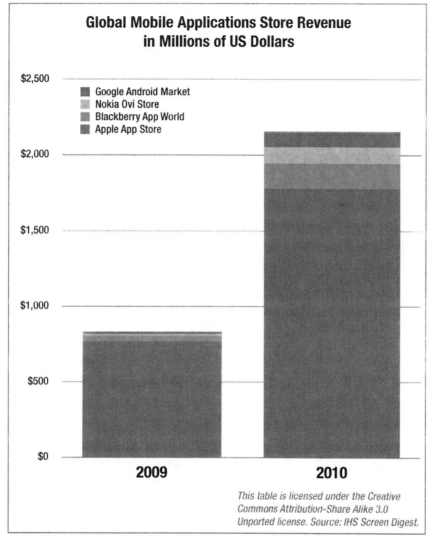

Figure 1–11. *Global mobile application store revenues*

Selling Apps at the App Store

The App Store revenue model is to split the proceeds from any sale: 30% to Apple and 70% to the app publisher (this is subject to change at any time). The model has proven immensely profitable for both Apple and many application producers. The term *app* (short for application) has also been used more broadly, and despite Apple being awarded a trademark for the term, it has been used in a similar context by others, such as Google (*Google Apps*) and Amazon.

NOTE: All native apps can be legitimately downloaded onto a mobile Apple device only through the App Store, unless the device has been jailbroken. *Jailbreaking* a device refers to using the process that gives access to the device's root filesystem, allowing modification and installation of third-party software components. It's not illegal, although Apple is sensitive to the topic and has stated that it may "void the warranty" for the device. Jailbreaking doesn't require any changes to the hardware and can be easily reversed.

More recently, Apple announced its new subscription-based service that allows application publishers to set the length and price of a subscription. Previously, this wasn't possible, and you were forced to sell each release on a per-release basis. The new service allows publishers to sell their content through their apps, and users can receive new content over a specified period of time.

A more significant change is that not only is the traditional model of selling through iTunes available, but Apple is also allowing app publishers to distribute their subscriptions directly from their own web sites, where the iTunes revenue model doesn't apply and so no revenue is shared with Apple. This obviously has the advantage of removing the obligation of contributing some of your application earnings to Apple, but it does mean that you lose the benefits of the App Store, such as audience reach and accessibility, and must rely on your own marketing campaigns.

Submitting an App to the Store

Here are the steps for submitting an app to the App Store:

1. Complete the development and testing for your app.

2. Create the supporting `info.plist` file for your app (more on this later).

3. Write a description for your app.

4. Choose a unique numeric SKU for your app.

5. Assemble your screenshots to be displayed on the App Store.

6. Prepare your iTunes artwork.

7. Submit through iTunes Connect.

Any application submitted is subject to approval by Apple, as outlined in the SDK agreement, for basic reliability testing and other analysis. Apple has a process for appeals, but it ultimately has the final decision. If your app is rejected, you can still distribute it ad hoc by manually submitting a request to Apple to license the application to individual iPhones (although Apple may withdraw the ability for you to do this at a later date).

The official *App Store Review Guidelines* for developers is a good source of material. We'll also discuss the details of submitting an application for approval and distribution rights in Chapter 9.

Summary

This chapter introduced the concepts of developing applications for Apple's mobile devices, specifically the iPhone, iPod touch, and iPad. We've looked at how to register as an Apple Developer, and why this is recommended, as well as some of the principles surrounding mobile application development. We then discussed the iOS operating system, which powers these mobile devices, and the iOS SDK and Xcode.

Following the introduction of these concepts, we took a look at some of the different options available to develop applications. These include not only Apple's own native languages and tools, but also a number of other third-party options, both open source and commercial.

We concluded with an introduction to the App Store—its purpose, revenue model, and support of various devices. You learned the mechanics of submitting a new application to the App Store for review and if approved, publication.

The next chapter provides a crash course in creating a simple application using Apple's native tools, the iOS SDK and Xcode. By the end of that chapter, not only will you have created your first iPhone application, but you will also have a better appreciation for some of the fundamental concepts in developing a mobile application, which you can reuse when you look at some of the other options available.

In Chapter 3, you will learn more about the third-party tools, such as the Mono family. After that, we'll focus again on the Apple tools and use these throughout the rest of the book to demonstrate how to apply your .NET knowledge and experience to creating compelling apps.

Chapter 2

Jump In: A Crash Course on Development Using the iOS SDK

The first chapter introduced both Apple's mobile operating system (iOS) and options for developing your own mobile applications. In this chapter, we'll get started with Apple's own software development tools: Xcode and the iOS SDK.

This chapter covers the following topics:

- The hardware and software you need to get started
- A guide to installing the relevant components
- An Objective-C primer
- An overview of Xcode and how to start your first project
- How to create your first iPhone application using the iOS SDK

Getting Started

Let's begin by taking a look at what you'll require to get started—not just the software components, but also the hardware you will need.

You'll also need to sign up to become a registered Apple Developer. Apple requires this step before you're allowed to download the iOS SDK. In Chapter 1, we discussed why you'll need to do this, the benefits, and how to go about it. As a reminder, you need to visit http://developer.apple.com/ to sign up.

NOTE: In Chapter 1, I mentioned some of the benefits of becoming a registered Apple Developer. One of these is a useful list of *Getting Started* guides that provide short introductions to a number of topics, such as graphics and animation, data management, and so on. You can find them and much more in the iOS Developer Library at `http://developer.apple.com/library/ios/navigation/index.html`.

Choosing the Right Machine

You will need an Apple Mac to get started. You may already have an old device and are wondering whether it is still suitable for developing modern mobile applications. The news is good: some of the older Apple Mac machines will run the required software. The important bit is the operating system.

To support development for the iPhone, iPod touch, and iPad, you will need Xcode 3.2.6 or higher (this includes iOS SDK 4.3). This version also provides support for packaging and submission of your apps to the App Store. This version of Xcode\iOS SDK requires Mac OS X Snow Leopard version 10.6.6 or later and an Intel-based Apple Mac machine. The important distinction here is the Intel processor.

In 2006, Apple discontinued the use of the PowerPC processor and announced the move for all future Macs to run on the x86 processor made by Intel. So, Mac devices made in 2006—specifically, the Mac mini, iMac, MacBook, MacBook Pro, and Mac Pro—will happily run Mac OS X Snow Leopard, or the more recently released Lion operating system, and development tools, provided that you have sufficient memory and hard disk space. The memory and space you need vary depending on the version of the operating system you are installing.

CAN I USE A PC?

What if you don't want to use an Apple device? What if you want to use a PC running an operating system like Windows? Well, this really depends on which tools you are planning to use to develop your mobile apps.

A number of the third-party options introduced in Chapter 1 are actually designed to run on a Windows-based PC, using languages other than Objective-C. But what if you want to use native Apple tools such as Xcode? That is not so straightforward. These tools will run only on Mac OS X Snow Leopard and Lion, and therefore you will need an Intel-based Mac. However, technically all is not lost! Through the use of virtualization software, such as commercial products like VMware or freeware such as VirtualBox, you could run Mac OS X Snow Leopard on an Intel-based PC within a virtual machine.

But wait! While running the operating system on a virtual machine is technically possible, and there are many examples of people successfully doing this (called Hackintosh) it is not permitted within Apple's license agreement for Mac OS X and is therefore illegal.

Choosing the iOS SDK

So you have a suitable machine, running Mac OS X Snow Leopard or Lion, which will allow you to download and install the required software. But what software? Chapter 1 introduced Xcode, which includes the iOS SDK and provides a complete tool set for building iOS applications. If you haven't already done so, you will need to download it from http://developer.apple.com/xcode/.

Since the release of Xcode 4, you currently have two options for obtaining and installing Xcode. As you've learned, Xcode 3.2.6 or higher supports development for Apple's mobile devices and is available free of charge. However, you may wish to use the most recent version, Xcode 4, which is available free to members of the iOS or Mac Developer Program or can be purchased from the App Store.

What's New in Xcode 4?

If you're familiar with Visual Studio as a development environment, you'll find yourself far more at home with Xcode 4 than with previous versions. So what are these new features?

- **New user interface**: The new integrated development environment (IDE) combines the separate windows from previous versions into a single window with different navigation panes, making it far easier to use. This includes the Interface Builder for creating new GUIs for your applications.

- **Assistance:** The software provides inline context-sensitive help as you write your source code—for example, prompting you with code for the class from which you may be inheriting. It's similar to Microsoft's IntelliSense, best known for its use within the Microsoft Visual Studio IDE.

- **New debugger:** This version provides an integrated debugging interface that allows you to step through your code and associated variables as you execute your application.

- **Instruments**: These allow you to gather information about how your application is performing and what effect it may be having on your operating system. For example, you can use some of the instruments provided to understand how your application consumes memory.

Apple iOS Dev Center Resources

Chapter 1 also referenced the iOS Dev Center (see http://developer.apple.com/ devcenter/ios/index.action) and a number of other resources. Now is probably a good time to take a look at some of these. The following are some resources that will support you through this chapter (and the rest of the book):

- **iOS Human Interface Guidelines**: Describes the considerations you should make when designing your interface and provides guidelines on how to create the best user experience.

- **App Design Strategies**: This is a particularly useful subsection of the guidelines, as it helps you to codify your thinking about the idea you have for your application, such as the features that you might include.

- **Getting Started**: A number of short but very useful guides on how to get started with a number of facilities, including the tools, the iOS SDK, and the programming language. I recommend the "iOS Starting Point" section (http://developer.apple.com/library/ ios/#referencelibrary/GettingStarted/GS_iPhoneGeneral/_index. html) as a good place to get started.

Installing Xcode and the iOS SDK

You should have decided by now which version of Xcode you'll be using, and therefore the associated iOS SDK. Given that we're looking to target the latest Apple mobile devices in this book, and I want to showcase the latest tooling options, I will use the latest version of Xcode available at the time of writing: Xcode 4. All of the examples in this book use Xcode 4, partly because of some of its improvements, and I recommend that you do the same.

One method for obtaining Xcode 4 is to take a look at the CD or DVD provided within your Mac. Xcode and the iOS SDK are often provided on separate media, and it's simply a matter of finding the CD or DVD, inserting it into the drive, locating the file devtools.mpkg, and double-clicking it to start the installation.

Another route is to download the app from the App Store, which is the most cost-effective solution for obtaining the very latest version. Simply open the App Store application on your desktop and search for Xcode. Finally, you could visit Apple's iOS Dev Center to obtain the developer preview of Xcode 4.2 and iOS 5. This is what we'll use in our book. Either by navigating to https://developer.apple.com/devcenter/ios/index.action, or by visiting Xcode on the App Store, you will see a screen similar to that shown in Figure 2–1.

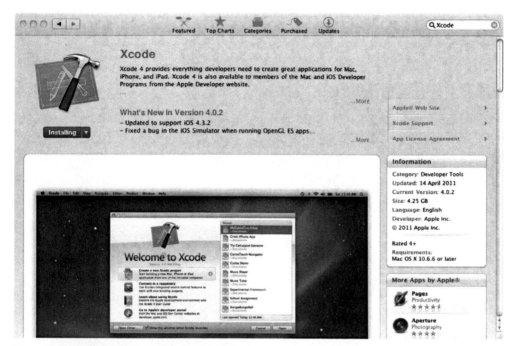

Figure 2–1. *Xcode available within the App Store*

Scroll down and select to download Xcode 4.2. Be warned: the file is large in size, so for all but the fastest of Internet connections, it will take a while to download. This is a sore point for many users, but once it's installed, the benefits you'll gain outweigh the wait.

After downloading Xcode, start it up to begin the installation. You should be presented with the screen shown in Figure 2–2.

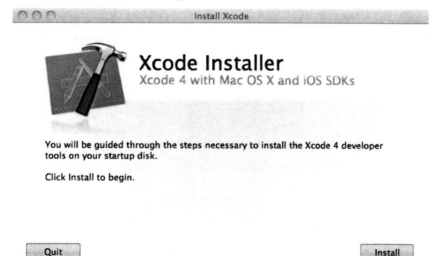

Figure 2–2. *Xcode 4 installation startup screen*

Follow the on-screen instructions and complete the installation of Xcode 4. Once the installation is complete, you should find the Xcode 4 application icon at the bottom of your screen. Click this icon to launch the program, as shown in Figure 2–3.

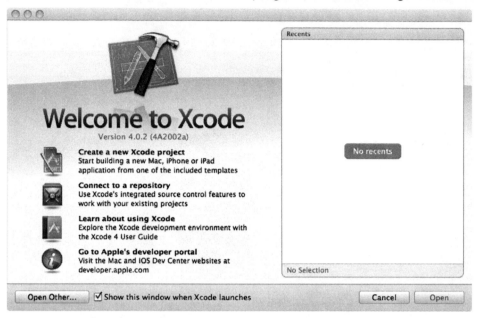

Figure 2–3. *Running the Xcode 4 application*

It's also a good idea to store all of your source code in a specific folder or repository of your choice. This should be somewhere in your own Home area. Set up this folder now, so it's ready to receive your first iPhone application. Create the folder in the Finder as preferred, and name it Projects.

When creating new projects in Xcode, you can direct your project location to this folder or create a local repository in this location instead, and use the version-control system to manage the changes you make as you develop your application. For version control, you have two options. You can use either Git or Subversion—both are installed as part of the Xcode installation. Subversion is typically server-based, although you could run the server on your local computer and create a local repository using the command-line interface, similar to the following:

Svnadmin create <repositoryname>

Once you've successfully created the repository in your desired location, you can add this to your Xcode repository list. To add the new repository, select **File ➤ Repositories**. On the screen presented, click the plus (+) symbol to display a pop-up menu, and then choose the **Add Repository** option. This will present the screen shown in Figure 2–4. Complete the fields, pointing at the repository you've just created. Click the Next button, and follow the on-screen instructions to complete the registration of your repository.

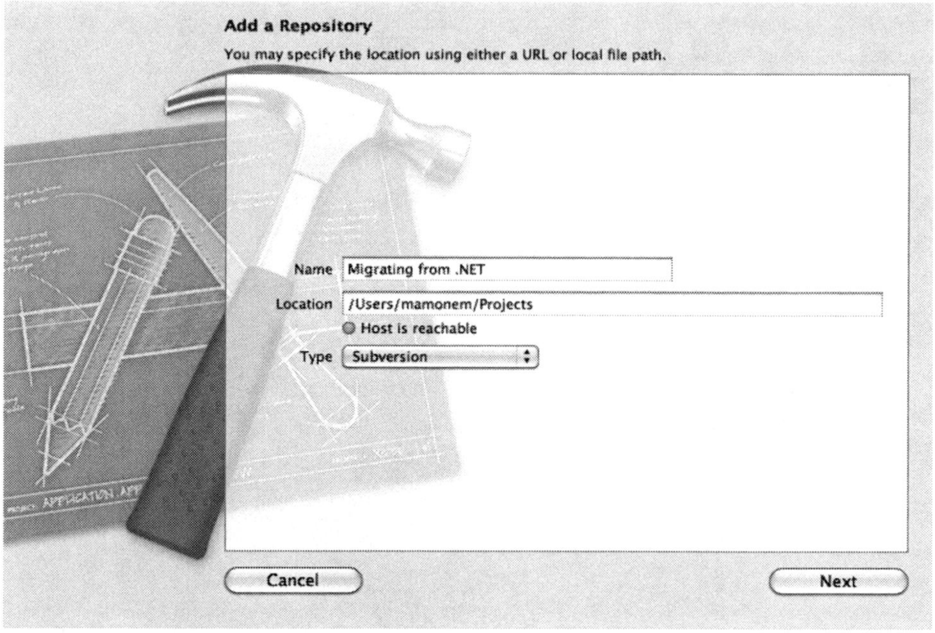

Figure 2–4. *Adding a repository*

Your empty repository organizer will be displayed, as shown in Figure 2–5. You are now ready to begin development of your first iPhone application using Xcode 4.

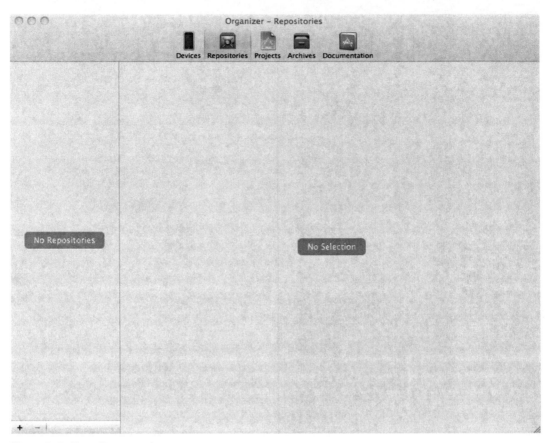

Figure 2–5. *Repository organizer*

Xcode's support for Subversion is built-in, provided that you're using version 1.5 or later. However, you must create your Subversion repository and import your project into Subversion on the command line before managing it in Xcode. For simplicity, our examples will not use a source code control subsystem. We're simply going to be using the filesystem. For detailed instructions on the use of Subversion, see the online book *Version Control with Subversion* (http://svnbook.red-bean.com/), which is endorsed by Subversion's developers.

> **NOTE:** You don't typically create the svn repository in the same directory from which you want to manage the project's source code. Instead, you can check out the repository "trunk," and that becomes a type of special folder on the filesystem (it has dot files that let Subversion know it is checked out). You can then create project files in that folder, and they can be added to the repository via Xcode's user interface.

Whatever you've decided to do, you should have now installed Xcode and selected your repository preference. You are ready to start your project and write code. But before we start building an application, let's take a brief look at the Objective-C language, focusing on some of the key tenets you will encounter in building your application.

An Objective-C Primer

Apple's Objective-C is the de facto standard language for app development on the iPhone, iPod touch, and iPad. Although new languages, such as those provided within .NET, are supported through the Mono implementation, the reality is that using Objective-C offers the fastest performing option. This becomes important if you're writing a particularly performant app, such as a game or computationally intensive app.

So what's Objective-C, and how does it compare with .NET languages, and specifically its closest .NET cousin, the C# language? Providing an exhaustive guide warrants a book in its own right. To get you started, we'll take a look at some of the most important concepts and immediate differences you should be aware of before writing your first program. As we progress through the book, some of the differences will be pointed out as we encounter them

The following list represents the key tenets for any Objective-C primer for .NET developers and those used by the application we'll create in this chapter. A brief introduction here will help you to understand some important aspects of your first application.

- Object model
- Square brackets
- Naming conventions
- Importing
- Class definition and implementation
- Exception handling
- Nil objects
- Memory management

> **NOTE:** This primer provides you with an introduction biased toward your existing .NET experience, but it cannot do justice to a comprehensive language such as Objective-C. If you're looking for further details, I recommend the book *Learn Objective-C on the Mac* by Scott Knaster and Mark Dalrymple (Apress, 2009), which can be found at
> `http://www.apress.com/9781430218159`.

Let's start with a brief introduction to some terminology.

Objective-C Terminology

Table 2–1 compares some of the NET C# programming language and Objective-C keywords. As you can see, they are different but still quite similar.

Table 2–1. *C# and Objective-C Terminology Comparison*

C#	Objective-C
#include "library.h"	#import "library.h"
This	self
private, protected, public	@private, @protected, @public
var = new Class();	var = [[Class alloc] init];
try, throw, catch, finally	@try, @throw, @catch, @finally
Interface	Protocol
Class	Interface
Null	Nil
True	YES
False	NO

Object Model

The object model in Objective-C bears a close resemblance to languages such as Smalltalk and C++. It is an object-oriented language that extends the C language by providing a strict superset of C. This means it is possible to include any C within your class, and it will compile quite happily (providing it is syntactically correct and libraries and other dependencies have been handled).

The object model's resemblance to Smalltalk will be instantly recognizable to those of you who are familiar with it (although its relevance goes back many years now). Essentially, it provides messaging-style syntax that involves passing messages to object instances, rather than calling methods on objects. It's a subtle difference but with implications.

This mechanism achieves the same goal as other object-oriented languages that are not loosely coupled, such as .NET. The main difference is that the association between the message being passed and the object is not resolved at compile time by being bound in code, but at runtime. Therefore, you need to be cautious about how this receiving object will handle the message. The object that is being sent the message (the *Receiver*) is not guaranteed to respond to the message, especially if it wasn't expecting it or doesn't understand it. In that case, at best the app will raise an exception. At worst, it will continue silently, making debugging applications a more laborious task. For this reason, you should also take note of the exception handling and `Nil` object tips provided later in this chapter.

Square Brackets and Methods

You will soon discover that square brackets are an important feature of the Objective-C language. As you've learned, the object model is based around the concept that objects are sent messages in order to invoke a method. Conversely, if you want to query a property of a method, the recommended route is to ask the object for a property value by sending a message, rather than by peeking inside it (which is seen as bad practice anyway). The square brackets indicate that you are sending a message to an object.

> **NOTE:** The examples here reflect the syntax and do not represent complete, compilable source code. You'll see the examples in working source code listings as the book progresses.

Calling a Method

So, if we had an object called `Engine`, we could "start the engine" by using its `start` method after first creating an instance of `Engine`. In Objective-C, the code would look like this:

```
// Create reference to an object of type Engine class called diesel.
Engine* diesel;

// Create an instance of the Engine object and point the diesel reference at it
diesel = [[ Engine alloc] init];

// Call the start method by passing the Engine object the start message
[ diesel start];
```

The same code in C# (without the comments) would look as follows:

```
Engine diesel;
diesel = new Engine();
diesel.start();
```

> **NOTE:** In the C# example here, notice that the new() command both allocates and initializes the object in a single call.

Passing and Retrieving

A similar syntax is used to both pass parameters when calling an object's method and to retrieve a value that might be returned by a called method. For example, to pass a flag or value indicating how much gas to apply when starting the engine, we would use the following syntax:

```
[diesel start: gas];
```

Alternatively, if we wanted to return the number of revs the engine is currently outputting, we could use the following syntax, presuming that we created a getter called revs to return such a value:

```
currentRevs = [ diesel revs ];
```

Naming Conventions

The naming convention used by Objective-C is much like other languages, using PascalCase for classes and camelCase for methods and properties. For those of you not familiar with either of these, PascalCase is concatenating capitalized words, always starting with a capital letter, as in PascalCase. The camelCase form is similar, with capitalized words being concatenated, but the first letter may be either uppercase or lowercase, as in camelCase. PascalCase is also known as UpperCamelCase.

If you were wondering, Microsoft's C# standard is PascalCase, which may be why the notation looked familiar.

Importing

With Objective-C, there are two ways of importing, just as with C/C++. The difference is that the syntax of one will force the compiler's preprocessor to look for the file in the system header directory, whereas the syntax using quotes will look in the current directory if you haven't specified an alternative location.

To look for your own header file in the current or specific directory, use the following syntax:

```
#import "myfile.h"
```

To look in the system header directory, use the following syntax:

```
#import <Foundation/foundation.h>
```

Class Definition and Implementation

As with most object-oriented languages, an object is defined by its class, and many instances of that object may be created. Every class consists of an interface, which defines the structure of the class and allows its functionality to be implemented. Additionally, each class has a corresponding implementation that actually provides the functionality. Typically, these implementations are held in separate files, with the interface code contained in a header file (.h extension) and the implementation held in a message file (.m extension).

> **NOTE:** A rumor (or fact maybe) I heard was that when the inventor of the Objective-C language was asked why the .m extension was used, he simply stated because .o and .c were already taken!

So, using our same `Engine` example, our source code in the respective files may look like the following:

Listing 2–1. *Engine.h*

```
@interface

- (int) revs;

@end
```

Listing 2–2. *Engine.m*

```
@implementation

- (int) revs (
        return revs;
}

- (void) start {
        // Start the engine at an idle speed of 900 rpm
        // - NOTE This is a comment
        revs=900;
{
@end
```

As you can see, in both cases, the code is preceded with either `@interface` or `@implementation` as appropriate, and concludes with an `@end` token. All interfaces and methods, respectively, must appear between these two statements.

Nil Objects

The way in which the object-oriented features are implemented in Objective-C means that calls to methods are implemented as messages being passed to objects whose correct identity is resolved at runtime. As discussed, this means that the type checking normally done at compile time, which would (usually) throw an error, will not occur.

In the case of a mismatch during runtime, either an exception will be thrown (best-case scenario) or the object will silently ignore the message (worst-case scenario). So, be extra careful about both ensuring your message\object interaction is valid and that good exception handling is added throughout. There is no easy or obvious way of replicating late binding in .NET.

Exception Handling

The exception handling syntax for Objective-C will be familiar to those of you who have used C# or exception handling in other languages.

```
@try
{
        // Code to execute and for which you wish to catch the exception
}
@catch ()
{
        // Do something after an exception has been caught
}
@finally
{
        // Clean up code here
}
```

Given the similarity, I won't replicate the C# equivalent code here. You should immediately recognize the syntax and be comfortable with its use. However, as noted earlier, the important thing to remember is that because of the way messages are passed to objects and resolved at runtime in Objective-C, it is critically important to ensure a defensive approach to coding is taken. You should anticipate exceptions, catching and handling them elegantly, as shown in the preceding example.

Memory Management

Just like the Common Language Runtime (CLR) in .NET, the runtime environment handles memory management for Objective-C applications for you. A reference-counting system is used by Objective-C. This means that if you keep track of your references, the runtime will automatically reclaim any memory used by objects once the reference count returns to zero.

Does this still sound complicated? Well it's not, providing you follow some simple principles. When writing applications for mobile devices, even with the larger memory footprints these devices have nowadays, the importance of memory management can't be understated.

If you've allocated memory using alloc(), remember to call release, unless you're using the autorelease mechanism. You may also wish to explore the use of @property and use the @synthesize feature, which will automatically create your setters and getters, although this doesn't remove the need for you to allocate space for your object.

In iOS 5, the new automatic reference counting (ARC) functionality automates memory management for Objective-C objects. ARC makes memory management much easier, greatly reducing the chance for your program to have memory leaks.

Creating Your First iPhone Application

The first step in starting a new project using Xcode 4 is to create a single Xcode project. In fact, it's compulsory to use a project with Xcode, as its under this project that your files and resources are collected. It is possible to have multiple but related projects, and we'll touch on this approach later in the book, but essentially, our book examples don't require it. The iOS SDK usefully provides a number of project templates to get you started, as you'll see shortly.

The following are the high-level steps for creating your iPhone application using Xcode:

1. Create your project.

2. Design your application.

3. Write code.

4. Build and run your app.

5. Test, measure, and tune your app.

The Xcode suite of tools can support you during all of these steps, from creating your project and managing the files associated with it to using the instruments provided to fine-tune your application's performance.

Creating a Project

Let's start by using Xcode to create a project using one of the templates provided by the iOS SDK, which will give us a head start. Providing project templates in this manner is similar to what you see in Microsoft Visual Studio and other IDEs such as Eclipse. These templates define, by default, some of the characteristics, files, and resources relevant to the project type you choose. You can see the similarity between Visual Studio and Xcode 4 in Figures 2–6 and 2–7.

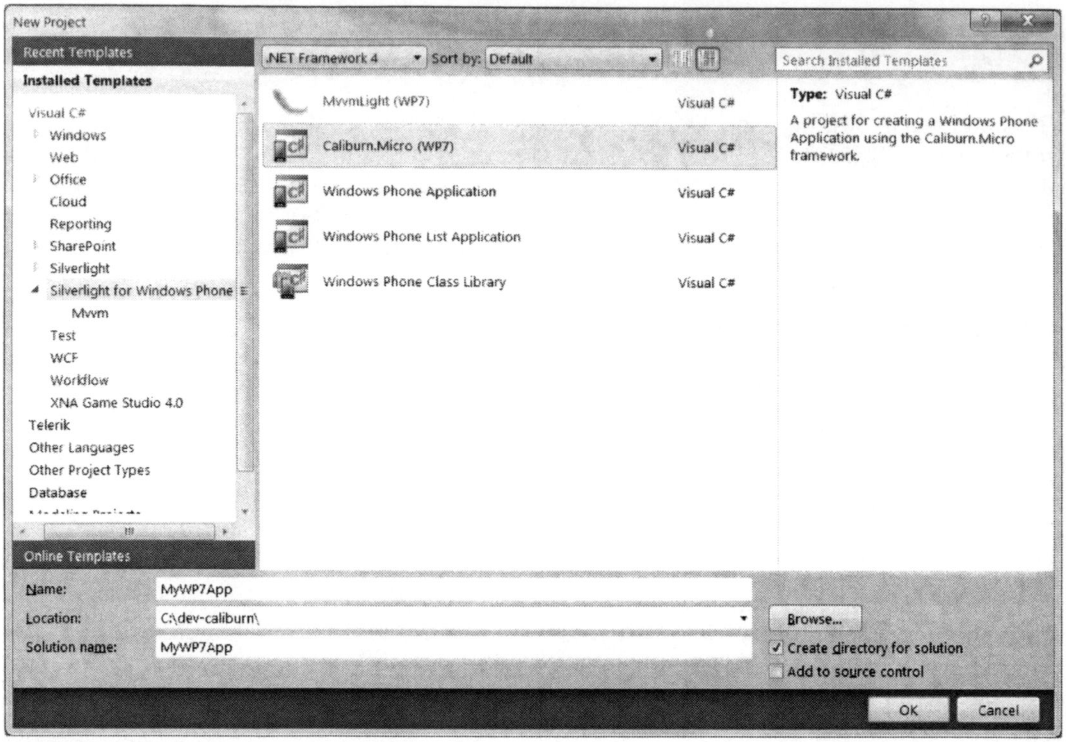

Figure 2–6. *Visual Studio 2010 project templates*

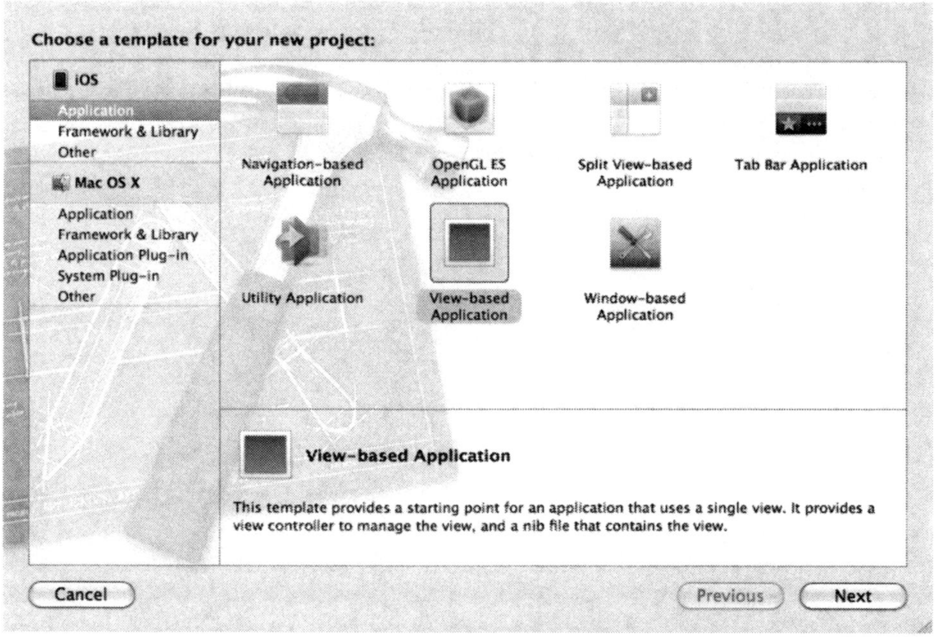

Figure 2–7. *Xcode 4 project templates*

There are many templates to choose from, and the "right" template really depends on the type of application you are building. Templates are not limited to applications either. Notice from the left pane in Figure 2–7 that Xcode provides a template to create libraries as well as applications, and the choice for the Mac OS X platform is even wider!

For this example, choose the View-based Application template, which uses a single view to implement its user interface. (We'll touch on views a little more when we look at creating a user interface later in this chapter.) You will be presented with the screen shown in Figure 2–8, asking that you set some of the options for your application, including the device family you wish to target. As shown in the figure, name the product HelloWorld and pick the iPhone as the device family. Then click the Next button.

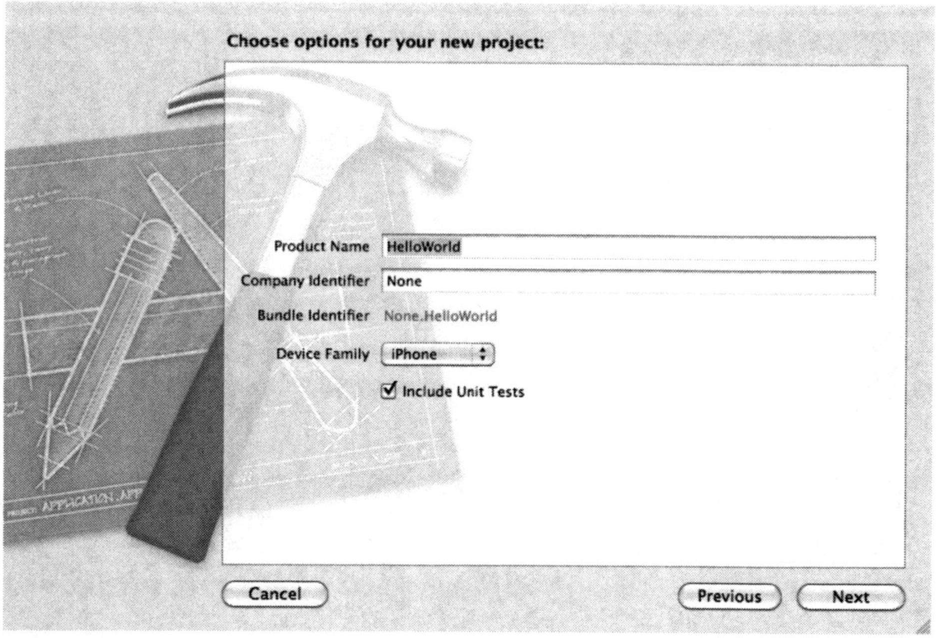

Figure 2–8. *Creating a new project*

You can now proceed with the creation of the project and its associated files and resources. When you're finished, you will have a new Xcode project, with the project and its file structure displayed, as shown in Figure 2–9.

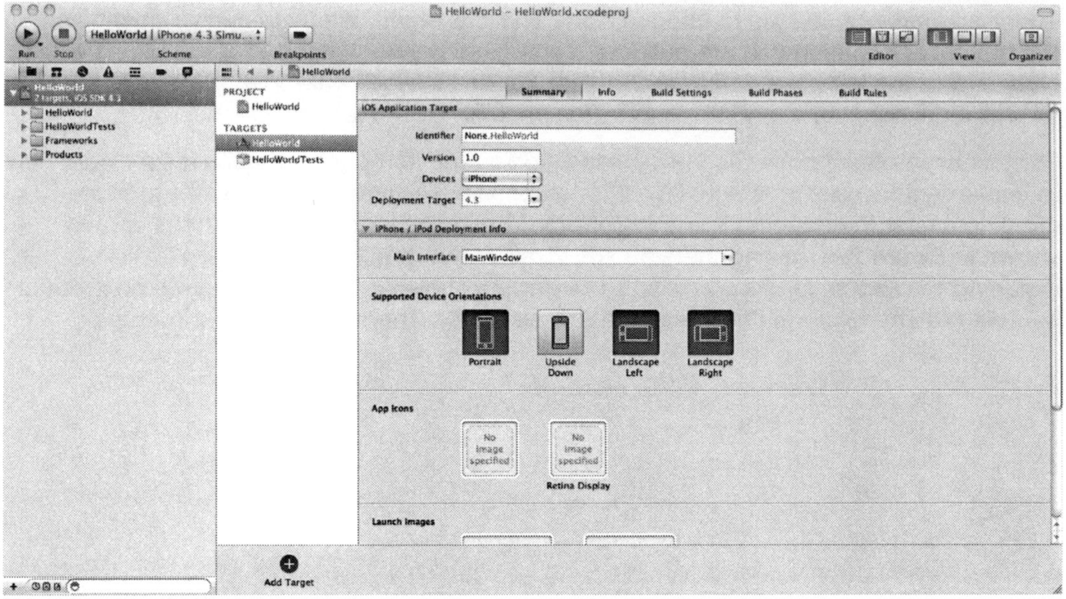

Figure 2–9. *Opening the HelloWorld project in Xcode*

Take some time to explore a little, looking at the project structure, the files created, and some of the menus. You will notice that some of the files have source code providing a default implementation. Don't worry about understanding everything yet.

Exploring Your Project and File Structure

Once created, your empty project will have a number of default files created for you, as I've mentioned. These files provide the default implementation for an empty view-based project that targets the device you chose—in this case, the iPhone.

Let's take a quick look at some of the project files created for you:

- **HelloWorldAppDelegate**: The *application delegate* is the controller that handles application initialization, including displaying the initial view for your user interface. It is also responsible for handling application termination when you exit your application. There is normally only one application delegate of object type UIApplication. This is called a *singleton* object.

- **MainWindow.xib**: This file represents the structure and resources for your user interface. It's the Mac OS X Interface Builder file, hence the .xib extension. In a typical application, mainwindow.xib is really a container for multiple views that you might have within your application, so it's common, and indeed Apple Best Practice, to have additional view controllers (and so .xib files) associated for every view. In our example, we have HellowWorldViewController to manage this view, and we'll reserve our main window for navigation across different views.

- **HelloWorldViewController**: The view controller class is always associated with a view, and this is where the logic for the user interface is implemented. This class completes the model-view-controller design pattern used by the iOS device to implement its GUIs. A view controller itself will contain properties that may be linked to the controls on your interface. For example, you may ask the user to enter text in a text field and wish to store this information somewhere using property getters and setters. You'll see examples of this in the source code we use throughout the book.

For each category, you will find you might have one or more of the following files, with some logically grouped. For example, an Implementation file will normally have an associated header file and vice versa. The key file types are as follows:

- **Header (.h)**: This is the header file that will contain references and interface definitions but not the actual. One reason for having a header file is that if your code references objects and their interfaces for which you don't have the source code, but you do have their implementation in a static library, you would simply include the appropriate header file for the implementation to be resolved at build time.

- **Implementation (.m)**: This is the implementation file, and essentially the same as a .c file in the C programming language or the .cs file in the C# programming language. The implementations for your interfaces and other items are provided within these files and referenced at build time.

- **UI resource file (.xib)**: This is a Mac OS X Interface Builder resource file, represented in XML. It is not a deployable file, but something used in the build of your application to create your executable. It profiles the XML representation of your user interface, and it is loosely coupled to your user-interface logic through the view controller.

In addition to these files, a number of supporting files complete an application. For example, you will find in the \Supporting Files folder a number of core files, including the main module with the starting function main(), which is described in the next section. Also included are references to the required precompiled headers to speed up the build stage of the application.

Initializing Your Application

Every mobile application running on an iOS-based device—the iPhone, iPod touch, or iPod—shares some common characteristics that set an expectation with the user, but also are strengths of the platform that have helped to make it so successful. For example, consider the immediacy of using your device to check your email, view any Facebook updates, or quickly check your current location on Google Maps. You don't need to wait; you simply unlock your device (if required), click the application's icon, and pow—it works!

Such an experience isn't by accident—it's by design, and your application should carefully consider this expectation. It should reflect the same sense of immediacy by not taking too long to launch, having an intuitive and response user interface, and so on.

Let's consider the structure of an iOS application, which will help you understand the roles some of the files created within our Xcode project play in implementing the application.

At the heart of your application is the main event loop, used to interpret events, either as a result of internal events being raised or user stimuli (such as touching the screen). These events are queued, and the queue is processed in a first-in/first-out basis, with each event being dispatched to the most appropriate event handler. In the case of user-interface controls, this is the window in which the user event occurred. The diagram from the iOS Developer Library shown in Figure 2–10 illustrates this perfectly.

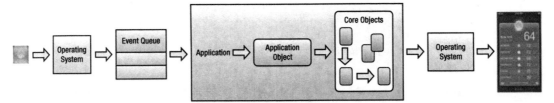

Figure 2–10. *Event processing sequence*

The diagram shows that user input is captured by the operating system framework and passed as a series of events to the application, along with its inherent objects. These objects then react to the events as required and provide the application's functionality.

The entry point for your iOS application is the same as that for any other application based on the C programming language: the main() function. Under the \Supporting Files folder, you will find the main.m implementation file, which contains the main() function, with the following implementation:

```
int main(int argc, char *argv[])
{
    NSAutoreleasePool * pool = [[NSAutoreleasePool alloc] init];
    int retVal = UIApplicationMain(argc, argv, nil, nil);
    [pool release];
    return retVal;
}
```

Let's examine the code it has created and its purpose. The first thing to note is that an object instance called pool is created based on the NSAutoRelease class. This provides the application's top-level memory pool from which objects can be associated and released. Every Cocoa -based application (Cocoa is one of the iOS SDK frameworks) always has an autorelease pool available. If it didn't, memory wouldn't be managed correctly, and your application would leak memory.

The next observation is the UIApplicationMain() function, which passes the argument count (argc) and arguments themselves (argv) to the main() function. The UIApplicationMain() function is used to create and initialize the application's key objects and start the event-processing loop. The application will not return from this function until the application quits. At that point, the pool instance is released itself, and the main function exits, returning the return value passed back from the UIApplicationMain() function.

Creating Your User Interface

In Xcode 3, the Interface Builder capability was implemented as a separate application, but with the release of Xcode 4, Interface Builder is fully integrated within the Xcode 4 IDE, so there is no need to swap applications. There are a few other improvements, especially tighter integration between the Interface Builder objects and source-code generation, which means fewer synchronization issues. This is especially evident in how the .xib files are now managed, or even more advanced features such as Storyboards. For more information about the differences between Xcode versions, see the excellent documentation on the http://developer.apple.com web site, which explain the details to a good standard. In addition, Chapter 10 of this book covers some of the more advanced features of Xcode 4 and iOS 5, such as Storyboards, used to manage the workflow of your application.

Using Interface Builder

Let's borrow the diagram from Apple's own web site, as shown in Figure 2–11. This does an admirable job of showing the different panes within Interface Builder and their purpose.

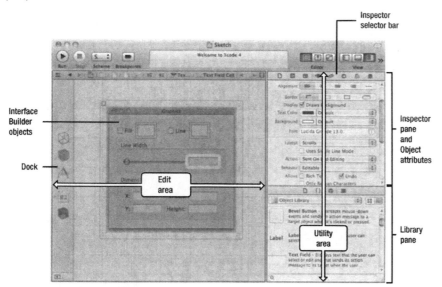

Figure 2–11. *Interface Builder*

The Interface Builder application is split into the following areas:

- **Editor area**: This contains the canvas and other elements that essentially present the graphical view of what your user interface will look like.

- **Inspector pane**: This displays the properties of a given object that is selected within the editor area, in keeping with the inspector chosen. Numerous inspectors provide a view of different properties. For example, the size inspector displays size, position, and related properties.

- **Library pane**: This provides access to a resource library available for you to use within your project. You can use the library selector bar to choose between the different types of resources such as code, objects, and media files.

You have already created your first iPhone application using the project template feature, although it's an empty shell. Some default implementations are provided, but it doesn't do anything functionally useful—yet!

Our application is going to be really simple. It will just display the text "Hello, World" in the middle of the user interface's canvas. So, building on our empty project and the default files, let's construct the rest of our application.

Initializing Your View

Our initial focus is the application delegate, which is responsible for a number of coordinating tasks, including initializing your user interface when the application has finished launching. This involves ensuring that you create an instance of the view, which implements your user interface, adding it to the list of available views within your application. In our case, we have only one view.

To initialize your view, the application delegate needs to be aware of your view class, which is accomplished by including the view controller header file, as follows:

```
#import "HelloWorldViewController.h"
```

The application delegate also ensures that the view is initialized after your application has finished launching. This is easily done by using the `didFinishLaunchingWithOptions()` method. For our example, our project has the following code added:

```
self.window.rootViewController = self.viewController;
[self.window makeKeyAndVisible];
```

The `self.window` reference points to the main `UIWindow` object referenced by the `window` property and automatically initialized by `MainWindow.xib`. When your application starts, this `.xib` file is loaded. Then the view controller and window are unarchived and loaded, mapping the XML key reference to your interface instance variable—in this case, `*viewController`.

The use of a synthesized property ensures that the getters and setters are provided automatically. We're telling our application that the main window for our application should point to the view controller for the view to which we'll be adding our controls.

This method finishes by passing the makeKeyAndVisible message to the window, making the view visible. It will be the main window through which to accept user input.

The application will now execute and display a blank window, so we're getting there. To complete the picture, we want to display the infamous text "Hello, World," well known to application developers across the world as one of the first apps anyone might write!

To display this text, we will place a UILabel object on our canvas and intercept an event that is called after the application has been loaded and the view initialized. This event will be used to set the label text to "Hello, World," which will display it on the screen. (Of course, we could display the text directly onto the canvas of the window using some iOS SDK objects and commands, but that would spoil the fun of later chapters.)

We will begin by adding the UILabel to our view. In Xcode, select the HelloWorldViewController.xib file (our view). This will display a visual representation of our view. From here, we can access the Controls Library to add our label control, as shown in Figure 2–12.

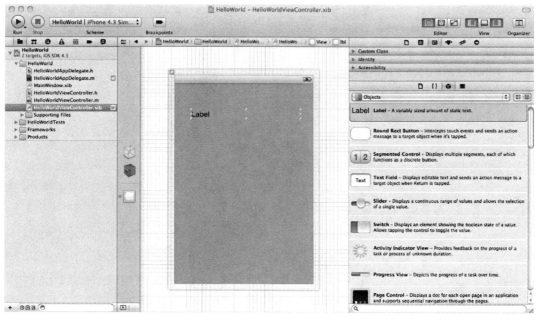

Figure 2–12. *Interface Builder canvas*

> **NOTE:** To match the setup shown in Figure 2–12, make sure that the standard editor view is shown, along with the Object Library utility and Project Navigator. Both of these can be displayed by selecting them from the View menu within Xcode.

You may have noticed that the Library pane can show different library types. You can expand and collapse the sections using the arrow icons. This allows you to navigate the many controls available in the library. For this example, we're using the UILabel control, which is toward the top.

Figure 2–13 shows the Object Library pane. From here, you can drag the label control to the view canvas and drop it into the position you wish.

It will show the default text of the label, which is the value we will change to display the "Hello, World" text.

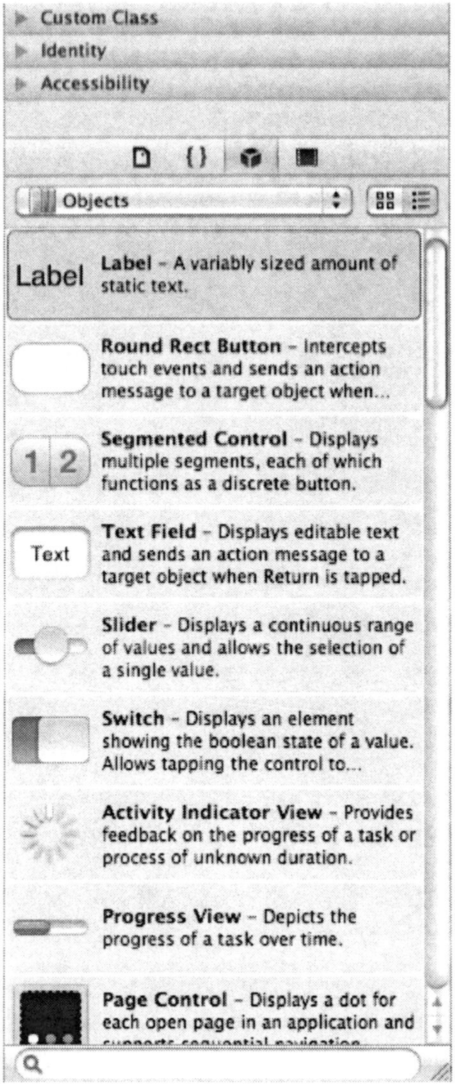

Figure 2–13. *Object Library*

Before we finish, let's change the label's name to something we can reference within our code. Select the Identity tab, and in the Label box, change the label name to lbl, as shown in Figure 2–14.

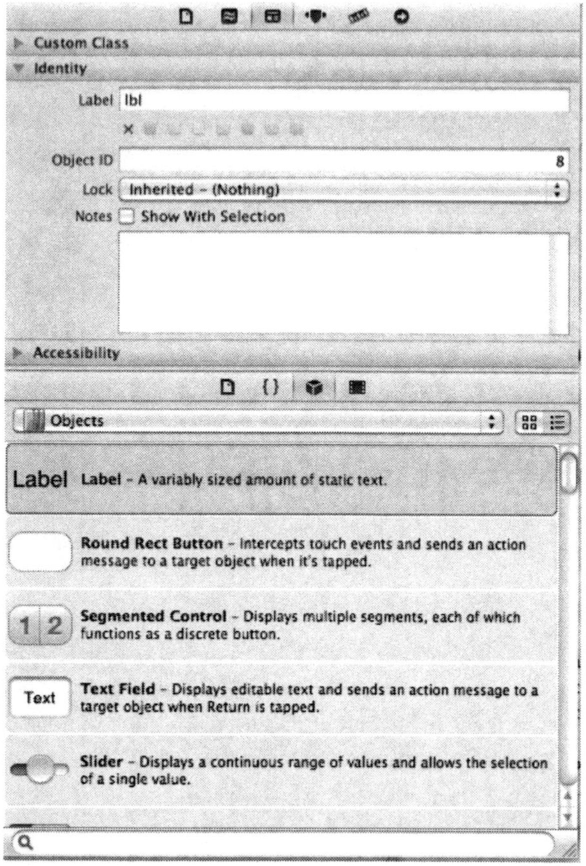

Figure 2–14. *Changing the label control's name*

In addition to adding this label control to our canvas, we need to be able to reference it within our code. To do this, we must bind an object to this control object. In the HellowWorldViewController header file, add a UILabel object reference called label, as follows:

```
UILabel *label;
```

Now let's create a property of the same name to point at the object. We'll make this a synthesized property to ensure that Xcode creates our getters and setters automatically.

```
@property (nonatomic, retain) IBOutlet UILabel *label;
```

Note the IBOutlet markup in this property definition. This acts as a marker for Interface Builder to identify properties, which can be linked to user interface elements, and Interface Builder will use these elements to display in the Outlets pane. So, our HellowWorldViewController.h file should now have the following implementation:

```
#import <UIKit/UIKit.h>

@interface HelloWorldViewController : UIViewController {

    UILabel *label;
}

@property (nonatomic, retain) IBOutlet UILabel *label;

@end
```

Of course, this isn't enough. We've simply provided the code for our header and defined our intent. Now we need to add the actual implementation in the HelloWorldViewController implementation file. We start by completing our property and ensuring that it is synthesized with the following line of code after the @implementation tag:

```
@synthesize label;
```

We also need to ensure that when our view controller object is removed from memory, we deallocate the memory taken up by the label. This is achieved by sending the release message to the label object. Your dealloc method should look like the following (with our new line highlighted):

```
- (void)dealloc
{
    [label release];
    [super dealloc];
}
```

Finally, we want to set the label's value to the text "Hello, World." A convenient event in which to do this is viewDidLoad, which is fired after the application has been initialized and the view loaded, but before it's displayed. We need to add a line of code to set the label's value in our viewDidLoad method. After the comments around it are removed, your code should look as follows (with the new line highlighted):

```
- (void)viewDidLoad
{
    label.text = @"Hello, World";
    [super viewDidLoad];
}
```

If you built your application now and ran it, it would work, but the label's text wouldn't change. Why?

We've defined our internal UILabel object called label, created a property to reference it by, and even set this property's text value to "Hello, World." But we have not yet associated the label on our user interface with our classes object. So it works, but it isn't pointing to our visible label.

This is easily fixed (in fact, even more easily fixed in Xcode 4 and the new Interface Builder than previous versions). You simply need to associate the two together graphically by dragging the outlet for the control to the actual control on the canvas, as shown in Figure 2–15.

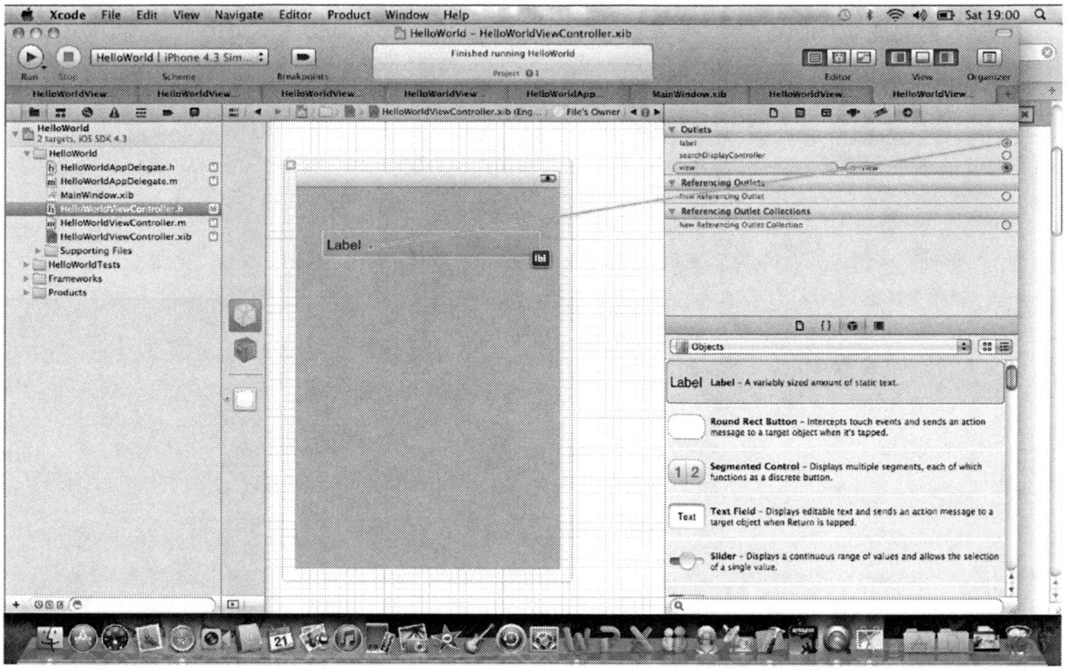

Figure 2–15. *Linking UI elements to your code*

This completes our application. We are safe in the knowledge that not only does it display the required text, but it is also behaving as a "good citizen" by releasing memory and object references when they are no longer required.

Let's build and run the application by using the ⌘R hotkey, which will launch the iPhone simulator to test it. It should compile without any problems, and the iPhone simulator should start with your new iPhone application running in it, as shown in Figure 2–16.

OK, so it's not going to make your rich if submitted to the App Store, since it doesn't do much. But what it does do is cover the basic principles of writing an iPhone application. This will provide a great foundation for upcoming chapters in the book, where you'll discover more about creating iOS applications with different tools and technologies.

Figure 2–16. *Running your first iPhone application*

Using Automatic Reference Counting

The example presented in this chapter has taken the traditional approach to memory management and has left the onus on the programmer to retain and release (or autorelease) the objects and the memory they consume. Xcode 4.2 and iOS 5 offer a new feature called *automatic reference counting* (ARC), which simplifies memory management.

Instead of you having to remember when to use retain, release, and autorelease, ARC evaluates the lifetime requirements of your objects and automatically inserts the appropriate method calls for you at compile time. The compiler also generates the appropriate dealloc methods to free up memory that is no longer required. Essentially, ARC is a precompilation stage that adds the necessary code you previously would have had to insert manually.

Why Use It?

If you're new to Objective-C, you will welcome ARC, because it greatly simplifies memory management. There is more than enough to learn without worrying about the complexities of memory management.

However, if you are comfortable with self-memory management, perhaps from experience in lower-level languages such as C or C++, then you might want to stick with it. One reason is that libraries that have yet to be converted to using ARC don't always play well with ARC-based code. In addition, manually managing memory, providing you know what you're doing, can be more performant.

Enabling ARC

To enable ARC, you must either choose it when you first create your project or add the appropriate compiler flag found by setting the value Objective-C Automatic Reference Counting in the compiler's build settings. It is possible to selectively choose which files use the ARC compiler features through the Compile Sources section under the project's Build Phases tab, although I don't recommend it unless you want to highly tune your application's performance.

Migrating to ARC

If you already have projects, or source code, you want to convert to using ARC but don't want to trawl through the source code removing all the memory management keyword references, then thankfully Xcode provides a migration tool to do the conversion for you. Open your project for conversion, select Edit ➤ Refactor, and then choose the Convert to Objective-C ARC... option. This will refactor (convert) your code so that it uses ARC features. Easy!

Programming with ARC

Once you've switched on ARC, you must follow certain rules. The rules can get quite complex, but the Apple documentation does a good job of explaining them. In summary, either you use ARC or you don't; you can mix flavors of memory management. For example, don't switch on ARC and then start to sporadically `retain` or `dealloc` memory. You can defined whether your property is strongly or weakly typed. `strong` (the default) is a reference that is retained for the lifetime of its scope (typically defined as the curly braces), and `weak` means it can be released at any time when no longer considered as used (and set to `nil` when released).

Summary

In this chapter, we began by taking a look at the requirements for running Xcode 4, by far the easiest method for developing iOS applications. We considered what kind of hardware you might need, and then proceeded to explore how to obtain and install the Xcode suite of applications.

Next, the chapter provided an overview of the Xcode suite and a primer in Objective-C, covering the basic tenets you should know for developing your first iPhone application. We even looked at some of the more recent features such as Automatic Reference Counting.

We then built an iPhone application. We used Xcode's project templates to get a head start. We also used some of Xcode's new features to link user interface components to code objects. Once everything was wired up together, we were able to build the application and test it within the iPhone simulator.

Phew! Now you're an iOS application developer using Apple's native tools such as the iOS SDK and Xcode 4. In the next chapters, you'll discover that this isn't the only development option. Now that you have a foundation in writing basic applications, we'll proceed to develop more functionally rich applications using some of the other options available.

Chapter 3

Understand Your Options: Using Third-Party Solutions and MonoTouch

In previous chapters, we've looked at the iOS operating system, the SDK and associated tools, and how you can use Xcode 4 with the iOS SDK to develop your first iPhone application. But as described in Chapter 1, options other than Apple's native tools are available for developing applications. This chapter elaborates on some of the third-party options introduced in Chapter 1 and describes how to create the Hello, World application using them.

We won't cover all of the third-party options available, not least because of space considerations, but also because it's a constantly changing environment, with new options being introduced all the time. In this chapter, we'll focus on some of the more common and longer-standing options:

- Using the .NET Framework with MonoTouch
- Using JavaScript with Appcelerator's Titanium Studio and Mobile SDK
- Using Xcode with the Marmalade SDK

After you've become comfortable with developing our Hello, World application using each of the options covered in this chapter, we can then look at different elements of the iOS and a more advanced application in more detail in the remainder of the book.

Understanding the Constraints

Before we get started with the third-party options, it's worth understanding some principle constraints:

▓ **Native apps require a Mac**: To write and execute native iOS applications, you will need a Mac.

▓ **SDK completeness**: Third-party options such as Mono provide a layer on top of the existing iOS SDK, but often have not gotten around to implementing *all* of its functionality. So if you want to have a complete implementation of the API, you need to either work around gaps in a third-party's implementation or attempt to write your own implementation.

▓ **Speed**: If you want to fully exploit the power of your iOS device, there is no substitute for writing your application in Objective-C directly on top of the SDK. While other options work, they introduce layers of abstraction that will slow down your application.

Having painted a relatively bleak picture of the third-party options, it is important to point out that some are extremely viable. This is especially true of the Mono implementation, which offers the most complete implementation of the iOS SDK's API in a familiar language. Speed is typically not an issue.

Developing with Mono and MonoTouch

You should know by now that the focus of this book is to support you in developing applications for Apple's mobile devices using a variety of methods, but with an emphasis on reusing your existing .NET knowledge and skills.

The success of the .NET Framework on the Microsoft Windows operating system didn't go unnoticed within the open source community. There are many who wished that .NET was available for not only Windows, but also for other operating systems, such as Linux and Mac OS X. Thankfully, someone did something about this. Miguel de Icaza took it upon himself, and then with community support, to bring .NET to these operating systems, allowing you write .NET applications for a multitude of platforms. And it didn't stop there. Soon the SharpDevelop IDE was ported to Mono, and MonoDevelop was formed, creating a Visual Studio-type IDE that is able to target not only .NET applications, but also C, C++, Python, and Java.

So, you have the .NET Framework, support for .NET languages such as C#, and a powerful IDE, and it was only logical for the mobile revolution to be supported! In fact, they went further. Not only was MonoTouch introduced, providing a mechanism to create C#- and .NET-based applications for the iPhone, but they also introduced MonoMac. MonoMac is an interesting development for creating Cocoa applications on Mac OS X using Mono. (For more information, visit http://www.mono-project.com/MonoMac.) MonoDroid has also been released, based on the same principles as MonoTouch but to target the Android operating system.

Enough of MonoMac and MonoDroid; let's look at MonoTouch. As stated, it allows you to use Mono to develop applications for the iPhone, iPad, and iPod touch with the API bindings to the iOS APIs.

Given that it's based on the .NET Framework and supports the C# programming language, you .NET guys and girls should be right at home! Let's take a look at obtaining, installing, and using the necessary components to write our Hello, World iPhone app using the Mono tools.

Installing Mono, MonoDevelop, and MonoTouch

To get started, you'll need to download and install the following components. These components can be accessed from the Mono projects home page (http://www.mono-project.com/).

- **Mono**: This is the actual Mono framework. It includes the open source implementation of the .NET Framework, language support, and supporting tools. You can download Mono from http://www.go-mono.com/mono-downloads/download.html.

- **MonoDevelop**: This is the IDE primarily designed for .NET and its languages such as C#. We'll be using this in the same way as we used Xcode in the previous chapter, or indeed, as you would probably use Visual Studio to help build your applications. You can download MonoDevelop from http://monodevelop.com/Download.

- **MonoTouch**: This is where the magic happens. MonoTouch is an SDK for developing applications for the iPhone using Mono. Using it, you will be able to write applications and test them on the iPhone simulator. You can download the trial version or purchase the full version from http://monotouch.net/Store.

Installing Mono

First, start by visiting the Mono project download page and downloading the Mono distribution appropriate for the platform on which you're developing. We'll be running Mono on the Mac OS X platform, as this is a requirement for developing iOS-based applications, but as you'll notice, Windows and a number of Linux and Unix distributions are also supported. Also notice that Mono conveniently separates the download options into both stable and long-term supported versions. The difference is essentially that the latest and greatest features are in the latest stable version.

> **NOTE:** At the time of writing, the latest stable version is 2.10.5 and requires either Mac OS X Leopard (10.5) , Snow Leopard (10.6) and Lion (10.7).

At the Mono downloads page, shown in Figure 3–1, select your platform and choose the SDK package appropriate for your chipset (for example, Intel or PowerPC) or choose the Universal option if you're unsure.

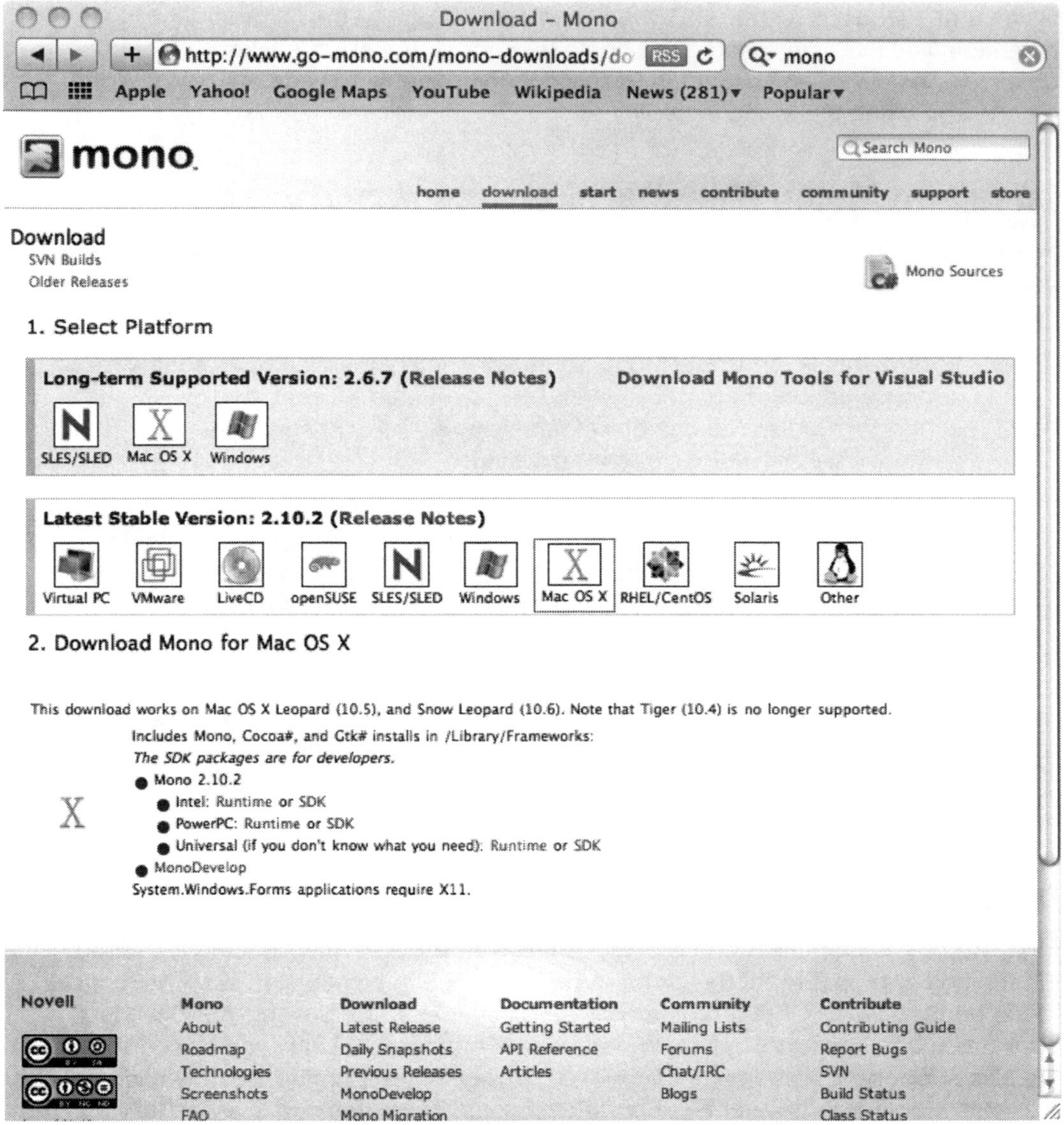

Figure 3–1. *Selecting a Mono SDK package from the Downloads page*

You'll notice options for both the runtime and the SDK. The runtime is used if you simply want to execute applications written for Mono, and the SDK is used if you want to execute applications and also write your own apps using the Mono API. It includes both the runtime and SDK development platform.

Once downloaded, clicking the icon in your downloads folder will start the installation, as shown in Figure 3–2.

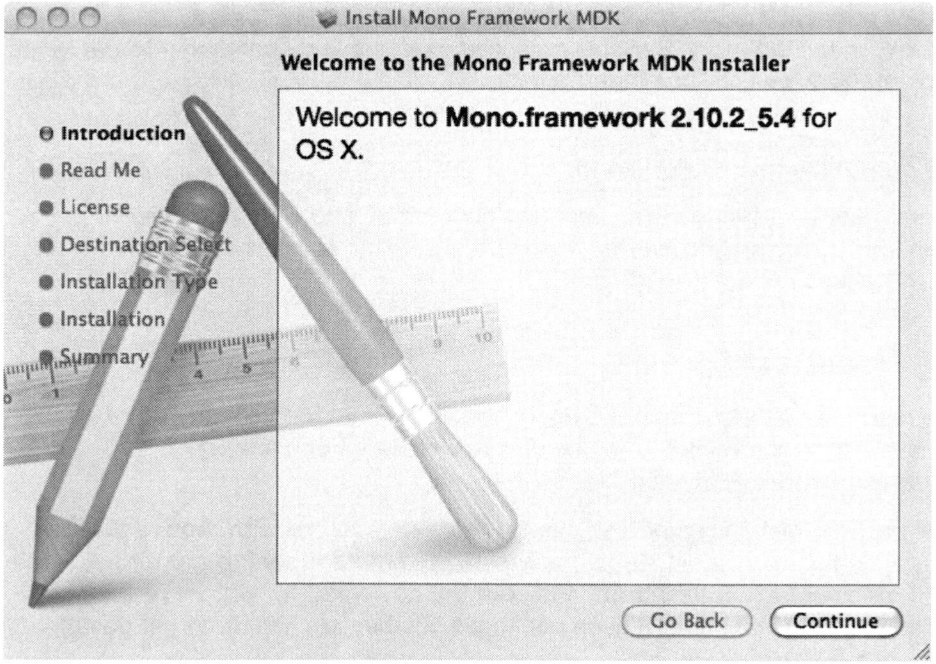

Figure 3–2. *Mono framework installation startup screen*

Follow the on-screen instructions to complete the installation. The software is not that large, and the installation should complete pretty quickly. After it's installed, you won't see any obvious desktop or toolbar icons.

Let's test the installation. We will create a console version of the Hello, World app and use the command line and a terminal window to do this (on the Mac).

Start by creating a folder to contain your source code and create a single file named HelloWorld.cs, with the following source code:

```
using System;

public class HelloWorld
{
        static public void Main ()
        {
                Console.WriteLine("Hello, World");
        }
}
```

This code's construct should be immediately obvious to any .NET developer. We are simply writing a text string out to the control that will display the text.

After this example is written to disk, you can attempt a compilation using the Mono compiler. While in the same directory as your source code, simply enter the following command at the command prompt:

```
gmcs HelloWorld.cs
```

If no errors are present, this will compile your source code silently, leaving
`HelloWorld.exe` in the directory. Run this compiled executable by sending it to the Mono
runtime (indicated by the mono command prefix):

`mono HelloWorld.exe`

This should output the text "Hello, World."

If all of this worked, your Mono installation was successful, and we can move on to
installing the MonoDevelop application. If it didn't, the mono support or community
pages should help you find a resolution.

Installing MonoDevelop

Now you're ready to download MonoDevelop. Make sure that the version you're
downloading matches the version of Mono you've installed. For example,
MonoDevelop 2.4.2 requires at least Mono 2.4 to run.

At the home page, shown in Figure 3–3, select the version you require. Again, the
choices usually include the latest stable release and the more recent, but unproven, beta
release. Choose the Mac OS X platform and start the download for whichever
installation mechanism you prefer (I used packages, as they are simple to get going).

Figure 3–3. *MonoDevelop home page*

After you've downloaded MonoDevelop, click the disk image. You will be prompted to complete the installation by dragging MonoDevelop to your `Applications` folder, as shown in Figure 3–4. This will complete your installation.

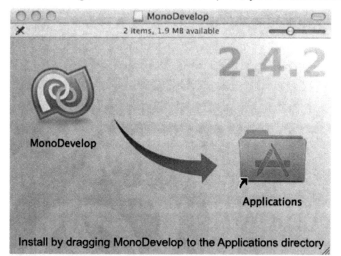

Figure 3–4. *MonoDevelop package installation*

Clicking the newly installed icon will launch the MonoDevelop application. This launches the MonoDevelop IDE, as shown in Figure 3–5.

NOTE: The installer may suggest that further MonoDevelop updates exist. If this is the case, installing them is optional, but if they are marked as stable, I recommend that you do so.

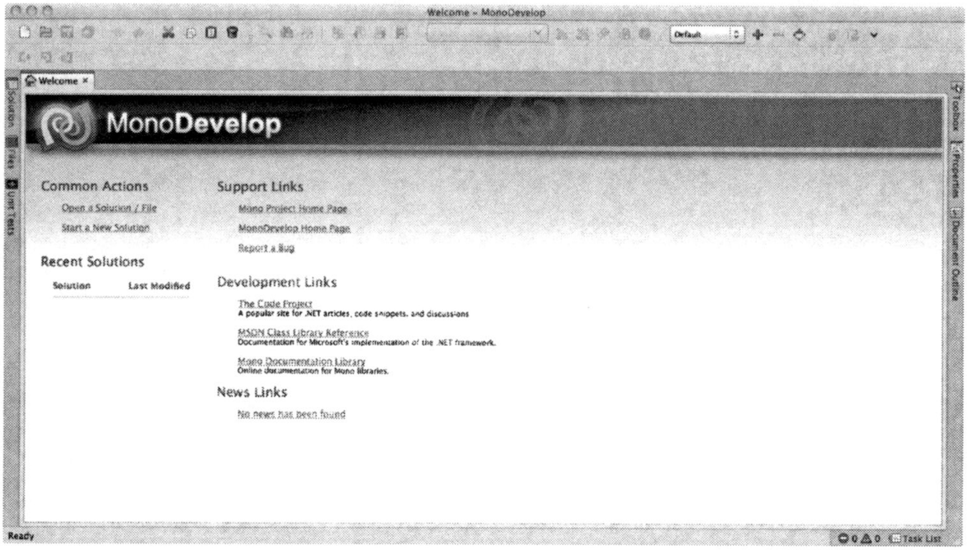

Figure 3–5. *Running MonoDevelop*

I recommend that you explore the application, taking a look at some of the links available. After you've done this, we can quickly create a console application similar to the one we used to test the Mono installation.

Start by selecting the Start a New Solution link, which will present you with a Project Template dialog box, in which you'll notice a C# Console project. Follow the on-screen instructions to create your project, selecting the location of your project and giving it a name. You'll be presented with an empty project and a default `main.cs` file with an implementation of Hello, World very similar to ours. Simply choose **Build ➤ Run**, and a terminal window will be displayed showing the text "Hello, World."

Now wasn't that easier!

Installing MonoTouch

Finally, to complete the "Mono trilogy," we'll look at how to obtain and install MonoTouch. The first thing to note is that MonoTouch is not free. Depending the version you require, it can cost anything from $99 to $3,999! Consider the chart in Figure 3–6, taken from the MonoTouch web site, which details the different features and the associated prices.

Compare Editions

Close this window

	Professional	Enterprise	Enterprise Priority
Deploy to your devices	✓	✓	✓
Publish to app stores	✓	✓	✓
Enterprise distribution		✓	✓
Priority support queue			✓
Guaranteed response time			✓
License expiration	Never	Never	Never
Update subscription	1 Year	1 Year	1 Year
License usage	Original User	Seat	Seat
Price (USD)	$399	$999	$2,499

Figure 3–6. MonoTouch version feature comparison

The key takeaway point here is that for you to use MonoTouch to create applications that are distributable via Apple's App Store, you need the Professional edition, which costs $399. A Student edition also is available, at a cost of $79. This edition allows you to create applications, but distribution onto Apple devices is possible only via ad hoc deployment—not the App Store." We'll discuss distributing your applications in Chapter 9.

For the moment, let's start with the trial version, which doesn't cost anything. Although it doesn't allow distribution via the App Store, it does permit you to test your application on the iPhone/iPad simulator. Visit http://monotouch.net/DownloadTrial, enter your email address, and click the Download button to obtain the trial version.

Start the installation by clicking the downloaded package. This will launch the installer, as shown in Figure 3–7. Follow the installation instructions. When installation is complete, the installer should take you to a web page containing the release notes for the version of MonoTouch just installed.

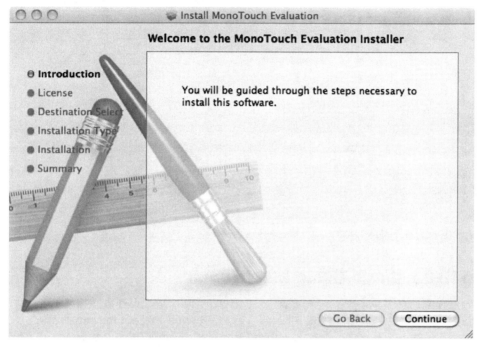

Figure 3–7. *Running the MonoTouch installer*

You can start to use MonoTouch immediately, but this requires that you use the command-line functions to ensure that the applications you develop are built against the MonoTouch licenses. If you prefer to use MonoDevelop, that is possible. However, you'll notice that within the version of MonoDevelop we installed, there are no such MonoTouch templates. At the time of writing, you will need to download and install a special version of MonoDevelop, updated to recognize the MonoTouch SDK. This is available from http://monodevelop.com/Download/Mac_MonoTouch. After it's downloaded and selected for installation, installing it follows a similar process to the installation of the other version of MonoDevelop you installed previously. You simply need to drag the new version onto your Applications folder, and after being prompted to replace the version you have, the new version of MonoDevelop will be installed.

Start MonoDevelop and choose Start a New Solution as before. This time, when you expand either the C# or VBNet projects, you will notice options for the iPhone and iPad projects of different types, as shown in Figure 3–8.

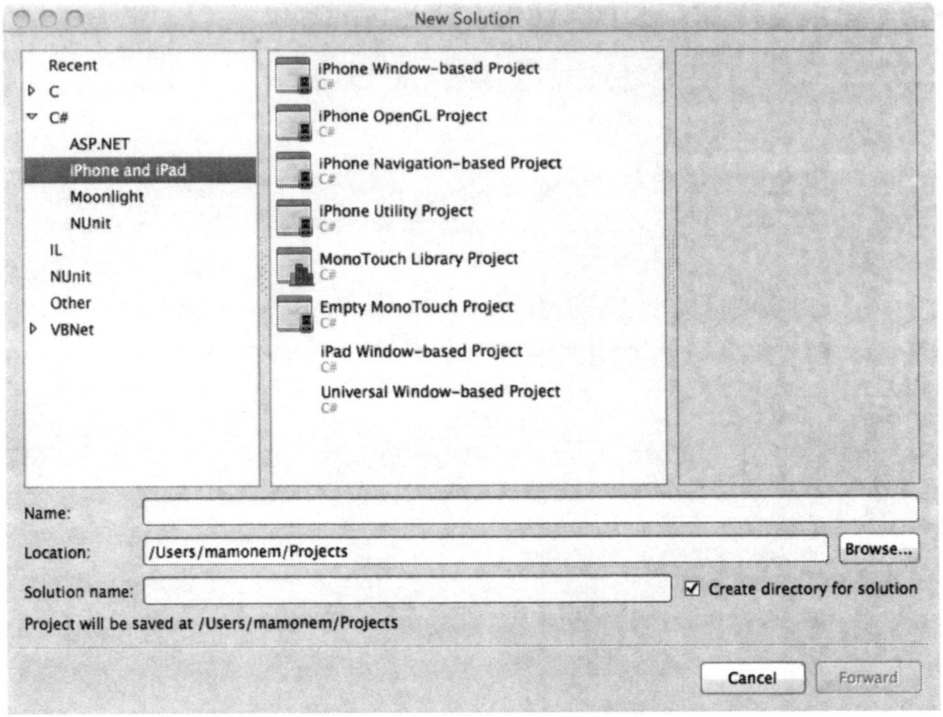

Figure 3–8. *MonoDevelop with MonoTouch project templates added*

Creating Hello, World Using MonoTouch

Let's build our Hello, World application. Just as you did when we used Xcode 4 in the previous chapter, start by selecting the iPhone Window-based Project and enter the name and location as you prefer. After you select Forward, a project with the default files and implementation for an iPhone Windows-based project will be created, as shown in Figure 3–9.

Figure 3–9. *Default iPhone Windows-based application in MonoDevelop*

A quick inspection will show some similarities to the Xcode project we created in Chapter 2. Both have a main.cs file with an AppDelegate instance created, making the default window key and visible. This shouldn't surprise you. It's using the Cocoa API, but with a .NET implementation.

Go ahead and build and run this application. It's not as fast as Xcode, but then again, it wouldn't be given the additional levels of abstraction. Your application will eventually launch in the iPhone simulator. Although it's a blank window (at the moment), it's your first iPhone app in .NET!

In keeping with our Xcode example, let's add a specific view and associated view controller to display our label and allow us to initialize it with the text "Hello, World." The key difference is that in this instance, we'll being working in .NET.

Thankfully, adding a view and view controller to our project is really easy in MonoDevelop. With the project selected, select the **File ➤ New ➤ File** menu option to open the New File dialog. Expand the C# tree, and then select iPad View with Controller, as shown in Figure 3–10. Then choose New to add these files to your project, again with a default structure and implementation for you to complete.

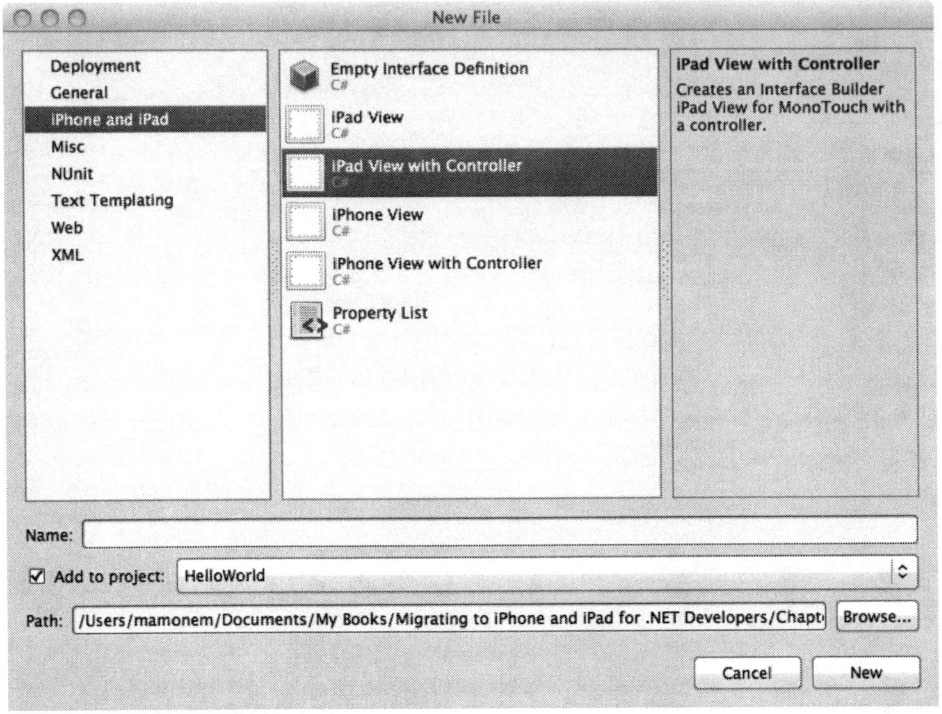

Figure 3–10. *MonoDevelop New File dialog*

As you did in the Xcode example, select the `HellowWorldView.xib` file. This will launch Interface Builder. Continue to add a label and hook it up as an outlet, as per the Xcode 4 example in the previous chapter.

Now we can set the text value. Once our code is hooked up, we can simply override the `ViewDidLoad()` method of the `ViewController` class, and within this, access the label user object by name, like so:

```
public override void ViewDidLoad ()
{
        base.ViewDidLoad();
        lbl.Text = @"Hello, World";
}
```

If you now run the application, your MonoTouch-based iPhone app will behave exactly the same as your Xcode 4 iPhone app, and display "Hello, World" on the device.

We've taken a look at how to install and create applications—including our now infamous Hello, World application—running on an iPhone (well, the simulator) using MonoTouch. But there are many more options available. In the rest of the chapter, we'll concentrate on how to create the same test application with a couple of the more stable and popular options available, using languages other than Objective-C and .NET that might be familiar to you, and in some cases, even running on a Microsoft Windows-based PC.

Using Appcelerator's Titanium Mobile

The Appcelerator Titanium Mobile platform was created to support the cross-platform development of native applications for mobile, tablet, and desktop devices using languages that are perhaps more common and leveraging the JavaScript-based API. The Titanium Mobile SDK works with the native SDK toolchains (in Apple's case, the iOS SDK) to combine your JavaScript source code, a JavaScript interpreter, and your static assets into an application executable that can be installed on an emulator or mobile device.

Note that, due to Apple's licensing agreement, Titanium Mobile has restrictions on which platforms can be used to target which mobile devices and operating systems. Table 3–1 summarizes the support options.

Table 3–1. *Titanium Mobile Operating System Support Options*

Operating System	Android Development	iOS Development
Mac OS X	Yes	Yes
Windows	Yes	No
Linux Ubuntu	Yes	No

Despite these restrictions, it is worth noting that it's free to get started, and we'll be focusing on the Mac OS X operating system. As with our MonoTouch example, we'll install Titanium Mobile and then use it to create our Hello, World iPhone application. The difference is that this time, we'll be writing our code in JavaScript.

Installing Titanium

The first step is to download the required software from the Appcelerator's Titanium home page at http://www.appcelerator.com/products/download/. After it's downloaded, install the application in the traditional Mac manner by dragging the Titanium Developer icon onto your Applications folder, which will invoke its installation. Follow the on-screen instructions provided by the installer, as shown in Figure 3–11.

> **NOTE:** Titanium Developer is the overarching GUI, which sits across the various SDKs that exist and acts as your single reference point. Once Titanium Developer is installed, the different mobile SDKs are installed within it. The first time it is run, it will automatically attempt to download the current versions of the Mobile and Desktop SDKs.

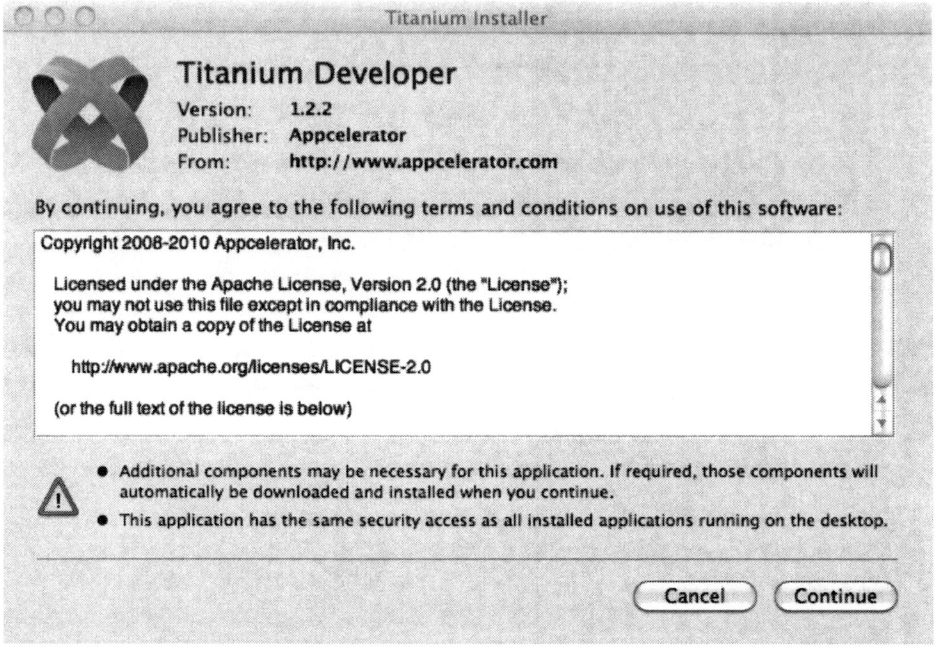

Figure 3–11. *Titanium Developer installer*

After you've installed Titanium, it is also worth registering as a Titanium developer, as this will grant you access to online resources to help you when developing your application.

Creating Hello, World Using Titanium

Start up the Titanium Desktop and allow it to update the Mobile SDK. Then you'll be presented with an empty GUI. The iOS SDK was automatically detected by the installation, so there was no need to install that package (unless you want to use a more current version). Let's get cracking.

Start by choosing the New Project option. This will present you with a dialog with some standard project properties to fill in, as shown in Figure 3–12. When completing the on-screen form, you may notice that under the Project Type drop-down list, the iPhone option uses the Mobile project type, whereas there is a specific option for the iPad. Once you've completed the form, choose the Create Project option to create the Mobile application.

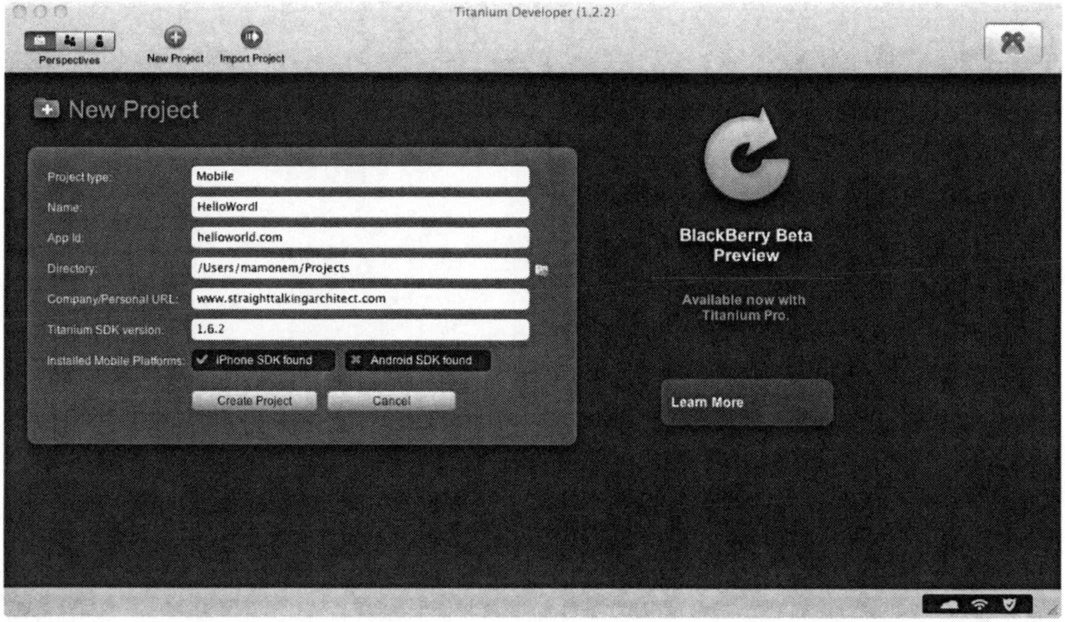

Figure 3–12. *Titanium Mobile New Project dialog*

NOTE: Notice that on my installation, I chose not to install the Android SDK. If you want to give that a try, the online resources provide you with instructions on how to do so.

The blank HelloWorld project will be shown, with options to visit the Dashboard, Edit, or Test & Package your application. On the Dashboard, you'll see a number of online resources to help you get started, as shown in Figure 3–13.

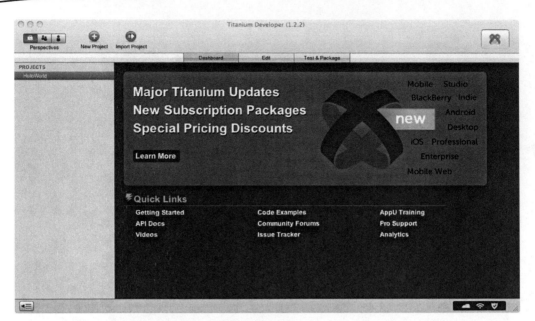

Figure 3–13. *Empty project Dashboard in Titanium Mobile*

If you jump straight to the Test & Package option tab, you'll see the screen shown in Figure 3–14. One of the options is the Launch button, which will build and run your application within the mobile device simulator matching the project type chosen, which is the iPhone simulator in our example.

Figure 3–14. *Test & Package tab in Titanium Mobile*

The default application generated by Titanium Mobile provides two tabs with a text label on each tab. We will modify this to show only one tab with our chosen text ("Hello, World") on it.

First, let's take a look at the folder structure and files created. In addition to the files created, the following folders were added:

- **\build**: This folder contains the files imported from the SDK and automatically generated files that typically are not modified, such as the main.m file. The binaries and libraries are also located here.

- **\resources**: This folder contains the resources that support your application, including source code. Here, you will find the app.js file, the main JavaScript application file used to start your application. We will make our modifications in this file.

Take a little time to examine the app.js file. It's pretty straightforward. As noted, the default implementation is to create two tabs, each containing a label, and add these to the main application window, and we're going to adjust this to display just the one tab and label.

Let's examine some of the highlights of the code. First, the most obvious thing to note is that an initial reference is made to the Titanium.UI namespace. This namespace contains the classes that provide access to the user-interface objects. It uses this information to initially set the background and also to create a tab group, as follows:

```
var tabGroup = Titanium.UI.createTabGroup();
```

The new Tab objects will be added to this group, with each Tab pointing to a window that will be displayed when chosen (although our code will implement only a single tab to show the "Hello, World" text). Consider the following code:

```
//
// create base UI tab and root window
//
var win1 = Titanium.UI.createWindow({
    title:'Tab 1',
    backgroundColor:'#fff'
});
var tab1 = Titanium.UI.createTab({
    icon:'KS_nav_views.png',
    title:'Tab 1',
    window:win1
});
```

This creates the main window and assigns it the caption of Tab 1, using a Tab object to which this window is assigned. When selected in the application, this tab will display this window.

Let's skip to the code that creates the new label, after creating a new window and assigning this to the new tab. Consider the following segment:

```
var label1 = Titanium.UI.createLabel({
      color:'#999',
      text:'Hello, World',
      font:{fontSize:20,fontFamily:'Helvetica Neue'},
```

```
            textAlign:'center',
            width:'auto'
});
```

```
win1.add(label1);
```

We simply create a label object and assign it the "Hello, World" text. We can then add this to the main window, referenced by the win1 variable.

Finally, we add our tab to the tab group and open the tab group, displaying the window and our tabs on the main application.

```
//
//  add tabs
//
tabGroup.addTab(tab1);


// open tab group
tabGroup.open();
```

In carrying out these actions, the application will also display our "Hello, World" text. And since it's built within the Titanium Developer IDE, it will also launch the iPhone simulator, as shown in our running application in Figure 3–15.

Figure 3–15. *Titanium Mobile HelloWorld application*

As you can see, the Titanium IDE is easy to work with and has a complete API. I'll leave further discovery for you to try out with the help of the online reference material and the Kitchen Sink application, which provides out-of-the-box examples to examine and modify.

Using the Marmalade SDK

The Marmalade SDK has the same goal as Titanium Mobile, which is to enable you to build your application against an API that is agnostic of the mobile device and its operating system. With it, you can develop cross-platform applications in a single hit!

The Marmalade SDK supports single-click deployment to a number of operating systems, including iOS, Android, Symbian, Windows Mobile, and more. We'll be using the Xcode IDE to create our Marmalade-based application.

> **NOTE:** While the Marmalade API supports core features for all types of applications, it has a bias toward games development. You will find a rich set of APIs that enable you to write compelling mobile games.

The Marmalade SDK can be thought of as the following two components:

- **Marmalade System**: This provides the operating system abstraction API, which when used with the associated libraries, allows you to build mobile applications for a variety of operating systems. It provides a suite of tools and the C API called the S3E API.

- **Marmalade Studio**: This provides a suite of tools and runtime components to allow a focused development on high-performance 2D and 3D graphics and animations.

Installing Marmalade

To start, you will need to register at the Marmalade SDK web site (http://www.madewithmarmalade.com/downloads). Once registration is complete, you will be sent an activation email message. After you've activated your account, you'll be able to download an evaluation copy of the software to try out. (Of course, you could purchase a copy, but I'm assuming you want to try it out first.) The evaluation version allows you to do everything apart from publicly distribute the applications you have written.

After you've downloaded the package, start the installation by selecting the icon. You will be presented with the installer, as shown in Figure 3–16.

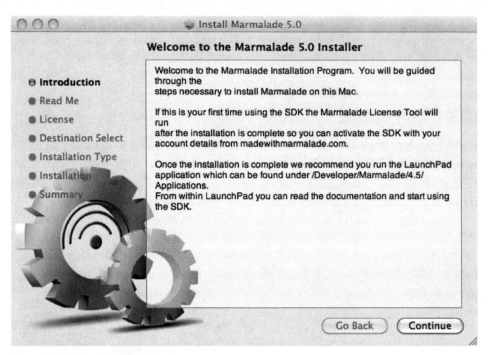

Figure 3–16. *Marmalade installer*

Follow the on-screen instructions, including entering your Marmalade account credentials in order to install under the 30-day evaluation license, which you obtained previously on the web site.

The default installation location is /Developer/Marmalade-SDK/<version>, where <version> is the version of the SDK you installed. After installation, you won't see any new icons, but you will find new files installed in the target location. The following are the key folders installed:

- **\Applications**: This folder contains the SDK's top-level applications.

- **\docs**: This folder contains documentation, including user manuals.

- **\examples**: This folder contains example applications.

- **\extensions**: This folder contains the Extensions Development Kit.

- **\Marmalade**: This folder contains additional tools used by Marmalade.

- **\s3e**: This folder contains the Marmalade System header files and runtime libraries.

- **\modules**: This folder contains all Marmalade Studio header files and runtime libraries.

Creating Hello, World Using Marmalade

Now that you've installed Marmalade, and perhaps had a look around its folders and the files, let's create our application.

Start by firing up Xcode (we could, of course, use the command line, but IDEs were invented to make our lives easier, so let's use them). We will use one of the examples provided, as they supply all the configuration necessary for Xcode 4 to deploy to the Marmalade simulator. This simulator is the tool used to debug native Marmalade executable files (with an .s3e extension).

The .s3e files are essentially dynamic-link libraries that are platform-agnostic. The Marmalade SDK allows you to build the same application for a number of different platforms, simply by reconfiguring the IDE. For the moment, we'll stick with deploying it to the Marmalade simulator, as we're just interested in how you might get started with such a feature.

Using the Finder application, locate the Hello, World example, which is under \examples\s3e\s3eHelloWord. In this folder, you will see the s3dHelloWorld.mkb file, which is essentially the project file. Open it by choosing **Open With** from the menu and selecting the **Mkb** application provided within the Marmalade SDK (in the \Applications folder), as shown in Figure 3–17.

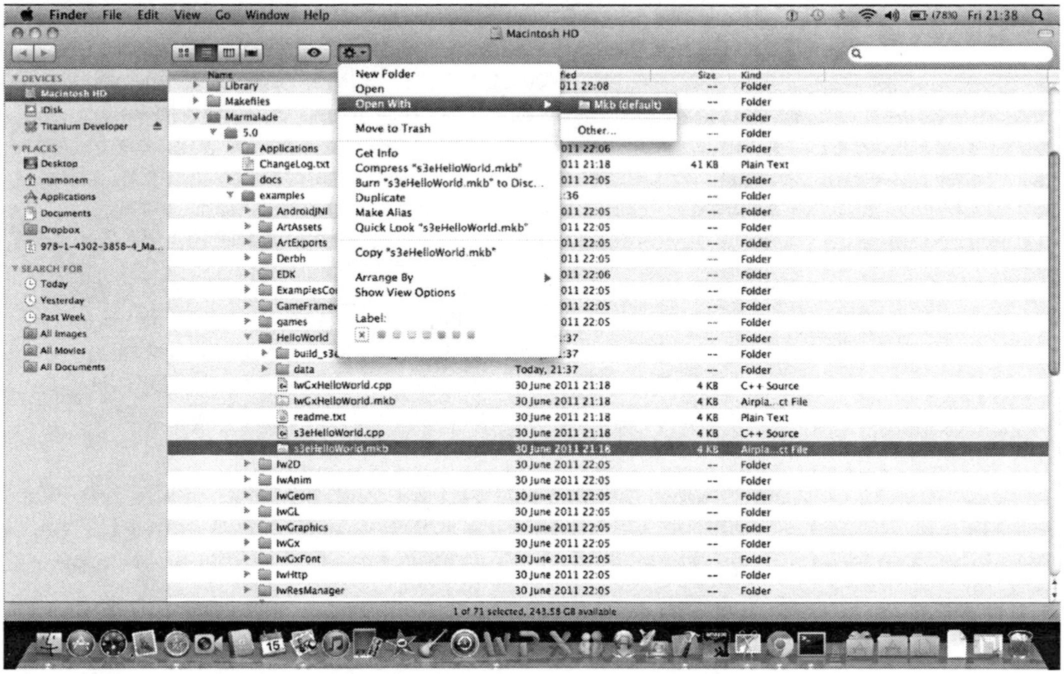

Figure 3–17. *Opening a Marmalade SDK project using Mkb*

This will launch Xcode, from which can choose the Debug Simulator option scheme from the top of the window, and then choose Build. Next, choose Run. This executes the application within the simulator, displaying our "Hello, World" text, as shown in Figure 3–18. From here, you can use the Marmalade SDK to target different platforms, including the iOS, to develop your apps.

Figure 3–18. *Marmalade simulator running our application*

Summary

This chapter built on the knowledge you have gained about using native tools in previous chapters by looking at the available third-party options. One of the most popular alternatives is Mono and MonoTouch, providing a .NET implementation of the Cocoa and Cocoa Touch APIs, but in the .NET language. This option provides you free and native-feeling access to iPhone and iPad development resources, complete with a Visual Studio-like IDE in the form of MonoDevelop.

As you learned, MonoTouch is not the only option, provided that you're happy to use languages other than .NET, such as JavaScript or C/C++. Other options available to you include Titanium Mobile and the Marmalade SDK. Each of these options allows you to write native applications, not only for the iPhone and iPad, but also for other devices. In fact, these platforms are built specifically to target cross-platform development, allowing you to develop against a single API but build applications that can target numerous mobile devices with different operating systems, including Apple, Android, and Symbian.

As useful as these third-party options are, apart from MonoTouch, the lack of support for the .NET language makes it more difficult to make the transition and reuse your experience. Clearly, the use of MonoTouch makes this far easier, but you will be dependent on the support MonoTouch has for the iOS and Cocoa Touch SDKs. If support is not provided, or features are incomplete, you will not be able to use this option—unless you write your own implementation!

So, apart from contributing toward the Mono project yourself, the other option is to map your C# and .NET Framework knowledge onto the iOS SDK and use Objective-C. The rest of the book will focus on doing just that and bridging the gap in your knowledge.

Chapter 4

Going Deeper: .NET, Objective-C, and the iOS SDK

Understanding the capabilities of Apple's mobile devices, the features of the iOS operating system, and the different options available to you for application development is only part of the story. Creating the Hello, World application using both native Apple development tools and numerous third-party options was cool, and the submission of it to Apple's App Store is possible, but it's not going to earn you million of dollars. It is very unlikely to attract good reviews, or even any downloads!

Now we need to look at how to create a more compelling application—one that will be the next "must-have" mobile app that *will* help you make some money. To do this, we need to explore the runtime frameworks in more detail, and the supporting design-time frameworks in even more detail. This will help you to create a rich user experience within your application.

We'll take the existing knowledge you have in .NET and apply that to Apple's own native tooling and SDKs. This will not only allow you to create the applications you desire, but will also give you a great head start in exploiting Apple's devices to full effect. The goal is to make the transition from .NET to Apple's native development environment much easier and faster.

In this chapter, we will take a more detailed look at the iOS SDK when compared with .NET's capabilities and the different languages supported. Specifically, we'll cover the following topics:

- Compare the relative capabilities of Apple's mobile devices

- Take a look under the hood of an application, reviewing its structure and life cycle

- Consider how you should approach designing an application and what Apple has done to help

- Compare the iOS SDK and the .NET Framework, both in approach and implementation

- Compare the development tools to support application development

- Review an Objective-C and Xcode 4 primer

We will start by building on the introductions given so far, and take a more detailed look at iOS and the iOS SDK side by side with the .NET Framework and programming model.

Comparing iOS Device Capabilities

We have already touched on the types of Apple devices you are able write applications for using the iOS SDK, and noted that not all devices are equal. It is important to consider the device or devices you intend to target, their respective strengths and weaknesses, and the capabilities exposed through the operating system. Such due diligence will ensure that the customer has the user experience you intend, and that you approach your application development in a way that embraces the capabilities the target device has and ensures you have a robust and dependable application.

The focus of this book is application development for mobile applications (although some of the tools and techniques can also be used for desktop applications). When considering the mobile devices available, our targets are the iPhone, the iPod touch, and the iPad. Table 4–1 lists some of their features based on the latest generation of each device.

Table 4–1. *Mobile Device Comparison*

Feature	iPhone	iPod touch	iPad
Generation	Fourth	Fourth	Second
Operating system	iOS 4.*x*	iOS 4.*x*	iOS 4.*x*
Display	3.5 inches 960 × 640 @ 326 ppi	3.5 inches 960 × 640 @ 326 ppi	9.7 inches 1024 × 768 @ 132 ppi
Storage	Up to 32GB	Up to 64GB	Up to 64GB
CPU	1 GHz ARM A4	1 GHz ARM A4	1 GHz dual-core ARM A5
Memory	Up to 512MB	Up to 256MB	Up to 512MB
Connectivity	GSM \ GPRS \ 3G \ Bluetooth \ 802.11n	Bluetooth \ 802.11n	GSM \ GPRS \ 3G \ Bluetooth \ 802.11n
Camera	Front and back	Front and rear	Front and rear
GPS capable	Yes	No	Yes (3G models only)

iOS Application Design

When starting to think about your application's design, in addition to looking at the capabilities of the devices you wish to target several other considerations, such as compatibility and tuning, are important when designing your application. Additionally, you should have an understanding of certain design patterns when working with the iOS SDK and Objective-C, as that will give you valuable insight as to why classes and APIs might be implemented in a given way. Design patterns also provide an excellent method of ensuring simplicity and elegance in your own applications.

We'll dig a little further into design considerations and design patterns in the following sections.

Design Considerations

In planning and developing your application, following a set of overarching principles not only helps to ensure that your application is well designed for its purpose, but also allows you to make the best use of the capabilities available on the device you target. As you move through this book, be sure to consider the following principles:

- Design your application to be as compatible with the broadest spectrum of devices as possible. This will maximize your market opportunity.

- Using the advanced capabilities of a device is OK, but if you can, provide options to automatically and\or manually turn off these features.

- Test on as many devices as you can, and not just using the simulator—test with real devices, if possible. We will explore the topic of testing in more detail in Chapter 9.

- Don't be tempted to leave your application unchanged when moving between significant form factors, such as iPhone to iPad.

- Tune for performance. Be aware of memory constraints and multithreading capabilities.

- Remember to consider costs. If your app requires a network connection, consider periodically scanning for Wi-Fi when using 3G.

As you build your applications, you should always be cognizant of these basic considerations. Now let's move to on to some design specifics in the form of iOS design patterns.

Design Patterns

The first thing to note when designing and implementing applications using the iOS SDK and Objective-C is Apple's use of design patterns. Design patterns are not a new concept, but not all operating systems or SDKs faithfully implement them. For example, the way that .NET's Windows Forms addresses user-interface design doesn't define or prescribe any kind of design pattern. This is left to the individual designing and implementing the application, if that developer chooses to do so.

A *design pattern* describes an approach to a common problem for which an elegant solution design has been created. The design is expressed in written form, often with diagrams depicting objects, their relationships, and their behavior.

A good example of a design pattern is the Singleton pattern. This restricts the instantiation of a class to a single object. The first time it is called, an object is created, but subsequent calls return a reference to the existing object. Its typical usage is for an Application object, where only one instance of the class can exist per application.

The use of design patterns by Apple is fundamental in helping to provide a framework around which your applications are written, and in doing so, helping to reinforce the user experience Apple is so protective of. Additionally, the use of patterns is good practice. It makes the implementation of applications easier, as some of the decisions around how to approach designing your application are already made for you.

The practice of using design patterns isn't implicit within the .NET Framework. It provides a Class Library with a set of APIs, but the architectural structure of your application and the implementation of design patterns are left to you—well, almost! As you can imagine, the .NET community is always happy to offer support, whether this is Microsoft itself through the Microsoft Developer Network (MSDN) at http://msdn.microsoft.com or third-party sites such as the dofactory at http://www.dofactory.com/Framework/Framework.aspx.

Table 4–2 describes some important iOS design patterns that you will use with your applications.

Table 4–2. *Significant iOS Design Patterns*

Pattern Name	Description
Model-View-Controller (MVC)	Divides your code into three distinct layers of encapsulated functionality, separating the user interface (the *view*) from the application's data and logic (the *model*), and bridge between the two (the *controller*).
Block objects	Allows you to encapsulate your code and local variables into a block, which can then be passed around as a value or called as a reference.
Delegation	Provides an alternative to subclassing, where the difference in behavior for an object is encapsulated within a delegate.
Target-action	Manages user interactions with desired actions in a controlled fashion, sending messages in response to user input to an object that implements the behavior associated with that action.
Managed memory model	Provides a reference-counting mechanism for managing the lifetime of an object, with an object having a usage count. When the count reaches zero, the runtime calls are invoked to reclaim the memory used. This pattern is a good example of one whose granularity is more specific and detailed than the others,

Now that you have had an overview of basic design considerations and design patterns, we'll delve into an application's structure and life cycle when running on iOS.

Looking Under the Hood of an Application

So, you've chosen which device or devices you wish to target and have an overview of their capabilities. Now let's take a look at how applications are structured on the iOS operating system, what to consider when designing them, and the fundamentals of how they are built.

Once you've designed your application, you can start to look at how to implement it. At this stage, it is important to understand how an iOS application is structured and runs internally. Consider the core application life cycle shown in Figure 4–1.

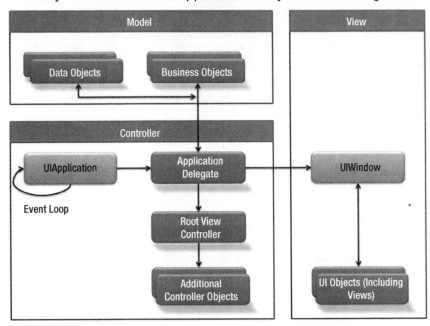

Figure 4–1. *iOS application life cycle*

As you can see in the diagram, the MVC pattern is at the heart of an iOS application, which is no surprise, given a user interface is displayed and human interaction is required.

Once your application has launched, the UIKit framework is responsible for managing the behavior of your application. It receives events from the operating system, and your application must respond to these events, which may be system-generated or user-generated. The behavior is similar to the Microsoft Windows messaging pattern, with a message queue from which events are retrieved and processed.

You don't need to physically process every message. A default implementation is provided for many messages, and the framework will therefore just process them. But when you require alternative behavior, or you want to change the default behavior in some way, then you can provide your own implementation for these events.

Next, let's take a look at the sequence of events that happen as part of the application's life cycle.

The Application Life Cycle

Once you have started your application, usually by tapping the icon on the screen, a sequence of events is started that should display your application on the mobile device (you can see this in the application lifecycle diagram in Figure 4–1. This is known as the application's *life cycle*.

We touched on some of the key functions involved in this life cycle when writing our Hello, World application in Chapter 2. After the main() function has been invoked, UIApplicationMain() is executed, and it won't return until your application exits. This class creates the application object and ensures the application delegate is instantiated, and then it looks to load the main .nib file that defines the application's main window.

The application knows which main .nib file to load by looking in the information property list file, Info.plist. This file contains a number of key\value pairs held in an XML file, each used to denote a configurable parameter. If you were to open Info.plist using Xcode, you would see something like the screen shown in Figure 4–2.

Key	Type	Value
Localization native development region	String	en
Bundle display name	String	${PRODUCT_NAME}
Executable file	String	${EXECUTABLE_NAME}
Icon file	String	
Bundle identifier	String	None.${PRODUCT_NAME:rfc1034identifier}
InfoDictionary version	String	6.0
Bundle name	String	${PRODUCT_NAME}
Bundle OS Type code	String	APPL
Bundle versions string, short	String	1.0
Bundle creator OS Type code	String	????
Bundle version	String	1.0
Application requires iPhone environmen	Boolean	YES
Main nib file base name	String	MainWindow
▶ Supported interface orientations	Array	(3 items)

Figure 4–2. *Info.plist values*

You can clearly see that the "Main nib file base name" entry is defined as MainWindow. So, if we look in our directory, we will see a file called MainWindow.xib, which is the main window resource file loaded by default. You could change this, but there is rarely a need to do so.

Loading the resource file will create classes for any objects that are contained within it and assign their associated properties by deserializing their values held in the resource file. The .xib file is essentially a serialized (saved-to-disk) version of your main window, user interfaces, and objects, which can be reconstituted (deserialized) at any time (much like adding water to dried noodles).

NOTE: You can use the Info.plist file to store your own application configuration values. Just add your values, either through the user-friendly Xcode editor or some other file editor.

After your main application is running, it is looked after by the application delegate, which uses *delegation* to overcome some of the complexities introduced by subclassing. This typically involves creating a new class that inherits from a parent class, and then maybe overriding methods provided within its parent. Our application delegate implements the UIApplicationDelegate *protocol*, which in C# terms, is the same as implementing an *interface*. Instead of a hierarchy of objects with inherited methods and overridden methods, we simply implement the methods specifically identified in the interfaces.

The final stage of the application launch process will see it entering the *active* state—one of many states the application will take on. This is indicated by the applicationDidBecomeActive method.

The application life cycle has a series of *states* that are defined by the iOS SDK, and you can manage your application's behavior based on its state. Let's take a look at the different application states that exist and how you should manage them.

Managing Application States

A key job of the application delegate is to manage the different state transitions the application goes through while it is running. Two new application states were introduced in iOS 4.0: the application can be running in the background or suspended.

Any state transitions require a response from your application as confirmation it is behaving correctly. For example, if the application state were set to the background by starting a new application, then it would make sense to stop updating its user interface.

When the application state changes, you respond accordingly using the method called within the application delegate. It is also worth noting that an application may be launched not as a direct result of the user asking it to, but through an indirect request. For example, your application might be invoked to deal with a push notification.

In all of these cases, the didFinishLaunchingWithOptions method is called with options providing a reason why it was invoked, and in some cases, such as due to a push notification, the payload of data relating to it.

All the states supported in iOS 4.0 and above are shown in Table 4–3.

Table 4–3. *Application States*

State	Description
Not Running	The application was running but has been terminated by the system, or it has not been launched.
Inactive	The application is running in the foreground but not receiving events. This is a state that is typically held only briefly, unless the device is locked or waiting for user input. This is similar to .NET's `Form.Deactive` event.
Active	The application is running in the foreground and is receiving events. The `applicationDidBecomeActive` method is called when entering this state. This is similar to .NET's `Form.Shown` event.
Background	The application is in the background and executing code. This is typically a brief state, as it normally precedes the application being suspended. The `applicationDidEnterBackground` method is called when entering this state.
Suspended	The application is in the background and not executing code. Note that the application may be removed by the system if resources are scarce, such as low memory.

An application doesn't just move from one state to another without sometimes going through transitory states. For example, if an application is interrupted because of an incoming phone call, the application will be told it's about to become inactive by calling the `applicationWillResignActive` method. This is your opportunity to prepare your application for being sent to the background. If you answered the phone call, the application would be sent to the background with the `applicationDidEnterBackground` method called. However, if you decided to ignore the call, the application would resume foreground focus and fire the `applicationDidBecomeActive` method again for you to handle accordingly. The same is true of an application that was previously running in the background and is sent to the foreground. In that case, the `applicationWillEnterForeground` method is called prior to moving to the foreground, and the `applicationDidBecomeActive` method is called when the application enters the foreground. These states are shown in Figure 4–3.

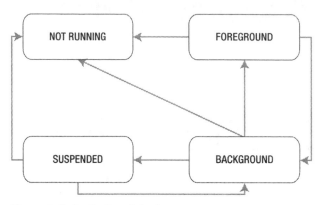

Figure 4–3. *Application state diagram*

Managing an Application's Behaviors

As you've seen, an application will typically spend time moving between different states, especially given typical usage. For example, it is common for a user to move between applications, checking email one minute, taking a telephone call the next, and surfing the Web after that. We've looked at handing state changes and the way the iOS SDK cleverly uses the Objective-C technique of delegation to have a method called, enabling you to provide your own implementation.

Clearly, how your application reacts to these state changes very much depends on your application, as each is different. But there are some application tasks that are the same for all applications. In this section, we'll take a brief look at these tasks, which will allow you to get started.

Dealing with Orientation Changes

Apple's mobile devices have mercury switches that understand the orientation of the device and so your application. Most iOS applications launch in portrait mode initially, and then will rotate your application to match the device's orientation; some will start in landscape mode if it makes sense for them to do so. It might not be appropriate for your application to work in different orientations, and it is up to you to manage this. For example, watching movies might suit only landscape orientation.

Before you start panicking and wondering how on earth you're going write all that inevitably complex code to rotate your application, stop! Thankfully *autorotation*, as it's called, is conveniently handled through a combination of the iOS and the UIKit framework—assuming you want your application to rotate. The iOS SDK supports autorotation through a method, which defines if the device has been rotated and whether your application should support it, and also through the Interface Builder, where you can define how the view manages the orientation of your user interface. We'll look further into this subject later in the book.

Files Within Your Application and the Application Sandbox

As with most operating systems, the filesystem is usually accessible by the application, although with some restrictions to ensure the security of your device. The iOS provides your application with access to an area of the filesystem that is accessible only by that application. It does this through the use of an *application sandbox*, which is implemented through the iOS as a security mechanism. The sandbox provides fine-grained control, limiting areas that it thinks could present a security problem if exploited, such as the filesystem and access to network resources.

The sandbox for an application is implemented when the application is first installed. The path to the Simulator's home directory is in the form `<//ApplicationRoot>/Applications/ApplicationID`, where `<Root>` is the following directory from the users home directory `/Library/Application Support/iPhone Simulator/<iOS Version>/` is an area on the filesystem where the applications are installed. The `ApplicationID` uniquely identifies the specific application. When combined, this is called the *application home directory*.

A number of important application subdirectories are created, allowing your application to write data and its preferences within the constraints provided by the iOS security system. These subdirectores are installed from the application's home directory. For example, `<Root>/Applications /ApplicationID/Documents` is where application data and documents are stored. The `/tmp` directory is for files that do not need to persist between application launches.

> **NOTE:** For more details about the sandbox, see the section "The File System" in the *iOS Application Programming Guide*.

Multitasking

We won't cover multitasking in this book, but this brief introduction of the capabilities made available in the iOS 4.0 may help you explore further using the online resources available.

The use of multitasking has long been supported in the .NET Framework, although for the iOS, it wasn't until version 4.0 that multitasking support was properly introduced to application developers.

Note that not all devices support multitasking. You can query the `multitaskingSupported` property of `UIDevice` to see whether the device on which the application is running supports it.

An application may process certain tasks in the background, although these are carefully controlled. The following types of background behavior are supported:

- Tracking a user's location, either continuously or periodically monitoring for updates. This is useful for location-based applications.

▓ Playing background audio. This is common for fitness-type
   applications.

▓ Completing finite-length background tasks. An example is saving data
   to disk to avoid corruption.

▓ Timed local notifications. This is used in alarm clock-type applications,
   for example.

Comparing the .NET Framework with iOS and the iOS SDK

Let's start with a comparison of the two environments and their frameworks, positioning
the runtime and design-time aspects of each relative to one another. This context will be
useful when understanding the architecture of your application and how the APIs are
used. Take a moment to consider the diagram in Figure 4–4.

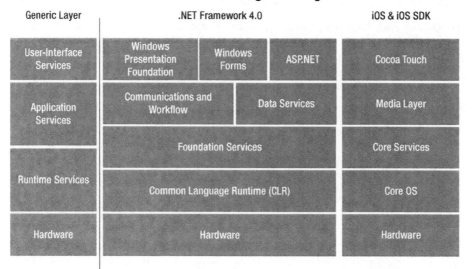

Figure 4–4. *.NET and iOS framework comparison*

If we consider the generic layers and which elements are covered by both the .NET
Framework and the iOS operating system and SDK, you'll notice the following
similarities:

▓ **User-interface services**: These are the services responsible for
   delivering the user interface and looking after user interactions, such
   as device input. The iOS SDK uses the Cocoa Touch extensions as
   well as aspects of other layers such as the Media Layer to accomplish
   this, especially the multitouch input. The .NET Framework includes
   both Windows Presentation Foundation (WPF) and Windows Forms to
   achieve this.

- **Application services**: This category consolidates a number of component parts in both .NET and Apple's frameworks, such as the iOS SDK. In iOS, the Cocoa API, Cocoa Touch, and Media layer are included, whereas for .NET, elements such as Foundation Services, Data Services, and communications and workflow would be included. Any API aspects that deal with the user interface and user input have deliberately been separated out into user-interface services.

- **Runtime services**: This is functionality that is provided to an application at runtime, and is typically contained within the operating system or runtime environments that run on top of the operating system. The .NET or Java runtime environments are good examples of runtime services sitting on top of an operating system. Runtime services include memory management, disk access, graphic card APIs, and so on.

- **Hardware**: This remains a constant in all our architectures, although the specification of it will change depending on the device, as will its capabilities. The software-based layers above the hardware enable an abstracted way of using it.

These similarities shouldn't be surprising. Over many years of device, operating system, and application evolution, best practices have surfaced leading to such similarities. So at a high level, it's easy to draw the comparison. But the devil is in the details. If we drop down a level, we'll start to see the nuances of each framework's implementation. We'll see features included in one framework but completely excluded from the other, or in other cases, implemented through different mechanisms.

Starting at the top of the stack, let's look at the different layers, comparing the frameworks and libraries within them. This will help you to understand the terms and structure in .NET and how its counterparts work in Apple's world.

We won't delve into the specifics of classes and methods within classes, which you can find in Apple's online iOS reference. By highlighting through comparison the equivalent capabilities in the iOS SDK, the usage of these should be straightforward. This will lay the foundation for upcoming chapters, where we will walk through some working examples.

User-Interface Services

The explosion of Web 2.0-based applications has significantly raised user expectations of how applications will perform. The gap between native applications and the capabilities of web-based applications has narrowed significantly. The same is true of mobile applications. The user experience associated with early mobile applications, including new protocols at the time, such as the Wireless Access Protocol (WAP), is vastly different from the intuitive, interactive, high-definition capabilities exposed by some of today's mobile devices, blending native functionality with Internet-based web or even cloud-based services.

This is possible in no small part due to the improved capabilities of the physical hardware, which now has faster processors, more memory, and higher-resolution screens that support touch-based input. However, software is at the heart of such functionality, and how this is organized and used is where key differences appear.

.NET makes provisions for user-interface design and implementation by providing the following runtime services through which functionality is exposed:

- **WPF**: This provides a complete API to creating highly visual user interfaces. It was introduced some time after Windows Forms to provide support for additional areas such as 2D and 3D graphics and video and audio.

- **Windows Forms**: This is the name given to the API that encapsulates Microsoft Window's native Windows API. Other APIs are required to deal with more advanced aspects, such as 2D and 3D graphics.

- **ASP.NET**: This includes ASP.NET, ASP.NET MVC, ASP.NET, and Ajax. It is Microsoft's Active Server Pages (ASP) technology that allows you to develop web sites using server-side programming.

We'll exclude ASP.NET from our comparison, as this is Microsoft's ASP technology used to deliver web-based applications, and our focus is on native applications. So, we are left with WPF and Windows Forms. Given that WPF effectively supersedes Windows Forms, we could easily exclude Windows Forms also, but given its popularity and the relatively recent introduction of WPF, we'll cover both in our comparison.

WPF exists as a subset of .NET Framework types that are for the most part located in the `System.Windows` namespace, just as Windows Forms does. But you'll notice that to accomplish more advanced graphical applications in Windows Forms, you need to step outside this API into things like the Windows Media Player and the Graphics Display Interface (GDI+).

Based on the assumption that WPF at least in part can be seen as a container for Windows Forms, the closest comparison for WPF, and Windows Forms for that matter, is Cocoa and Cocoa Touch. We'll start with Cocoa Touch, which includes the following frameworks:

- **UIKit (`UIKit.framework`)**: Provides the capabilities necessary to implement graphical, event-driven applications.

- **Message UI (`MessageUI.framework`)**: Provides support for composing and queuing email messages. In iOS 4.0, this extends to include Short Message Service (SMS) support.

- **Map Kit (`MapKit.framework`)**: Provides support for a scrollable map interface that can be integrated into your application.

- **iAd (`iAd.framework`)**: Provides support for banner-based advertisements within your application.

- **Game Kit (GameKit.framework)**: Provides support for peer-to-peer networking capabilities. It allows you to create complex multiplayer networking games.

- **Event Kit (EventKitUI.framework)**: Provides support for viewing and editing calendar-based events.

- **Address Book UI (AddressBookUI.framework)**: Provides support for viewing, editing, and creating new contacts.

Application Services

The applications of today not only require a more intuitive and interactive user interface, but are generally more demanding in the features and functionality they provide. The day has long gone where an application ran on the device, isolated from the rest of the world, or where the application's interactive features were based on text and simplistic graphics.

Today's applications demand video, music, high-definition graphics, parallel processing in the form of multitasking, and a speed and responsiveness that was unheard of only a few years ago—and this is on a *mobile* device! Such functionality is exposed, in part, through the application services provided within the iOS, which include the following features:

- Multimedia capabilities

- Storage and management of data

- Network and communication access

- Workflow and communication

- Access to device-specific features such as the GPS

Such features are provided for within .NET through the .NET Framework Class Library. These include some of the class libraries we've already mentioned in the discussion of .NET's user-interface capabilities. The following features support application services:

- **Windows Communication Foundation (WCF)**: Provides functionality to support service-oriented applications, which collaborate over a network connection.

- **ActiveX Data Objects for .NET (ADO.NET)**: Provides support for accessing data and data services, such as native database libraries, or abstracted drivers, such as ODBC.

- **Windows Forms and WPF**: in the context of application services, WPF provides similar user-interface capabilities to those in the iOS UIKit framework, as well as multimedia and audio capabilities, along with 3D and animation support.

- **Language Integrated Query (LINQ)**: New to .NET Framework 3.5, LINQ provides native data-querying capabilities.

In the iOS SDK, such services (and others) are encapsulated within the Media and Core Services layers. Let's take a look at the key frameworks provided within these layers to map onto the capabilities we've touched upon in the .NET Framework Class Library.

Media Layer

The Media layer contains the graphics, audio, and video technologies that support you in building applications that look and sound great. It contains the following frameworks:

- **AV Foundation (AVFoundation.framework)**: A comprehensive set of APIs that support playing, recording, and managing audio content in iOS. In iOS 4.0, this includes movie-editing support and precision controls for playback.

- **Core Graphics (CoreGraphics.framework)**: Supplies support for 2D graphics by providing a vector-based drawing engine.

- **Core Text (CoreText.framework)**: Provides a comprehensive and performant set of APIs for laying out text and using fonts.

- **Image I/O (ImageIO.framework)**: Supports importing and exporting image data and its associated metadata.

- **Media Player (MediaPlayer.framework)**: Allows you to embed support to play audio and video content from within your application. This includes support for accessing the iTunes library and for coping with resizable video.

- **OpenAL and OpenGL ES (OpenAL.framework and OpenGLES.framework)**: Cross-platform frameworks included within iOS to provide close-to-hardware, high-performance audio and video functionality.

Core Services

Core Services provides fundamental system services that all applications use, either directly or through other frameworks. Its key frameworks are as follows:

- **AddressBook (AddressBook.framework)**: Provides an API that allows programmatic access to the contacts stored in the mobile device.

- **CFNetwork (CFNetwork.framework)**: Provides high-performance and low-level access to the network protocols available to the device.

- **Core Data (CoreData.framework)**: Provides functionality along with Xcode to manage your application data using a schema that is visually defined in Xcode and a support API to manage the data. This is ideally suited to the MVC pattern and can significantly reduce the amount of code required.

- **Core Telephony (CoreTelephony.framework)**: Provides functionality for interacting with the telephony features of a compatible mobile device.

- **Event Kit (EventKit.framework)**: Provides support for accessing calendar events on your device.

- **Foundation (Foundation.framework)**: Provides an Objective-C–based API around support for core data types and functions.

- **Store Kit (StoreKit.framework)**: Provides support for purchasing content and services from within your application, such as additional content.

- **Systems Configuration (SystemsConfiguration.framework)**: Provides access to network configuration details of your device such as Wi-Fi or cellular connection capabilities.

Runtime Services

The frameworks and class libraries we've discussed so far can't exist without the support of a core platform on which they run. In the case of the .NET Framework, low-level runtime services are provided through a combination of the CLR, low-level Core Services, and the operating system. In the iOS SDK, such capabilities are provided by the iOS and the Core OS layer that exposes the same kind of low-level functionality supported in the low-level runtime services and the CLR.

Here, we start to see some of the key differences. For example, the .NET Framework creates applications that run in a managed environment provided by the CLR. They are not native applications, but interpreted applications. Using the iOS SDK, this creates native applications that are not interpreted by any kind of runtime, but instead rely on the operating system- and SDK-provided services directly to support the application's execution.

The following are examples of the capabilities provided within the CLR:

- **Memory management:** Provides the automatic allocation and reclaiming of memory used by applications. This kind of memory management goes a step further than the reference counting provided within the iOS, where you programmatically free up resources no longer required.

- **Type management**: Ensures the runtime type safety of core data types and is an essential ingredient in cross-platform, multilanguage capabilities.

- **Security:** Provides security features, such as the signing of code and access-control features.

- **Multitasking:** Supports multithreaded applications where multiple tasks can appear to run simultaneously and be scheduled across multiple processors.

- **Exception handling:** Provides support for exception trapping and handing.

- **Delegation:** Improves on the existing inheritance and interface capabilities to provide delegation enabling you to implement pointers to functions for runtime execution.

Similar capabilities to those just listed are provided for within the iOS SDK, but they do not completely match. This is partly due to the fact that we are dealing with native applications that run directly on top of the operating system rather than a container/runtime like the CLR—unless you're using Mono and MonoTouch!

Let's take a look at some of the key frameworks within the iOS SDK:

- **System:** Provides the lowest level capabilities above the operating system and exposes the kernel environment, drivers, and the UNIX interfaces of the operating system. This includes memory allocation, threading, filesystem access, math computations, locale information, and more.

- **Security (`Security.framework`):** Enhances the built-in features of the device to provide programmatic and application security features, such as signing applications for authenticity, cryptographic key management, and support for keychain sharing.

- **External Accessory (`ExternalAccessory.framework`):** Supports communicating with external hardware connected to your device.

- **Accelerate Framework (`Accelerate.framework`):** Provides support for computationally intensive applications by providing interfaces for complex math, big number calculations, and so on.

Objective-C Primer, Part 2

Chapter 2 provided a short introduction to some of the essentials required to start developing your mobile application. Before we start to really put the iOS SDK to work and focus on the specific aspects of mobile applications, you'll need to understand a few more essentials of the Objective-C language. Learning about some of these slightly more advanced features will better prepare you to not only write your own applications, but also to understand how the iOS SDK itself is constructed.

In the following sections, in order to assist your transition from .NET, I'll introduce each by its .NET language term, rather than the Objective-C term, and make comparisons between the languages.

Class Declaration

Both .NET and Objective-C are object-oriented languages, and so the definition of a class is a key construct for the language. Consider the following Objective-C and .NET C# examples, shown together.

.NET C#	```Class AClass : Object
{
   int aValue;

   void doNothing();
   String returnString();
}``` |
| **Objective-C** | ```@interface AClass : NSObject
{
   int aValue;
}
- (void)doNothing();
+ (NSString)returnString();
@end``` |

Both of these code segments declare a new class object that inherits from an object class. It has a default integer member variable called aValue, and two methods. One method is called doNothing() and returns nothing and takes no parameters. The other method is returnString(), which returns a string but also takes no parameters.

You may also notice that different characters precede the method declarations. This is significant, as you'll learn in the next section.

Method Declaration

An obvious companion to the class is the methods that provide the necessary functionality for the class. Methods may be defined as *instance methods* or *class methods*, as indicated by the character that precedes their declaration, as follows:

- A class method is indicated by a plus (+) character. It is the same as a C# static method. Only a single implementation exists, and it is associated with the class type.

- An instance method is indicated by a minus (-) character. Here, the method is associated with an instance object associated with the class.

The following are .NET C# and Objective-C examples.

| .NET C# | ```
public static void aClassMethod();
public void anInstanceMethod();
``` |
| Objective-C | ```
+ (void) aClassMethod;
- (void) anInstanceMethod;
``` |

Now let's look at how to pass parameters to the method. Consider the following examples.

| .NET C# | `String addStrings( String a, String b);` |
| Objective-C | `- (NSString) addStrings (NSString *) a secondParm2:(NSString *) b;` |

This syntax creates a method called addStrings, which concatenates strings given as two parameters and returns a string value. The way you invoke the method is important, too. The parameters are *order-sensitive*, and so the following call is invalid because the second parameter, indicated by the name secondParm, must be the second value passed.

```
// This is invalid

[ addStrings secondParm:s1, s2) ];
```

However, the following example demonstrates the correct invocation syntax.

```
// Correct invocation
[ addStrings s1, secondParm:s2 ];
```

Because you're working with a reflective message-driven programming language, the sequence and type of parameters passed are important.

Properties

The use of properties has long been the mainstay for accessing class objects, and in doing so, managing how they are accessed and what they return. Such class members are known as *instance variables*, as the property manages access to the actual value associated when an instance of the class is created. They can also be used to control scope and to hide any complexities associated with returning the property value.

Objective-C can also help by *synthesizing* (automatically creating behind the scenes) the accessor methods (the *getter* and *setter*) and creating the instance variable required. It also ensures that the memory management surrounding instance variables is handled appropriately. Consider the following examples.

.NET C#	```
	// Definition of your instance variable either within the class, or as
	// a minimum, in the scope of the class
	string _name;
	
	// Definition of your property accessor methods are within the class
	public string name
	{
	    get { return _name; }
	    set { _name = value; }
	}
	``

Objective-C	```
	// Definition of your property within your class header file (.h)
	@property (nonatomic, retain) NSString *name;
	
	// Synthesis of your property in the implementation file (.m)
	@synthesize name = _name;
	``

You'll notice in the C# example that C# has no equivalent to the synthesis model for accessing an instance variable. You must write accessor methods manually. This is reminiscent of the Objective-C found in Xcode 3.*x*, which is still valid for Xcode 4 but not the best practice. I recommend writing accessor methods in Xcode 4 only when necessary, usually in cases where more complex processing is required when returning property values.

Strings

Because Objective-C is based on the C programming language, you are free to use and manipulate strings in the C way, through the use of pointers and strings essentially being character arrays. There is no C# comparison, as C# doesn't support pointers, so we'll use strings, string constants, and more advanced features, such as string localization as comparisons.

Consider the following examples for representing a string constant, which is a static string value that cannot be changed.

.NET C#	```
	// Define a constant string using the following syntax.
	const string example="This is a constant string"
	
	// Using this syntax to set a string attribute
	window.title = example;
	``

Objective-C	```
	// Define a constant string using the following syntax.
	// @"This is a constant string"
	
	// Using this syntax to set a string attribute
	window.title = @"Main Window Title";
	``

The following examples show the definition of a string using the respective string class provided within the language. Note that using the class with the @ symbol creates an *immutable* string—that is, a string that cannot be changed.

.NET C#	```String string1 = @"This is an immutable string";```
	
	```// Both of these statements are the same```
	```String string2 = "This is a mutable string";```
	```String string3 = new string("This is a mutable string");```

Objective-C	```NSString *string1 = @"This is an immutable string";``` ```NSString *string2 = "This is a mutable string";```

In Xcode 4, you can also create a `Localizable.string` file that contains the string resources, assigned both a name and value, which then are referenced at runtime in your code. This allows your string values to be configured for the locale in which you're deploying your application. Store the values in your `Localizable.string` file in the following format:

```
"LOCAL_MAIN_MENU_TITLE" = Main Menu";
```

And then reference the string in your code using the following syntax:

```
NSLocalizedString(@"LOCAL_MAIN_MENU_TITLE", @"");
```

Interfaces and Protocols

An Objective-C *interface* is actually a C# class, and an Objective-C *protocol* is actually a C# interface—confusing, eh? Let's put these into context with some examples, and in doing so, remove the confusion.

We'll start with a C# and the definition of a class, with member variables and methods. C# uses the `class` keyword and syntax to define a class; Objective-C uses the `@interface` compiler directive. We looked at this earlier within the class declaration section.

If we focus on what C# calls an *interface*, which Objective-C refers to as a *protocol*, this uses a different syntax. In Objective-C, a protocol declares methods that can be implemented by any class, or indeed, be used as a variable.

Consider the following example. It defines an interface, which is then implemented by a class. You use angled brackets within the interface declaration to declare your class implements the named type for implementation or specialization.

| **.NET C#** | ```csharp
// Definition of your interface template
interface IEquatable<T>
{
    bool Equals(T obj);
}

// Implementation of your class
// which realizes the interface
// defined above
public class MyClass : IEquatable<MyClass>
{
    // Implementation of IEquatable<T> interface
    public bool Equals(MyClass c)
    {
      // implementation here
    }
}
``` |
| **Objective-C** | ```objc
// Definition of your interface template
@protocol IEquatable
- (bool) Equals : (NSObject*) a ;
@end

@interface MyClass : NSObject <IEquatable>
{
    // Some methods here
}
@end

// Implementation of your class
// which realizes the interface
// defined above
@implementation MyClass

// Implementation of IEquatable<T> interface
- (bool) Equals : (NSObject*) a
{
    // implementation here
}

@end
``` |

A class definition can declare an implementation of more than one interface simply by separating the interfaces by a comma, like so:

```objc
Public class MyClass : NSObject <IEquatable, AnotherProtocol>
```

As you can see, it's quite similar. One key difference is where Objective-C uses protocols as variables or as an argument to a method, which is often the case when an interface's implementation is used as a callback function. Consider the example in Listing 4–1, which defines a protocol that in turn defines a method that will indicate via a Boolean value whether success was achieved.

Listing 4-1. Protocol Declaration Code

```
#import <Foundation/Foundation.h>

// Define our protocol, with a single method
@protocol ProcessDataDelegate <NSObject>
@required
- (void) processSuccessful: (BOOL)success;
@end

// Create an Interface using the Protocol, and notice the use of the ID type that points
// to a generic type that will be unknown at compile time and resolved at run-time
@interface ClassWithProtocol : NSObject
{
 id <ProcessDataDelegate> delegate;
}

@property (retain) id delegate;

-(void)startSomeProcess;

@end
```

The implementation section for the interface defined in Listing 4–1 synthesizes the delegate instance variable and then calls the method defined in the protocol as needed. Its implementation is shown in Listing 4–2.

Listing 4-2. *Using a Protocol Declaration in the Class Example*

```
#import "ClassWithProtocol.h"

@implementation ClassWithProtocol

@synthesize delegate;

- (void)processComplete
{
   [[self delegate] processSuccessful:YES];
}

-(void)startSomeProcess
{
  // Create a time which uses the processComplete interface to signal when complete
  [NSTimer scheduledTimerWithTimeInterval:5.0 target:self
    selector:@selector(processComplete) userInfo:nil repeats:YES];
}

@end
```

For the sake of brevity, assume you have a class that is performing some kind of action. Further, assume this class is called from another class to begin the processing. At some point, the caller will want to be notified that the class processing the data is finished, and the protocol is used for this very purpose, as shown in Listing 4–3.

Listing 4-3. *Using the Class in the Example*

```
@interface MyDelegate : NSObject <UIApplicationDelegate, ProcessDataDelegate>
{
        ClassWithProtocol *test;
```

```
}
@end

@implementation MyDelegate
-(void) processSuccessful:(BOOL)success
{
        NSLog(@"Finished");
}
@end
```

Delegation

The use of delegation in the iOS SDK is common, predominately because it is introduced as an elegant solution to the problem of complex subclassing. Instead of having complex object hierarchies, where you need to create many more classes whose behavior may change only slightly from one another, you can pass delegates to an object to perform the modified behavior on your behalf. Modern best practice in today's programming languages is to avoid deeply nested class hierarchies, and Objective-C helps with this through delegation.

The general rule is that delegation is an alternative to subclassing, good practice is to use it, as it creates far cleaner code. Let's start by defining our protocol in Objective-C, as in the following examples.

| .NET C# | ```// Defining the delegate in C# is different
public delegate void jobComplete();``` |
| --- | --- |
| Objective-C | ```// Definition of your interface template
@protocol jobComplete
    (void)jobFinished;
@end``` |

We next define an object variable within our class pointing to the protocol defined for our delegate and name it. We'll also expose a property of the same name that we can call to reference our protocol, as follows.

| .NET C# | ```public class MyClass
{
// Create our delegate
    jobComplete jc = new jobComplete(jobFinished);
}``` |
| --- | --- |
| Objective-C | ```@interface MyClass : NSObject {
        id <jobComplete> delegate;
}
@property (nonatomic, retain) id <jobComplete> delegate;
@end``` |

Our class would then invoke the delegate as a suitable point, using the following syntax, and must @synthesize the delegate property as part of its implementation.

| .NET C# | ```csharp
public void SomeMethod()
{
    // Invoke our job complete delegate
    jc();
}
``` |
|---|---|

| Objective-C | ```objc
-(void) SomeMethod
{
    // Signal that the job is complete by calling the delegate
    [delegate JobComplete];
}
``` |
|---|---|

The only thing left to do in our class is implement the delegate's jobFinished method, as in the following, which will be called as shown previously.

| .NET C# | ```csharp
public void jobFinished()
{
    // do something to signal the job has finished
}
``` |
|---|---|

| Objective-C | ```objc
-(void) jobFinished
{
    // do something to signal the job has finished
}
``` |
|---|---|

I encourage you to play around with some sample code to test your understanding of delegates.

> **NOTE:** On the Apple Developer Program web site, you will find some more information about how to use delegates and delegation. If you're interested, take a look at
> http://developer.apple.com/library/mac/#documentation/General/Conceptual/DevPedia-CocoaCore/Delegation.html.

Comments

Last, but definitely not least, is the syntax used to embed comments within your code.

The use of naming conventions like camelCase helps, but there really is no substitute for good comments within your code. The syntax needs to conform to the form described here, but it's also important that the comments themselves describe the intent and approach taken by the developer, and not just a verbatim narrative of the syntax (the code and its naming should do that).

For single-line comment, you can use the following structure.

.NET C#	`// this is a comment`
	
	or
	
	`/* this is a comment */`

Objective-C	`// this is a comment`
	
	or
	
	`/* this is a comment */`

For multiple lines, in Objective-C, you can use the /* *(open comment)* and */ *(close comment)* structure, but not in C#, as follows.

.NET C#	`// this is the starting line`
	`// this is a second comment line`
	`// this is a terminating third comment line`

Objective-C	`/* this is the starting line`
	`** this is a second comment line`
	`*/ this is a terminating third comment line`

Comparing .NET and Xcode Tools

So far, we've compared the Apple devices, the application life cycle, and the respective class libraries in both .NET and the iOS SDK. But as we've covered in previous chapters, tooling is equally important, and Xcode is a worthy equivalent to Visual Studio, as is MonoDevelop if you decide to pursue the MonoTouch path. But there are other tools to consider as you start your development journey, as listed in Table 4–4.

Table 4–4. *Tool Comparison*

Domain	Microsoft .NET	Apple
IDE	Visual Studio	Xcode or MonoDevelop
Device simulator	Windows Phone 7 emulator	iOS simulator
File Comparison	Visual Studio (not Express)	Version editor
Debugger	Visual Studio	Xcode using LLM debugging engine
Static code analysis	Visual Studio	Xcode 4
Unit testing	NUnit	Xcode 4
Source code control	Team Foundation Server includes Visual SourceSafe	Subversion or Git
IntelliSense	Visual Studio (not Express)	Xcode 4

The tools listed in Table 4–4 are provided out of the box. Visual Studio and Xcode can be extended with additional tools, both commercial and open source.

XCode 4 Primer

We've already taken a very simplistic look at the new Xcode 4 editor in Chapter 2 when creating our Hello, World application. If you were familiar with previous versions of Xcode, you'll have noticed a big difference: Xcode 4 now works within a single window and is far more integrated. If you're familiar with Visual Studio, you'll be far less impressed, and may need to take some of Xcode's features in stride.

In this section, as in the Objective-C primer, we'll dig a little deeper into Xcode 4's features, so that you are better prepared to start coding in earnest in future chapters.

We've already looked at the general structure of the Xcode interface, with its various functional panes, and we've created a new project, which highlights both the project templates available and the project explorer tree, which is the name given to Xcode 4's project structure view.

As noted, the IDE shipped with Xcode 4 is a substantial improvement on previous versions, and a real comparison to Microsoft's Visual Studio IDE. It includes a number of new features. One is the way in which you navigate around the application. The multiple windows of Xcode version 3.x are replaced with a single window that has different workspaces and other areas. The following sections describe the key aspects of the IDE.

The IDE Workspace and Its Editors

In Xcode, every window within the IDE is a workspace, and as such, provides an elegant solution to supporting multiple projects. Each workspace has tabs, which represent a given context and, when selected, adjust the windows that appear below it, showing what you need to see.

In supporting workspaces, Xcode has also introduced a number of editors, including ones for source code, property list files, rich text files, and NIB files, among others. (*Editor* refers to the dialog box that allows you to edit the values given against certain parameters.) To open or display any of these editors, select a file of that type in the project navigator (see the upcoming "Navigators" section). The editor opens automatically in the editor area of the workspace window. Table 4–5 shows how to access the different editors.

Table 4–5. *Ways to Access the Xcode Editors*

Editor	Toolbar	Shortcut
Standard editor	☰	⌘↵
Assistant editor	⧉	⌥⌘↵
Version editor	◩	⌥⇧⌘↵

Code Completion and Support

Those of you familiar with Visual Studio will be right at home here, because the code-completion capabilities in Xcode 4 have been enhanced. The IDE prompts you to not only complete the statement you are typing, but if options exist, it already provides you with the options available—complete with Quick Help documentation to support any highlighted option, should you have the Quick Help Inspector open.

A useful shortcut is control-spacebar, which toggles the code-completion feature on and off. Press the escape key to cancel any operation.

If you're using the LLVM compiler to build your code, the Fix-It feature will also be enabled. As you are typing, the Fix-It feature will look for errors in your code. If it finds something that seems like an error, it will highlight the problem using a red underbar and an error symbol in the gutter bar, in the left pane of your IDE. It will also provide some suggestions on how to fix the problem, offering to repair it for you.

Schemes and Scheme Editors

A useful addition to Xcode 4 is the concept of a *scheme*, which can be used to define a collection of targets to build, a configuration to use when building, and a collection of tests to execute. Each scheme is associated with a debug or release build, and changed using the scheme popup window. From this same menu, you can manage the schemes you have—editing an existing scheme or creating a new scheme.

Essentially, the creation of a scheme allows you to associate a set of configuration items to the scheme name and select it at the click of a button. The scheme editor then allows you to configure the schemes and their settings.

You can have as many schemes as you want, but only one can be active at a time. The schemes you create can be stored in a project and be available in every workspace that includes that project. Alternatively, schemes can be stored in the workspace and be available only in that workspace.

Schemes are a powerful feature. I recommend that you spend a little time playing with different scheme configurations using the scheme editor.

Project Editor

The project editor window allows you to adjust core configuration information about the project itself, under the Summary tab. You can also adjust the build settings, phases, and rules.

In most instances, the values such as those found in the summary information will not need to be changed from the default settings provided with the template. But if you do need to make any changes, you can do it here.

As noted in the previous section, you can set the target, build configuration, and executable settings using schemes. In Xcode 4, selecting a scheme will automatically provide default settings for all three areas.

Inspectors

In Xcode, *inspectors* are panes in the utility area that you can use to read or enter data about files and Interface Builder objects. These inspectors are listed in Table 4–6 along with their shortcut keys.

Table 4–6. *Inspectors and Their Keyboard Shortcuts*

Inspector	Shortcut
File Inspector	⌥ ⌘1
Quick Help	⌥ ⌘2
Identity Inspector	⌥ ⌘3
Attribute Inspector	⌥ ⌘4
Size Inspector	⌥ ⌘5
Connections Inspector	⌥ ⌘6

These inspectors also are available under the Utilities menu item within Xcode. Note that the menu is context-sensitive, and all of the inspectors are relevant only when you're viewing user interfaces provided in an XIB file. When viewing code, fewer inspectors are available.

Navigators

The Xcode IDE introduces a number of *navigators*, which display different workspaces within the main window and allow you to jump to different areas of your project with ease. Navigators are a useful tool for navigating the Xcode interface, and understanding how to use them will make developing applications within Xcode far easier.

Seven navigators are available to help you navigate to various aspects of your project:

- **Project navigator**: This navigator provides a standard view of your files and groups. It shows your classes, frameworks, resources, products, and so on. Xcode 4 offers some nice improvements over the previous version. At the bottom is a filter bar with three preset filters for recently changed files, unsaved files, and files with an SCM status. It also includes a search field that you can use to filter files across all projects in the workspace.

- **Symbol navigator**: As its name suggests, this navigator allows you to view and navigate the various symbols created within your application. It lets you view the symbol in a hierarchical format (parents and children) or a flat format, displaying classes, methods, attributes, and so on.

- **Search**: This navigator provides a workspace-wide find-and-replace feature. The navigator itself is a standard find-and-replace panel. It also provides a feature for doing mass replacements, through the Preview button. Using this feature slides down a sheet that gives you the differences for every change and lets you select which changes to put into effect.

- **Issue**: As its name suggests, this navigator shows you issues that the compiler or syntax checker has detected and allows you to view the complete issue text.

- **Debug**: This navigator displays your program-execution information, including the stack, when you stop in the debugger. You can view multiple threads at once and have Xcode filter out threads that are not relevant. It also has a stack-compression feature, provided by a slider at the bottom of the debug navigator. When you slide it from right to left, Xcode takes out stack frames that may not be relevant, so you can adjust the slider to show information to the level of detail you want.

- **Breakpoint**: This navigator displays all breakpoints set within your application, both active and inactive. If you have set a breakpoint and it is inactive, you will see the symbol, allowing you to switch it on in the code. This doesn't do any harm, since it's not affecting your code. However, if you want to remove the fact that the debug breakpoint ever existed, delete it from the navigator list.

- **Log**: This navigator displays the history surrounding the project's run and debug sessions. It can be used to view output sent to the debug console using the NSLog method.

Figure 4–5 shows the Navigator toolbar.

Figure 4–5. *The Navigator toolbar, with (from the left) Project, Symbol, Search, Issue, Debug, Breakpoint, and Log buttons*

Each time you choose a navigator, the navigation window will appear on the left side of the window, along with the relevant inspector on the right side of the window, with the details displayed for the object selected (if any) in the navigation tree. The navigation tree and the inspector window are only displayed if you have already switched off the Navigator view (⌘0 to toggle). You also can choose a navigator with the shortcut keys shown in Table 4–7.

Table 4–7. *Navigator Keyboard Shortcuts*

Navigator	Shortcut
Project	⌘1
Symbol	⌘2
Search	⌘3
Issue	⌘4
Debug	⌘5
Breakpoint	⌘6
Log	⌘7
Hide navigator	⌘0

Views

In addition to the different navigators, you can manage the different views that are displayed:

- **Navigator view**: Provides access to navigators that let you navigate your project structure, or object hierarchy.

- **Debug area view**: Allows you access to breakpoints and object watchpoints as part of Xcode 4's debug functionality.

- **Utilities view**: Provides access to things like the help pages and object inspectors.

You can switch these views on and off, in order to free up screen space.

Table 4–8 shows ways for accessing the three views.

Table 4–8. *Tools for Toggling Between Views*

View	Toolbar	Shortcut
Navigator		⌘0
Debug area		⇧⌘Y
Utilities		⌥⌘0

Using Other Xcode Tools

Xcode provides a number of other tools to assist in the development of your code. Here, we'll look at two: one that enables static analysis of your code and another that enables you to drag and drop code snippets.

Static Analysis

Static analysis can help you to reduce bugs and inefficiencies within your code. The Xcode 4 IDE allows you to perform the analysis, examine your code, and take corrective actions as necessary—all within the same workspace window. Once the project you wish to analyze is selected, simply choose **Product ➤ Analyze** to start the analysis.

Once complete, Xcode opens the issues analyzer window to highlight the results of the analysis. Any problems are labeled in blue and marked. When you click one of these, Xcode will highlight the faulty code for your analysis and correction.

Code Snippets

A useful feature, and one that has been extended, is the ability to drag code snippets into your project, thus providing a default implementation for common code features such as implementing a protocol.

This Interface Builder feature can be used to select the library of items, including code snippets. Then you can highlight and drag an item onto your source file. For example, in the case of a protocol code snippet, this will implement the default code in your editor for you to complete.

Summary

In this chapter, we began by considering the relative features of Apple's mobile devices. You'll notice that the iPhone and iPod touch are very similar, whereas the iPad starts to introduce some key differences, mainly due to its tablet form factor.

We next took a look at design patterns that are used as approaches to application development, including how the code is structured. We considered an iOS application's life cycle, mapping this on the MVC pattern, and you should have started to notice some similarities with the Microsoft Windows method of running GUI-based applications.

Then we compared the class frameworks, which again are similar in features if not in structure, and compared the Objective-C language and the Xcode tools with their .NET counterparts. Objective-C is similar to C# in many respects. However, one of the key differences stems from the fact that iOS apps are not managed applications. Because the language is based on C, you see memory management, pointers, and non-same-typing being the norm within the language.

You should now be more familiar with the Xcode 4 environment, Objective-C as a language, and the similarities with Microsoft .NET in code, framework, and tools—at least in the key areas. We didn't go through a step-by-step comparison of everything—the breadth of the language and the class frameworks is far too large—but it isn't necessary. Using a combination of the Xcode development environment, online resources, and the following chapters, we'll start to dig into the details. You'll see more specific examples of how to use both the language and the SDK's features, making the comparison with .NET's classes clearer. In doing so, the transition to Objective-C and the iOS SDK will become easier and more apparent.

Chapter 5

Get to Work: Creating Your First Application

In the chapters so far, we've covered a multitude of topics, including an introduction to the iOS, the iOS SDK, the different devices available, and how to use development tools such as Xcode and MonoDevelop to create your initial application. But it's going to take more than a Hello, World application to satisfy your users.

Now we will begin to build on the knowledge you've gained so far and create a compelling application that is more feature-rich and functional. We will delve into the details of objects contained within the frameworks you've read about in previous chapters and how to use those objects. You'll also learn how to structure your application within Xcode to better support the build, debug, and deploy phases of your project, along with a more detailed look at the simulator for predeployment testing.

To demonstrate all of these features and capabilities, we will create a copy of the simple Lunar Lander app, using a similar style of graphics and physics that made it famous in the 1980s. We'll start the app in this chapter and continue to enhance it throughout this book.

To get started, we will cover the following topics in this chapter:

- Designing your application, considering the key issues to address before you start to build it

- Setting up your project and its structure in Xcode, including the settings that are most relevant in building and debugging your application

- Understanding the options for presenting the user interface to the user, including how to render simple graphics with collision detection

- Exploring the different methods for navigating the features of your application, such as difficulty level and high scores

- Interacting with the outside world, both through the Internet and through interactions from the user

- Exploring the iPhone simulator to test your application

As we work through the construction of the application, I'll continue to highlight the features found in the .NET Framework for comparison. I'll also point out common "gotchas" and how to avoid them.

The App Planning and Design Process

In the previous chapters, we looked at a few factors to consider before designing your application. For example, we compared the features of each device, which you need to consider when deciding which is best suited to your application. You need to understand some of the key differences that will need to be accommodated in your application. Such considerations are important, but there are also many more aspects you should think about before you start to write code.

In most professional organizations, the process of building an application usually starts with the *requirements capture stage*. This involves collecting the requirements of the users, or in the case of an undetermined audience, the features of your application. These are then prioritized, enabling you to drop those features you consider to be less important if time runs out.

The nonfunctional requirements are equally important as the functional requirements. An example of a nonfunctional requirement is how fast certain actions are expected to perform, or how much data you want your application to be able to handle. The actual devices you wish to target are also noted at this point, along with the features of the devices you wish to use.

Once you've captured and documented the requirements, the next phase is to start the design process. This involves defining how the core structure of your application will look—which aspects you will write in your own bespoke code, and which frameworks you will integrate together to achieve the desired functionality. This is known as the application's *architecture*.

The application's architecture is like the foundation and frame of your house. It provides the necessary structure, and from there, you can create your rooms and install the wiring, water, and heating. An application is no different.

You then build up the architecture with detailed implementation of your application's functionality using code. The end result is a working application that realizes the requirements you defined—much like your house, built with the features you expected.

Capturing the requirements for your application and designing the structure of your application will provide valuable guidance for when you write code, and will ensure that your application is more flexible and robust. You won't need to keep bolting bits of code on to accommodate features you had not considered earlier. So, while it's not mandatory, following a pragmatic version of the planning and design process, as described here, is considered good practice.

Apple iOS Design Resources

The process of designing your application relies heavily on your own imagination and brainpower—that's part of the fun. However, if you're confused when it comes to understanding how to best design your user interface or use the frameworks provided in the way in which they were intended, you are not alone!

The iOS operating system exposes the core features of the devices on which it runs. Therefore, understanding the characteristics of the device and knowing how Apple intended it to be used are important. Apple has also spent a lot of time creating and tailoring user-interface elements to particular tasks, exploiting the touch and gesture user interface.

For example, date and time entry are achieved by using the Date and Time Picker control, for which a more generic Picker control is available. This allows you to spin the wheel (or wheels) of the picker until the value you want is displayed. In the case of the date, the day, then the month, then the year appear. This is a good example of a control that has been specifically developed to suit the touch and swipe gestures of the device.

This really isn't that different to the principles adopted by Microsoft when it created the Windows SDK, and the existence of different user-interface controls as part of the .NET framework. Initially, these controls were suited to the mouse and keyboard as input, and then extended to cope with the introduction of tablet devices, such as the electronic-ink (e-ink) concept. And with the introduction of Windows Mobile 7, the process continues.

Apple provides a number of helpful guides at `http://developer.apple.com`. For user interface design, the main resource is the *iOS Human Interface Guidelines*. Its guidance includes the following:

- **User-Interface guidelines**: For example, a focus on building applications where the emphasis is on user experience and user collaboration

- **Usage guidelines on iOS user-interface controls**: A breakdown of the different user-interface controls, in which scenarios they are best used, and how to use them.

iOS Human Interface Guidelines does cover many more topics. I recommend you familiarize yourself with this guide. Also, take the time to browse the site and its associated content.

Other Design Resources

Many resources on the Internet provide example applications—some simple and some very complex. A particular favorite of mine is the source code and narrative of the journey taken to port the Doom game to the iPhone, available at `http://www.idsoftware.com/doom-classic/`. (Using something as complex as that as our example application would be fun, but unfortunately, impossible. I hope Lunar Lander is the next best thing.)

The following are some other useful resources you may wish to reference:

- *Objective-C for Absolute Beginners* (ISBN 978-1-4302-2832-5) is a great book that takes you through the details of Objective-C. It serves as a useful reference as you familiarize yourself with the language.

- Pttrns.com (`http://pttrns.com/`) is a useful resource for demonstrating user-interface patterns—not in a programmatic sense, but in a visual sense. It's a useful resource for giving you visualization ideas.

- *Pro Objective-C Design Patterns for iOS* (ISBN 978-14302-3330-5) provides design patterns to help you implement some of the more complex designs that you may want to use in your applications (it's more on the advanced side).

- Many resource management tools are available, some of them open source. If you're dealing with a large number of requirements for your application, you may find these tools useful. An example is available at `http://sourceforge.net/projects/osrmt/`.

Planning and Designing the Lunar Lander Application

So, let's practice what we preach. We will follow the phases of the design process described in the previous section. First, we'll capture and document the requirements, and then we'll design the application.

Requirements Specification

The requirements specification defines the scope of the application and provides the details on which the design is based. It is also usual to classify your requirements in terms of priority, allowing you to make the hard decisions should you run out of time. A common mechanism for doing this is to use what is known as the MOSCOW notation, for those requirements you **M**ust have, **S**hould have, **C**ould have, and **W**ould like to have. This is a simple but effective approach.

Table 5–1 shows a summary of requirements specification for our Lunar Lander game.

Table 5–1. *Requirements Specification for Lunar Lander*

ID	Description	Priority
01	The game will replicate the same graphical style as that adopted by the original Lunar Lander game.	M
02	There will be three difficulty levels: Easy, Medium, and Hard. Each will use a combination of space available for landing, the target angle, and the terrain to achieve different difficulty settings.	M
03	The top-five high scores will be stored locally.	M
04	The top-five high scores will be stored on the Internet for pan-Internet competition.	C
05	The keyboard will be used to provide user input.	M
06	The iPhone's accelerometer may also be used for user input.	C
07	When the lander strikes terrain, or attempts to land with a speed greater than the specified tolerance, it will explode.	M
08	The game will support five different terrains.	M
09	The game will start with a tank full of fuel, which will decrease by the number of seconds the engine is held in thrust mode (used to counteract gravity).	M
10	When the fuel supply runs out, the game will stop responding to user input.	M
11	The screen will show the score (fuel remaining added for every successful landing), the fuel remaining, the altitude, and the horizontal and vertical speed	M

Clearly, the requirements could be elaborated to provide further details, but for brevity, I've reduced the specification to the key requirements and associated data. This is enough information to allow us to create the game, which is the focus of this chapter.

Lunar Lander Application Design

Once you've decided the type of application you're developing, and what attributes make the most sense, you are ready consider some of the details. For example, a productivity tool (such as a calculator), a game (graphical), and a messaging (textual) app will all need a different look and feel.

User Interfaces

The application will present two distinct user interfaces:

- **Main menu**: This will be the default screen when the application is launched, and will provide a menu from which settings such as difficulty can be chosen. Also, the game can be started through this menu system. It will show the high scores in the middle of the screen and present a graphical picture of the lunar lander cabinet as a backdrop.

- **Game view**: This is the main view for the game, supported by its own controller. On this screen, the terrain will be drawn and the lander will be displayed, along with the game, statistics such as score and fuel remaining, and so on.

Game States

The game can be in one of the following five states, each of which responds to user input as relevant to its state:

- **Menu**: At the main menu, waiting for the user to quit, select a difficulty level, or start a new game.

- **Running**: The game has started and is responding to any user input.

- **Paused**: The game has either been paused or suspended and is waiting for the user to signal a restart.

- **Crashed**: The game has been running but the user has crashed. A new game can be started from this menu.

- **Won**: The game has been running and the user has successfully landed the lander. The next level is ready to commence when the user presses a key.

Other Game Design Elements

Other elements included in the game design are as follows:

- The game will use a simple timer to manage the on-screen graphic updates. However, this could be changed later to use multiple threads, which would provide for smoother game play.

- The Lunar Lander graphic will have three core states: flying with no thrust, flying with thrust, and crashed. The rotation is managed by using the iOS's graphic API.

- The terrain is predefined as a series of points, drawn at runtime using simple line graphics.

■ On-screen toolbar buttons will initially be used as user input. The left and right arrow keys rotate the lunar lander ship, and the up arrow key signals thrust. This could be changed to use the touch and gesture interface, topics that are explored in Chapter 10.

Building the Lunar Lander Application

With the requirements and design phases complete, we're ready to dive in and build the Lunar Lander game.

The Lunar Lander application will be written initially as an iOS application that targets the iPhone device. We'll talk about how you would change this to suit other devices using the iOS orientation features in Chapter 7.

We'll use the iOS View-based Application project template, allowing it to create the initial view and view controller for the main menu. We'll then create a separate view and associated view controller to manage the game's view. This will provide a head start and also build on the earlier examples we've already covered.

We'll also include other resources within the project, such as graphical images for the lunar lander image. So, let's get started.

Creating the Application Project

You know the drill: Choose a location on your disk for the project and fire up Xcode. Create a project using the View-based Application project template. I named the project LunarLander. Create the following files:

■ LunarLanderAppDelegate (.h and .m files)

■ LunarLanderViewController (.h, .m, and .xib files)

■ MainWindow.xib (which will use the LundarLanderViewController.xib view)

These will provide our single application delegate, which will launch the view controller that will use the LunarLanderViewController.xib as the view for the game's main menu. Your project structure should look like that shown in Figure 5-1.

Figure 5–1. *Initial LunarLander project files*

Before we go any further, let's add the main game view—again, a view controller and a view. To do this, choose **File ➤ New** (or use the ⌘N shortcut), and from the Cocoa Touch iOS templates, choose a UIViewController subclass. On the next few screens presented, ensure it subclasses the UIViewController class and is given the name GameViewController. Also remember to check the "With XIB for user interface" option. We'll use a NIB file to handle the game's main user interface—at least the view canvas and static items. After doing this, your folder structure should resemble that shown in Figure 5–2.

Figure 5–2. *LunarLander project with GameView class*

These files will provide a sufficient foundation to start the core mechanics of our Lunar Lander application. Before we add any more files, let's work with these initial files to start our game's implementation. We'll begin with the main menu view and some elements of our foundation architecture. Other resources will be added to the project as required, and we'll extend the application's logic as specific topics are introduced later in the book.

Building the User Interface and Flow Logic

The user interface uses the initial window, with a simple button that starts the game. We could also use this screen to display the high score and decorate it with pretty graphics. The main Lunar Lander view controller and XIB file will be used to manage this view. When the Start Game button is selected, it will load and display modally the game view with its own controller. This initial game screen is shown in Figure 5–3, with the Start Game button already added.

Figure 5–3. *Initial Start Game screen*

Our application delegate will be used to load this screen. As shown in Listing 5–1, in the header file, we declare two properties (highlighted in bold): one of type Window and the other a pointer to the LunarLanderViewController class instance. We'll use these in the application delegate code to display the window.

Listing 5–1. *LunarLanderAppDelegate.h*

```
#import <UIKit/UIKit.h>

@class LunarLanderViewController;

@interface LunarLanderAppDelegate : NSObject <UIApplicationDelegate> {

}

@property (nonatomic, retain) IBOutlet UIWindow *window;
@property (nonatomic, retain) IBOutlet LunarLanderViewController *viewController;

@end
```

And then we provide a supporting implementation file, in the form of
LunarLanderAppDelegate.m, as shown in Listing 5–2 (relevant code in bold). Here, you'll
notice we synthesize the properties, and in the dealloc() method, we free the member
these resources are occupying.

Listing 5–2. *LunarLanderAppDelegate.m*

```
#import "LunarLanderAppDelegate.h"

#import "LunarLanderViewController.h"

@implementation LunarLanderAppDelegate


@synthesize window=_window;
@synthesize viewController=_viewController;

- (BOOL)application:(UIApplication *)application didFinishLaunchingWithOptions:↵
(NSDictionary *)launchOptions
{
    // Override point for customization after application launch.
    self.window.rootViewController = self.viewController;
    [self.window makeKeyAndVisible];
    return YES;
}

….. default implementation code goes here and is unmodified

- (void)dealloc
{
    [_window release];
    [_viewController release];
    [super dealloc];
}

@end
```

The interesting part is in the didFinishLaunchingWithOptions() method, where we set
the rootViewController instance variable of the main window to be that of our Start
Game view controller (that is, the LunarLanderViewController class), and this is then
made visible as per the default implementation.

Although we start with this initial screen, it is the game view that will be used to manage the actual game playing. This very simple flow is shown in the diagram in Figure 5–4.

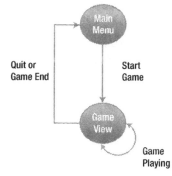

Figure 5–4. *Game state flow*

So, the LunarLanderViewController.xib file that we created earlier will have a simple user interface like that shown in Figure 5–3. This screen has nothing other than a view (of type UIView) and a button (of type UIButton), with the text of the button saying "Start Game." In .NET, this would be exactly the same as creating a form using Windows.Forms and placing a button on the screen.

We will also need to attach an action for the button click to display and start the game. This is no different from how we started our simple actions in the previous chapters.

Let's now look at hooking up the Start Game button to an action that is meaningful—that is, loading our main game view so that you can provide a location for the actual game mechanics. First, take a look at Listing 5–3, which is the header file for the view controller that handles the start game interaction.

Listing 5–3. *LunarLanderViewController.h*

```
#import <UIKit/UIKit.h>

// Inform the compiler that our GameViewController reference is to a class
@class GameViewController;

// Define the main class, or interface as it's known in Objective-C, inheriting from
 UIViewController
@interface LunarLanderViewController : UIViewController {

    @private GameViewController *pgameViewController;
}

// Property we'll use to refer to our ViewController
@property (nonatomic, retain) GameViewController *gameViewController;

// Event we'll use to attach to the Start Game button for the user to commence game play
-(IBAction)startGame:(id)sender;

@end
```

The implementation is held in LunarLanderViewController.m, as shown in Listing 5–4.

Listing 5–4. *LunarLanderViewController.m*

```objc
#import "LunarLanderViewController.h"
#import "GameView.h"
#import "LunarLanderAppDelegate.h"

@implementation LunarLanderViewController

// Synthesize our GameViewController pointer to the internally held variable
@synthesize gameViewController = pgameViewController;

- (void)dealloc
{
    // Release the custom controller
    [self.gameViewController release];

    // Call inherited
    [super dealloc];
}

- (void)didReceiveMemoryWarning
{
    // Release the view if it doesn't have a superview.
    [super didReceiveMemoryWarning];

    // Release any cached data, images, etc. that aren't in use.
}

#pragma mark - View lifecycle

// Implement viewDidLoad to do additional setup after loading the view, typically from
 a nib.
- (void)viewDidLoad
{
    [super viewDidLoad];
}

- (void)viewDidUnload
{
    [super viewDidUnload];
    // Release any retained subviews of the main view.
    // e.g. self.myOutlet = nil;
}

- (BOOL)shouldAutorotateToInterfaceOrientation:(UIInterfaceOrientation)
interfaceOrientation
{
    // Return YES for supported orientations
    return (interfaceOrientation == UIInterfaceOrientationPortrait);
}
-(void)startGame:(id)sender{
    // Do Something

    self.gameViewController = [[GameViewController alloc] initWithNibName:@"GameView"
 bundle:nil];
    [self presentModalViewController:self.gameViewController animated:YES];

}
@end
```

In summary, we will have achieved the following parts of our game's functionality:

- Created a GameViewController property and managed its memory
- Wrote an event handler for the Start Game button click that loads and displays modally the game view interface

These essentially allow the main game screen to be displayed. To that screen, we'll attach the menu and display the high score. We will react to the Start Game button click by displaying and starting the game.

So, creating the property uses the same method as described in previous chapters. However, here we are specific about assigning the property to the class member variable, allowing us to use different names for each.

Let's start at the beginning, in the header file:

```
@class GameViewController;
```

This tells the compiler that GameViewController is a class, and it means we don't need to include the full class declaration at this point. We just need to inform the compiler that it is a class. The semantics of the messages and attributes it supports will be provided at runtime by the iOS framework.

Next, we define our internal class member variables with the following line:

```
@private GameViewController *pgameViewController;
```

Most of this is similar to previous examples, but notice the @private declaration. This is a *visibility modifier*, and it defines the visibility (or *scope*) of the member variable. A number of options are available for specifying the visibility of the variables, which you place after the declaration. Also available are @public and @protected, which behave the same as the .NET equivalents with the same names and syntax (preceding the variable), but without the @ symbol.

Having a property allows us to control elements of that variable, such as its ability to be retained in memory until we decide it's no longer required. But we do need to remember to release it. In the dealloc() method, we release our gameViewController variable and its associated memory by sending it the release message. Also note that we call the inherited dealloc() method with the [super dealloc] call. This is known as *passing the call along the chain*, and using it is called being a *good citizen*. This behavior is provided for within the default implementation of methods created by Xcode. You can see all of this happening in the following code:

```
- (void)dealloc
{
    // Release the custom controller
    [self.gameViewController release];

    // Call inherited
    [super dealloc];
}
```

We need to react to the Start Button being pressed. So, if you have not already added the Start Game button, do that now.

Within the XIB file, you need to ensure the Start Game button's Start Touch Down event is hooked up to the `startGame` event property we created in code. You can do this using the drag-and-drop feature within the Connections Inspector. With the `LunarLanderViewController.xib` file open and the view visible (you'll see the Start Game button), you need to show the Connections Inspector to see the outlets available. From there, simply drag the `StartGame IBAction` (rember our definition in code) onto the Start Game button. This will wire it to the button's Start Touch Down event, which will fire when we first click the button.

The definition for the IBAction required to be visible on the Outlets page within the Interface Builder is as follows:

```
-(IBAction)startGame:(id)sender;
```

The `(IBAction)` declaration is key to telling Xcode 4's Interface Builder it's an action available for wiring up to an event.

Finally, we need to provide an implementation for the event, which, in our case, will load and display the `GameView` interface and its associated controller. This will manage the game-play mechanics for our Lunar Lander game. Here is the code:

```
-(void)startGame:(id)sender{
    // Set up our gameViewController pointer to our loaded GameView class
    self.gameViewController = [[GameViewController alloc] initWithNibName:@"GameView"↵
bundle:nil];
    // and display it modally.
    [self presentModalViewController:self.gameViewController animated:YES];
}
```

Our first line allocates the memory for our `GameViewController` class `[GameViewController alloc]`, and then we embed this within a message call to the `initWithNibName` method, passing the name of our XIB file. Finally, we display the window by sending the message `presentModalViewController` with a pointer to the view controller—in this case, `gameViewController`.

The syntax of this code will be more familiar to C++ developers than to .NET developers; the allocation of the `GameView` class is the same as calling new in C#. Indeed, the following syntax is also valid in Objective-C: `[GameViewController new]`. Once the class has been created, invoke the `ShowDialog()` method in .NET, using code similar to the following—this is the equivalent to the preceding objective-c code:

```
// C# Form creation and display using Windows Forms
Form MyForm = new MyForm;
MyForm.ShowDialog();
```

After implementing the event, go ahead and build the executable and start your application. It will display the main window with the Start Game button. If you select this button, a blank game window will be displayed. To help me make sure it was being displayed properly, I added a simple label to the game window user interface.

Implementing Navigation in Your Application

So we've built our application to display two simple forms, with a button click linking the two. But the game isn't much use if once you've completed it, you cannot get back to the main menu to start again or exit. So, we need to continue building our game screen implementation to provide a mechanism for returning to the main menu or the parent window.

We'll start by building on our existing game interface screen. We'll add a toolbar to conveniently allow us to place buttons on it. We'll also add some on-screen labels, which we'll use to display status information.

Go ahead and add the Toolbar, Button, and Label controls to create the interface shown in Figure 5–5. Use the standard features of Xcode 4's Interface Builder, as you've done in previous examples. Any code surrounding these items is automatically generated.

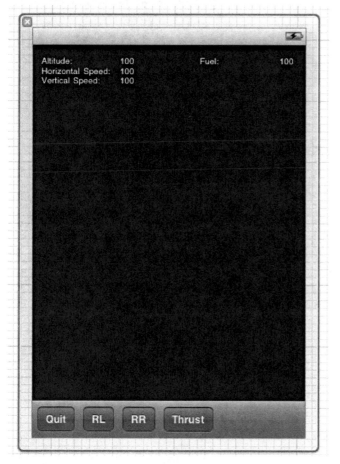

Figure 5–5. *Game interface screen*

We will improve this screen, but for the moment. It serves its purpose: to provide a Quit button that will return us to the main menu. To do this, we'll use techniques similar to those we've employed previously.

We need an IBAction property, which is used to provide the event property that is fired when selected. Also, we need to hook up the action on the Connections Inspector tab as before and provide the following event implementation code:

```
-(void)quitGame:(id)sender
{
    // No longer require the game window, go back to parent
    [ self dismissModalViewControllerAnimated:YES ];
}
```

This code will do the reverse of what the code that initially displayed the GameView view as a dialog box did. It will send the dismissModalViewControllerAnimated message to the view. This will cause the window to be unloaded and focus returned to the parent view from which it was launched—in our case, LunarLanderViewController. In .NET, this would be the same as calling the Close() method on the form, although no animation would be performed on the closing window, as is the case with the iOS SDK.

We won't do anything with the other buttons yet. (They will be used to test our game's physics before we look at more advanced user-interaction mechanisms in later chapters.) The labels are placeholders for the moment, and while we won't update their values yet, they start to make the game take shape.

Building the Core Game Engine and Enabling User Interaction

So far, we've displayed our initial game screen with the button that will start our game. Now we need to create the main game's mechanics. Next, we'll add to our application's functionality by starting to implement the core game engine. We will build on the GameView class, and explore some further iOS and Objective-C concepts in the process.

Examining the Game View Header

The GameView XIB files and the associated GameViewController class provide the implementation of our core game engine. First, consider the GameView.h file shown in Listing 5–5. I'll highlight the key segments of the code before we look at the code (a complete explanation follows the listing). In the header file, we do the following:

- Define our class with an NSTimer class member to provide a timer.

- Declare a number of methods that we will use to respond to on-screen button presses, namely Quit, Rotate Left, Rotate Right, and Thrust.

- Declare a method that our timer will execute at the desired frequency.

- Define a number of enumerated types to hold state, and a number of constants, which will be used within the game's physics.

- Declare our GameView that will hold three images to map onto the state of our thruster: Thrust, No-Thrust, and Crashed.

- Declare instance variables that represent state or instance variables, for which we will use our already defined enumerated types and constants.

- Declare a property to hold our lunar lander image and IBActions for each of the buttons so that we can wire them up to the methods that provide the implementation.

Phew. Now take a look at the code and see if you can spot all of these features in Listing 5–5.

Listing 5–5. *GameView.h*

```
#import <UIKit/UIKit.h>

// GameView class manages the game's view controller
//
@interface GameViewController : UIViewController {

    NSTimer *gameLoop;  // Core game timer
}

// Declare class events for our view controller
- (void)timerLoop:(NSTimer *)timeObj;   // Timer event loop
-(IBAction)quitGame:(id)sender;
-(IBAction)rotateLeft:(id)sender;
-(IBAction)rotateRight:(id)sender;
-(IBAction)thrust:(id)sender;

@end

// Declaration of some enumerated types to avoid lots of messy constant definitions
typedef enum { NOTREADY, READY, RUNNING, WON, LOST, PAUSED } GameState;
typedef enum { EASY, MEDIUM, HARD } GameDifficulty;
typedef enum { THRUSTERS_ON, THRUSTERS_OFF } ThrusterState;

// Declaration of other constants used to manage the physics
static const int FUEL_INITIAL = 200;
static const int FUEL_MAX = 200;
static const int FUEL_BURN = 10;
static const int MAX_INIT = 30;
static const int MAX_SPEED = 120;
static const int ACCELERATION_DOWN = 35;
static const int ACCELERATION_UP = 80;
static const double GRAVITY = 9.8;

// GameView class manages the main game
//
@interface GameView : UIView {
```

```
    // Images to hold the lander state
    @private UIImage            *plander_thrust;
    @private UIImage            *plander_nothrust;
    @private UIImage            *plander_crashed;

    // Other game member variables
    @private GameState          gstate;
    @private GameDifficulty     level;
    @private ThrusterState      thrusters;
    @private int                fuel;
    @private int                speed_x;
    @private int                speed_y;
    @private double             rotation;

    // Define our lander's X and Y on-screen coordinates
    @private int loc_x;
    @private int loc_y;
}

// Declare our member properties
@property (nonatomic, retain) UIImage *lander_nothrust;

// Declare our class methods
- (void) newGame;
- (void) updateLander;
- (void) rotateLeft:(id)sender;
- (void) rotateRight:(id)sender;
- (void) thrustEngine:(id)sender;

@end
```

Did you spot them all? If not, don't worry. We'll walk through the important parts of the implementation.

The game will support a number of states. These will be used to invoke functionality that is appropriate for its state. For example, when the game is running, we'll update the screen with the on-screen graphics. However, if the game has yet to start or a recent game has just finished, there will be no need to constantly update the screen. We will also use a timer to drive the core game, update the game physics, and invoke the code necessary to update the on-screen graphics and detect user interactions.

A more detailed view of the game's engine flow is shown in Figure 5–6.

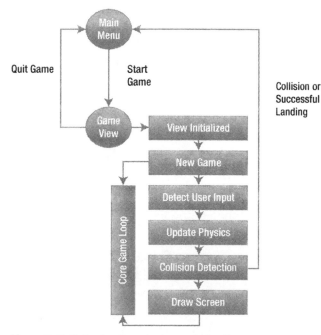

Figure 5–6. *Following the core game engine flow*

You can see from the flow that once the GameView is initialized, we will initialize the game settings, such as loading graphics and setting default values. Then we proceed to detect user input, update the game's physics, and check collision detection, which may indicate a successful landing or a crash.

At this point, we'll force the screen to be repainted. But this screen painting actually happens automatically by linking such updates to a timer, which will fire every one-quarter second. If the game isn't in the correct state—it's yet to start or you have crashed and it's waiting for you to reset the game—then the screen will not be updated.

As with most designs, we could improve on this application, and we'll do this as the book progresses. For now, our current design is sufficient to introduce some key topics.

Examining the Game View Implementation

Before we start to discuss some of the header code's implementation, let's look at the main source code file, which defines the header's implementation, as shown in Listing 5–6. As before, I'll introduce the key tenets of the code's implementation, and then provide a more detailed explanation following it. In the GameView implementation, we achieve the following through bespoke code:

- Provide an implementation for our timer, which will update the lander's position using the UpdateLander() method and set the screen to be dirty to force it to be redrawn.

- ▪ Provide a `QuitGame()` implementation that dismisses the modal dialog box, taking us back to the Start Game screen that presented it.

- ▪ Provide implementations for `RotateLeft()`, `RotateRight()`, and `Thrust()` button clicks, which simply call methods of the same name within the core game engine.

- ▪ Provide code for the initialization of the class—in our case, display the lander after having first loaded the image.

- ▪ Provide a default implementation for `NewGame()`, which resets our game variables.

- ▪ Provide a placeholder for the `UpdateLander()` method, which is where we would apply the games physics in response to the time spent firing and keys being pressed.

- ▪ Provide empty methods for the `RotateLeft()`, `RotateRight()`, and `Thrust()` methods, which will implement the game mechanics.

Again, see if you can spot all of these features in Listing 5–6.

Listing 5–6. *GameView.m*

```objc
#import "GameView.h"

@implementation GameViewController

- (id)initWithNibName:(NSString *)nibNameOrNil bundle:(NSBundle *)nibBundleOrNil
{
    self = [super initWithNibName:nibNameOrNil bundle:nibBundleOrNil];
    if (self) {
        // Custom initialization
    }

    return self;
}

- (void)dealloc
{
    [super dealloc];
}

- (void)didReceiveMemoryWarning
{
    // Release the view if it doesn't have a superview.
    [super didReceiveMemoryWarning];

    // Release any cached data, images, etc. that aren't in use.
}

#pragma mark - View lifecycle

- (void)viewDidLoad
{
    // Create an instance of the timer every (0.025) 1/4 of a second, to fire the↵
```

```
'timerLoop' function
    gameLoop = [NSTimer scheduledTimerWithTimeInterval: 0.025 target:self selector:↵
@selector(timerLoop:) userInfo:nil repeats:YES];

    [super viewDidLoad];
    // Do any additional setup after loading the view from its nib.
}

- (void)viewDidUnload
{
    [super viewDidUnload];
    // Release any retained subviews of the main view.
    // e.g., self.myOutlet = nil;
}

- (BOOL)shouldAutorotateToInterfaceOrientation:(UIInterfaceOrientation)↵
interfaceOrientation
{
    // Return YES for supported orientations
    return (interfaceOrientation == UIInterfaceOrientationPortrait);
}

// timerLoop - main Timer event function
-(void)timerLoop:(NSTimer *)timerObj
{
    // Update the lander's position
    [(GameView *)self.view updateLander];

    // Redisplay the whole view
    [self.view setNeedsDisplay];

}

// User has indicated that want to fire the thruster engines; pass this onto the game
//
-(void)quitGame:(id)sender
{
    // No longer require the game window, go back to parent
    [self dismissModalViewControllerAnimated:YES];
}

// User has indicated that want to fire the thruster engines; pass this onto the game
//
-(void)rotateLeft:(id)sender
{
    [(GameView *)self.view rotateLeft:sender];
}

// User has indicated that want to fire the thruster engines; pass this onto the game
//
-(void)rotateRight:(id)sender
{
    [(GameView *)self.view rotateRight:sender];
}

// User has indicated that want to fire the thruster engines; pass this onto the game
//
```

```objc
-(void)thrust:(id)sender
{
    [(GameView *)self.view thrustEngine:sender];
}

@end

@implementation GameView

@synthesize lander_nothrust = plander_nothrust;


// initWithCode - called when we programmatically initialize our XIB resource
//
- (id) initWithCoder:(NSCoder *)aDecoder
{
    if (self == [super initWithCoder:aDecoder]) {

        // Initialize the sprites
        //
        NSString *imagePath = [[ NSBundle mainBundle] pathForResource:@"lander"↵
 ofType:@"tiff"];
        self.lander_nothrust = [UIImage new];
        self.lander_nothrust = [UIImage imageWithContentsOfFile:imagePath];

        // Set initial game state
        [self newGame];

    }
    return self;
}

-(void)dealloc
{
//    [self.lander_nothrust release];
    [super dealloc];
}

// newGame - Initializes a new game
//
-(void) newGame
{
    gstate = READY;
    level = EASY;
    thrusters = THRUSTERS_OFF;
    fuel = FUEL_INITIAL;
    loc_x = self.frame.size.width / 2;
    loc_y = self.frame.size.height / 2;

    // Set the game as RUNNING
    gstate = RUNNING;
}

// updateLander - Updates the lander position\state based on gravity and any user input
- (void) updateLander
{
    // *TODO
```

```
}

// drawRect - Redraw the screen
-(void)drawRect:(CGRect)rect
{
    // Only draw when we're ready to draw
    if (gstate != RUNNING)
        return;

    [self.lander_nothrust drawAtPoint:CGPointMake(loc_x, loc_y)];
    self.backgroundColor = [UIColor redColor];
}

// rotateLeft - rotate the lander left
- (void)rotateLeft:(id)sender
{
    // Do Something
}

// rotateRight - rotate the lander right
- (void)rotateRight:(id)sender
{
    // Do Something
}

// thrustEngine - fire the thruster on the engine
- (void)thrustEngine:(id)sender
{
    // Do Something
}

@end
```

Using a Timer to Invoke Key Core Events

The first thing to notice in Listing 5–6 is that as part of the ViewController class, we defined a timer that will implement our game's core loop. Our timer uses the iOS NSTimer class, which is similar in functionality to the System.Threading.Timer class in the .NET Framework. The full definition is as follows:

```
NSTimer *gameLoop;  // Core game timer
```

In the GameView class, we won't need the time initialized until the view is loaded. Remember that our GameView class encapsulates the essence of the game. While we could initialize it in other places, the viewDidLoad event is as good as any other. as it's executed after the view successfully loads (as its name suggests). Our implementation of this is as follows:

```
- (void)viewDidLoad
{
    // Create an instance of the timer every (0.025) 1/4 of a second, to fire the⏎
 'timerLoop' function
    gameLoop = [NSTimer scheduledTimerWithTimeInterval: 0.025 target:self selector:⏎
@selector(timerLoop:) userInfo:nil repeats:YES];

    [super viewDidLoad];
```

```
    // Do any additional setup after loading the view from its nib.
}
```

Examining the code further, you can see that we use the `scheduledTimerWithTimeInterval` method. We pass it the interval at which the timer is fired (in seconds, and you can use fractions), the target for the callback, and the callback method we'll use to host the bespoke code we'll execute every time the event is fired. The remaining parameters allow bespoke information to be passed in the form of `userInfo` and specify whether the timer event repeats or is a one-off. In our case, we won't pass custom information and the time is repeating.

You'll notice that for the callback method, we use the `selector` parameter and the `@selector` notation, passing the name of our method. It returns an object type of SEL, expected by the method for the callback. In .NET, delegates are used to provide type-safe function pointers, equivalent to our functionality here.

The end result after being successfully initialized is that the `gameLoop` member variable now points to an instance of an `NSTimer`, which when fired at the prescribed interval, will call our `timerLoop` class method in the `ViewController` class. Let's take a quick look at the implementation of this method, which is pretty straightforward.

```
// timerLoop - main Timer event function
-(void)timerLoop:(NSTimer *)timerObj
{
    // Update the lander's position
    [(GameView *)self.view updateLander];

    // Redisplay the whole view
    [self.view setNeedsDisplay];

}
```

In our game engine's main loop, whose implementation is encapsulated within the `timerLoop` method, we do a number of things. First, we call a method that handles the game's physics and recognizes user interaction detected by further events being called. This method will simulate the effects of gravity, fire the engines if you're telling it to, and rotate the craft as you dictate. It will also decrease the fuel being used and look for either a collision or a successful landing.

You'll notice that the method to handle all of this magic is called `updateLander`, but because `self` in this instance points to a `UIView` (look at your XIB file), we're going to cast it into the `GameView` class of which we know it's an instance. In order for the cast to work, with the `GameView` view open in Xcode's Interface Builder, ensure that in the Identity Inspector, the Custom Class class name is set to `GameView`. We can then do the cast, because the `UIView` class is used in the Interface Builder to define the view. In our code, we extend the functionality of this class and call it `GameView`. If you reexamine `GameView.h,` you'll see code like the following, so we know it's safe for us to perform such a type cast:

```
@interface GameView : UIView {
// Implementation goes here
}
@end
```

The notation in .NET depends on the language. But using C# as a comparator, the syntax is similar, using the colon and then the parent class to denote class inheritance. So, use a cast (GameView *) to type cast the view property of our view controller, this then allows us to refer to the defined updateLander() method.

The final point to note, and not really related to timers per se, is that once we've updated the game's physics, we will need to update the display to reflect the change in the lander's position or state. To do this, we use the setNeedsDisplay method and pass this message to the view object—in this case, our GameView object. This will force a refresh of the display (the whole display), during which we will do updates such as redrawing the lander.

Self-Documenting Code

Before we continue with the GameView class's implementation, I want to touch on the concept of *self-documenting code*. The principle behind this term is that your code should be self-explanatory through its implementation. A good example is the use of well-named variables and methods, employing the camelCase convention we discussed earlier in the book. Another concept is that while you can hard-code values into your code, they won't necessarily mean anything to the person who picks up the code for debugging or to extend it. To improve readability, where possible, avoid the use of hard-coded literal values by replacing them with a constant or an enumerated type.

Using Constants

An example is the best way to demonstrate the use of constants. Imagine we're setting our initial fuel tank value to its full capacity, which is actually 200 liters. We could do this by assigning the literal value of 200 to our variable, like this:

```
int fuel = 200;
```

Or, we could define a constant, like this:

```
static const int FUEL_INITIAL = 200;
```

And then use this constant to assign a value to our variable, like so:

```
int fuel = FUEL_INITIAL;
```

Notice that while it takes an extra line to define the constant, it makes our code more readable without the use of comments. Also, if we need to reset the value to use this same value within the same context, we can simple use the constant again. The syntax for C# is exactly the same.

Using Enumerated Types

Another coding method, similar but subtly different from using a constant, is to use an enumerated type. This not only provides predefined literal values with a more meaningful name, but it also supplies an object type that can only be a value in the set of values defined. This ensures your code is more reliable and robust by keeping it type-safe.

Again, let's use an example. Consider the requirement that our game can be in six different states: Not Ready, Ready, Running, Won, Lost, and Paused. We could use literal values, or even define six different constants. But, highlighting the value of type safety, if we used numbers stored in an int, as is the case with constants, nothing would stop us from setting it to a value that was an invalid state, thus causing an error. So, rather than that, we'll use an enumerated type:

```
typedef enum { NOTREADY, READY, RUNNING, WON, LOST, PAUSED } GameState;
```

When placed in the header file (not within a class definition), this will define a new type (hence the typedef command) of enumerated values (hence the enum syntax) with valid values of NOTREADY, READY, RUNNING, WON, LOST, and PAUSED. The incremental order of the set values means that NOTREADY will automatically be assigned a value of 0 (zero), with PAUSED holding a value of 5. This is then given a tag name of GameState, meaning we can use this to refer to the type.

So, after defining our enumerated type, we can create objects of that type that can only hold values defined in the set we've defined—that is, valid states. Here's an example:

```
GameState state = NOTREADY;
```

You'll notice that within our application, we use both constants and enumerated types to help create more readable code—*self-documenting code*. We do so not just for the GameState, but also the game's difficulty level (as GameDifficulty) and the lunar lander thruster's state (as ThrusterState).

The C# equivalent of enumerated types is very similar and uses almost exactly the same syntax. The following code line shows this, with a small difference in the exclusion of the typedef specified and the tag name in a different place:

```
enum GameState { NOTREADY, READY, RUNNING, WON, LOST, PAUSED }
```

Programmatically Initializing an XIB Resource

You know that the GameView user interface, contained within our GameView.xib file, is displayed as a result of starting the game. In our case, we want finer-grained control over this process, and so we used the initWithNibName command to load the GameView.xib programmatically. This has the effect of calling the initWithCoder method, kind of like a constructor, which we'll use to not only load the XIB file, but to also do some application initialization. Consider the following implementation of this method:

```
- (id) initWithCoder:(NSCoder *)aDecoder
{
    if (self == [super initWithCoder:aDecoder]) {
```

```
        //// Initialize the sprites
        //
        NSString *imagePath = [[ NSBundle mainBundle] pathForResource:@"lander"↵
 ofType:@"tiff"];
        self.lander_nothrust = [UIImage new];
        self.lander_nothrust = [UIImage imageWithContentsOfFile:imagePath];

        // Set initial game state
        [self newGame];

    }
    return self;
}
```

Our implementation is pretty simple. Although it's incomplete at this stage, it's starting to take shape.

First, we call the parent method using the [super initWithCoder:aDecoder] command, which will ensure the inherited foundation object is created first and assigned to the calling class, referenced by self. If this works, and is not nil, then we move into our bespoke code and finally return the newly created object. This is typical object initialization code, and you'll see it repeated with many other objects that use inheritance to provide their own implementation.

Our initialization code does two things. First, we initialize a property of type UIImage, which will hold one of the many thruster states. In this case, it's the image of the lunar lander with no thruster being fired, hence the property called lander_nothrust. Remember in Listing 5–5 we defined our property as follows:

```
// Declare our member properties
@property (nonatomic, retain) UIImage *lander_nothrust;
```

And remember to synthesize it in our implementation, as we did in Listing 5–6:

```
@synthesize lander_nothrust = plander_nothrust;
```

However, this is an empty property and needs initializing. Once the image has been initialized, we'll also call one of our own bespoke methods called newGame, which as its name suggests, initializes the application to start a new game. This is achieved with the [self newGame] command.

Let's take a closer look at the image initialization code. At this point, we're using three separate UIImage objects to hold the different states of our lunar lander craft: with the engine thrusting, without the engine thrusting, and crashed. We could use an array of images or one of the bespoke iOS classes to achieve this, but at this point, we're keeping it simple.

So, after we've added our Lander.tiff image to the project (go ahead and do this), we can reference this resource using the pathForResource method, passing the file name, including its extension. The following command achieves this, returning a string to our image resource:

```
NSString *imagePath = [[ NSBundle mainBundle] pathForResource:@"lander" ofType:@"tiff"];
```

We can then create an instance of our UIImage using the slightly different notation of new, as follows:

```
self.lander_nothrust = [UIImage new];
```

You'll notice that this syntax is similar to C#, in that were using the new keyword to instantiate a new object. We can then use the imageWithContentsOfFile method to load our image using the fully qualified path to the resource. Here's the full line:

```
self.lander_nothrust = [UIImage imageWithContentsOfFile:imagePath];
```

If you examine the newGame method's implementation, you'll see that it's straightforward, It simply starts to initialize some of the class member variables to their default values for a new game.

Manually Drawing the User Interface

In most cases, you won't need to worry about drawing your user interface, because it's typically handled automatically by the iOS framework as part of the control's functionality. However, in some instances, you might want fine-grained control over your user interface. This is especially the case if your application is a game, because the controls provided as part of the iOS framework provide only some of the functionality required.

In such circumstances, you can override the method called whenever your application's window requires a refresh. This method is called drawRect and passes the region that requires redrawing as a CGRect structure. This structure contains the starting point and size of the rectangular area that requires redrawing. This area is known as *dirty* if it requires redrawing. Redrawing is necessary when something has changed, such as an area previously being obscured by a window or a control updating the way it looks. Consider the following method and its implementation:

```
// drawRect - Redraw the screen
-(void)drawRect:(CGRect)rect
{
    // Only draw when we're ready to draw
    if (gstate != RUNNING)
        return;

    [self.lander_nothrust drawAtPoint:CGPointMake(loc_x, loc_y)];

}
```

You'll notice that we query the state of the application first—if it's not running, there is no need to update the screen. Assuming that it is running, at this stage, we simply draw our lunar lander image at the x and y location defined during game initialization and using the lander_nothrust image. At this stage, that's all we're doing. However, as the game's physics are reflected and the user interactions are taken into account, we'll update the location of the lunar lander, check for collisions, and so on—all within this method—and draw the visuals that make sense. This will mean the lander will fall if no thrust is applied, climb if thrust is applied, and so on. So, it's pretty straightforward, but effective!

Using Bespoke Methods

As with most programming languages, the structure of your application typically uses subroutines, or class methods in an object-oriented world to define bespoke functionality. When called in the correct order, this functionality implements your application—in our case, the Lunar Lander game. The structure and naming of these routines are part of your application's architecture.

Our game provides placeholders as follows:

- newGame: Initializes the game. This method is called after the user interface has been initialized.

- rotateLeft: Rotates the lunar lander craft to the left. This is in response to the user indicating he wants to rotate left. In the first instance, this is achieved by a toolbar button. Discussed in Chapter 7, and Later on, we'll look at swipes and gestures, discussed in Chapter 10.

- rotateRight: Rotates the lunar lander craft to the right. This is in response to the user indicating he wants to rotate right. Again, here we're using a toolbar button; later, we'll look at swipes and gestures.

- thrustEngine: Fires the lunar lander's thruster engine, which in turn will slow down the rate of ascent, and even increase altitude if held down for long enough. It will also indicate a change in the engine's state, allowing our drawing method to reflect this in what the user sees.

- quitGame: Quits the game by dismissing the modal GameView displayed. This method and newGame are the only ones we'll implement in this chapter.

Using Simulators to Test Your Application

Given that we are now starting to develop our application in earnest, we'll be using the simulator much more. We could start looking at deployment and testing on a real device, but we'll leave that complication for the moment, partly because it's not yet necessary.

Targeting the simulator during the early stages of application development can save you a great deal of time. You don't need to wait for applications to be installed on your physical device before seeing the effects of changes in your code. It also is not necessary to buy and install a developer certificate to run code in the simulator.

Don't get me wrong—using the simulator is not perfect and has its own challenges. For example, it can't display OpenGL graphics, simulate multitouch events, or provide readings from some of the iPhone sensors such as the GPS. That said, for most apps, it has enough features to be a valuable part of your development process.

One gotcha to be aware of is that you can't guarantee that your simulated app performance will resemble your real application performance. The simulator tends to run silky smooth, helped by the power of your Mac on which it runs. Real applications will almost certainly have more limited resources, affecting the user experience. Be sure to test your app on all the physical devices it targets, so that you know your expectations are in line with reality.

The following are some of the simulator's features:

- **User input**: The mouse can be used to simulate a fingertip. Holding down the option key (⌥) will display two circles, which then can be used to simulate multitouch events.

- **Rotation**: This can be achieved using the hardware menu.

- **iOS versions**: You can choose different iOS versions to test your application.

- **Low memory**: This can be simulated, so you can send this status to your application to see how it behaves.

- **Hardware keyboard**: The simulator allows you to use your Mac's keyboard to provide keyboard input.

So, after all that hard work, what does your game look like running? In Figure 5–7, you can see the game running within the simulator, with the two circles representing the touch gestures in the simulator.

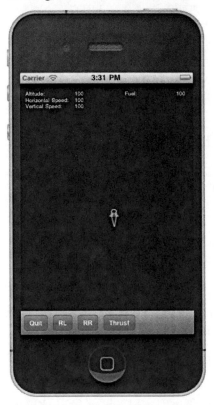

Figure 5–7. *Game running within the simulator*

Summary

In this chapter, we've taken the foundation provided by previous chapters and started to develop a real application—something closer to fulfilling the rich user experience expected by most iPhone and iPad users. OK, so our Lunar Lander game won't suit everyone, and yes, I'm still hankering after my youth, but mobile game applications should be fun. It also gives you a chance to build on some of the lessons you've learned so far and elaborate on them.

We covered some recommendations on how to begin application development, starting with the basics, such as capturing the requirements and thinking about application design. We then started to build on the visual and programmatic aspects of our application.

While building the application, you were introduced to the use of more than one view in presenting user interfaces, including the programmatic display of our game application. We added some navigation controls and tapped into the events these controls provide. We also looked at using utility type classes, such as the NSTimer class and the UIImage class, to start to implement our functionality.

We also looked at how to write more readable, self-documenting code, as well as how to use our own bespoke methods to implement a meaningful architecture whose structure should be easily understood by most developers. Finally, we considered the simulator as a good test resource.

In the next chapters, we'll build on this application, fleshing out its functionality. In doing so, we'll explore other aspects of the iOS, such as more advanced user interfaces and data persistence.

Chapter 6

Build Your Skills: Enhancing Your Application with a Dynamic User Interface

Apple has always placed an important emphasis on the experience a user has when using an Apple iOS-based device, especially because it was one of the first companies to implement an operating system that used a graphical user interface (GUI) as its focus for user interaction. The Macintosh wasn't the first personal computer to use a GUI but was the first to provide such comprehensive support to the developer community. This included Interface Guidelines, which you've already discovered exist in the OS X of today through some of the Apple Developer resources provided. Apple's take on user experience isn't just the graphical user interface, of course. It also includes things like the physical characteristics of the device and touch-based user input. However, the design of your application's user interface is pivotal in providing the engaging user interface Apple expects and which works harmoniously with the other attributes that make iOS devices some of the world's leading mobile devices.

So with your iOS device in hand, and limited only by your imagination, the only hurdle is unlocking the magic held in your device and converting your ideas to reality through the application. This chapter focuses on how the iOS SDK helps you do just that. Specifically, you look at the following:

- The capabilities of your device and how to embrace them, such as autosizing

- Different application types, and view controllers available to support them

- The user-interface elements provided by the iOS SDK to help you build your user interface

- Working examples of how to use the iOS SDK to implement typical UI Element application features

- Apple resources provided to support you, and some tips of how to get the best from them

You start by exploring some of the key features of the iOS devices and typical applications.

Understanding Platform and Device Constraints

The user experience starts with the device being used, and therefore the devices you target and the physical characteristics of each device your application is written to exploit. Note that I deliberately use the words *target* and *exploit* because certain features such as device orientation and the ability of your application to rotate its user-interface are not automatically adopted by your application—you need to specifically write your application to be aware of them. You cover this later in the book.

Let's take a look at some relevant platform characteristics.

Display Size and Resolution

The screen resolution of the different iOS devices is very relevant when designing your application. There is an important distinction between a unit of measure used to describe the size of a device's screen (a *pixel*) and the measure used to describe the area that is drawn onscreen (a *point*). Table 6–1 details the screen resolutions available for the different iOS devices in pixels.

Table 6–1. *iOS Device Screen Sizes*

Device	Portrait	Landscape
iPhone 4	640 × 960	960 × 640
iPad	768 × 1024	1024 × 768
Other iPhone and iPod Touch devices	320 × 480	480 × 320

Note: All measurements are in pixels.

At this point, it's worth noting that when you look at the graphical system frameworks provided as part of iOS SDK, they require you to use a logical coordinate system that uses points, not pixels. You look at why, but the conversion between pixel and point depends on your display type. A standard display has is a 1:1 ratio; but on the Retina display, a 1:2 ratio is used.

Example Applications That Take Full Advantage of the Device's Form Factor

Good examples exist of applications that take advantage of the different device sizes and format. Some example applications change the display orientation to one that makes more sense for its usage. For example, in Figure 6–1, the YouTube application on the iPhone uses portrait to display its lists because landscape mode adds little value.

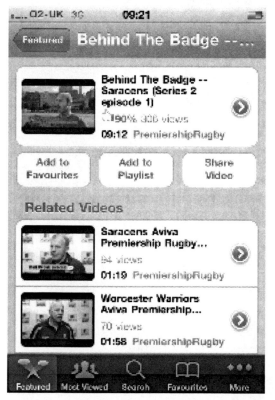

Figure 6–1. *YouTube video list represented in portrait orientation*

But when you play a particular video, the landscape orientation is better suited. You see the application switch to playing the video in landscape mode, as shown in Figure 6–2. It still has the option for portrait, but that mode is less effective.

Figure 6–2. *YouTube defaulting to landscape mode to play a video*

The iPad in particular gives you even more opportunity to take advantage of its dimensions. The *Financial Times* iPad app uses the device's form factor to present the look and feel of the newspaper that it's digitally emulating, as you can see in Figure 6–3.

Figure 6–3. *The* Financial Times *iPad application in all its portrait glory*

An alternative is the BBC's iPad application, which takes full advantage of landscape mode to display news and corresponding video side by side using a Split View controller (something you build an example of later in the chapter). You can see the application in Figure 6–4.

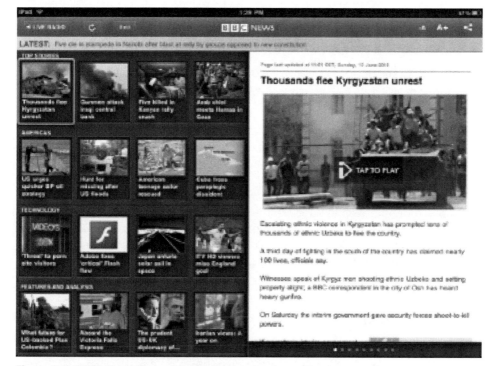

Figure 6–4. *BBC's News iPad application taking advantage of Landscape mode*

Points Compared to Pixels

The point measurement unit is used to describe the area that is drawn onscreen, whereas pixels describe the size of a screen or the size of an image such as an icon. Why bother? Apple provides you with support to enable your application to be consistently presented regardless of the device on which it is running. It does this through the use of points and a logical coordinate system that, when also used by the iOS system frameworks to interpret a physical device location, ensures the content you draw appears the same size regardless of device. Microsoft employs a similar logical coordinate system as part of its GDI+ framework. You'll soon find it's as easy to deal with points as pixels, and the logical equivalence across devices often means it's easier.

Other Considerations

There are some obvious considerations when looking at screen size. An iPad clearly has a much larger screen than an iPhone, so your application can make use of this and your artwork quality can also reflect that the size difference. For example, don't just use the same size graphical content and scale it up unless you are happy to sacrifice the quality of your artwork.

Also keep in mind that the Apple Human Interface Guidelines suggest that certain user interface elements remain the same despite the size of the screen. For example, the guidelines suggest that tappable elements in your user interface are most comfortable for users at a size of 44 × 44 points.

> **NOTE:** Typically, the pixel density on a mobile device is higher where it is designed to be viewed up close. This is true of an iPhone 4, which has a pixel density of 326 pixels per inch (PPI), vs. an iPad 2, which has 132 PPI.

Supporting Device Orientation

The iOS provides support for rotating your application based on the device's orientation. Whether your application chooses to support this is of course a design consideration. In some cases it makes no sense for your application to rotate into a certain orientation because the user experience would be sacrificed. For example, a game with some kind of scrolling landscape would look squashed and compromised if rotated to portrait mode.

Handling Device Orientation

As you may have come to expect, the iOS SDK fires an event to notify your code of a device orientation change. Take a look at the event's signature:

```
(void) didRotateFromInterfaceOrientation(UIInterfaceOrientation)fromInterfaceOrientation
```

When this event is fired and your application catches the event by implementing this method signature in your code, it is passed the orientation from which the device has been rotated. So you just have to implement the event, right? Wrong—in addition to providing an implementation for the rotation method, you also need to tell your application to support different orientations and fire the event in the first place. If you examine the code created when you build your view controllers, you notice the following code commented out:

```
/*
// Override to allow orientations other than the default portrait orientation.
- (BOOL)shouldAutorotateToInterfaceOrientation:(UIInterfaceOrientation)↵
interfaceOrientation {
    // Return YES for supported orientations
    return (interfaceOrientation == UIInterfaceOrientationPortrait);
}
*/
```

You need to both uncomment this code, indicating to the application that it now supports different orientations, and ensure that you return the value YES if the orientation fired (in the example, portrait) is supported or an unconditional YES if all orientations are supported. You also need to implement the rotation event discussed earlier.

If you want to know whether the device has been rotated into portrait orientation, you look to see if it has moved from landscape orientation and reflect the change by using a view controller that is oriented to that orientation:

```
if((fromInterfaceOrientation == UIInterfaceOrientationLandscapeLeft) ||
    (fromInterfaceOrientation == UIInterfaceOrientationLandscapeRight))
  {
    //  Load the view controller oriented to the Portrait mode
  }
```

You can also test for UIInterfaceOrientationPortrait and UIInterfaceOrientationPortraitUpsideDown, in all cases returning YES or NO depending on whether your application has been written to support a particular rotation.

Let's test it. If you leave your code commented out or return a flat NO, your application supports only portrait and not landscape orientation. So, if you run the application in the simulator and use either the rotate left (⌘←) or rotate right (⌘→) command from the Hardware menu, the device rotates. Rotate it to the left, and you should see a screen similar to the one in Figure 6–5.

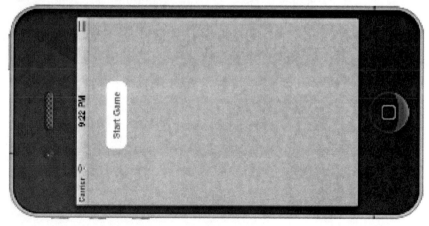

Figure 6–5. *Device rotated left*

This clearly doesn't look right, and it's no surprise because you've indicated that your application doesn't support any orientation other than portrait. Just to illustrate the point, let's uncomment the code and return YES as the value regardless of the orientation. After you change the code, re-run the application, and follow the same left orientation, you should see a screen similar to the one in Figure 6–6.

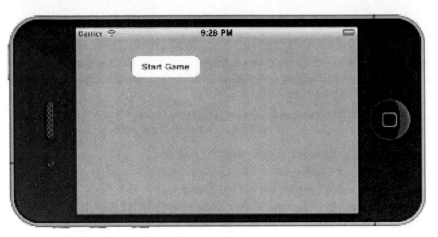

Figure 6–6. *Device rotated with landscape support*

Better, but not right. As you can see, the button isn't centered on the screen as it was in portrait mode. No matter: this is easily fixed because Xcode and the iOS SDK support autosizing using control attributes. Open your project and LunarLanderViewController.xib to display the start screen. Select button using Size Inspector (⌥⌘5), and you're presented with the Size Inspector shown in Figure 6–7.

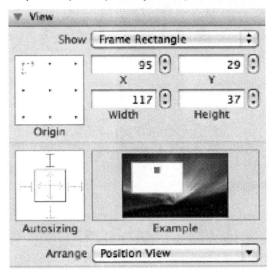

Figure 6–7. *Size Inspector*

First, don't be baffled by the display; it's pretty straightforward. Let's focus on the Autosizing pane. The box on the left is where you modify the attribute's values; the box on the right is an example animation depicting the effect of your change—a really useful visual tool to confirm you're making the right changes.

Looking more closely, notice two things:

- A set of red arrows in the inner square that represent horizontal and vertical space inside the selected object

- A set of *I* shapes outside the inner box that represent the distance between the object selected and the outside of the view that contains it

In both cases, a dashed line means the space is flexible: that is, it adjusts based on the orientation of the screen. A solid line means the space is fixed. So, if you want your button to be flexible along the horizontal axis and center itself, you need to ensure that the left *I* shape is dashed, not solid, as it is by default. This change is shown in Figure 6–7, and the animation shows the button moving to be centered on the landscape screen when rotated—exactly what you want. Make the change and run the application, and you should see a screen similar to that in Figure 6–8. Much better!

Figure 6–8. *The screen rotated left with autosizing adjusted*

Autosizing isn't the only option available to you. The iOS SDK provides a method that gives you precise control over the control's look and feel through code by adjusting its properties just before the rotation has completed. The method signature to change is as follows:

```
(void)willAnimateRotationToInterfaceOrientation:(UIInterfaceOrientation)
```

The final option available gives you exact control over what your screen looks like in a given orientation but without the effort of doing it programmatically. To achieve this, you have a view for each orientation you want to support, and in the same method just described you adjust the view using the self.view property. This means your view can define the look and feel of your user interface at design time for a given orientation, without you having to programmatically adjust the user-interface controls in code. Simple!

Enough of rotation and orientation. Although they're important, they aren't the main focus of this chapter. Let's look beyond the attributes of the device and consider the type of application you may be building and the SDK support provided to give the user a familiar but rich experience.

Application Types and Associated View Controllers

So far, this book has introduced the concepts of views and view controllers, and even suggested how an application might have multiple views that are programmatically displayed as a result of the user interface. I make distinctions between *application types*: that is, applications that exhibit certain behaviors and so use view controllers in a certain way. Consider the following application types:

- Utility applications
- Tab bar applications
- Navigation applications

In this context, I class the Lunar Lander as a utility application. The game is played predominately from a single view, and it also shows a configuration\startup screen. However, this is the simplest of user interfaces. It also displays the view controller modally, because the design of the application displays the main game screen as the only screen available while the game is being played or is terminated. Displaying a view modally is typically implemented to stop the flow of your application and force it to return before flow continues. Another typical example is to obtain key information required before you can continue. The alternative is that flow doesn't stop, and views are coordinated through controls such as tab bars.

As you can see, there are many innovative and often complex ways for users to interact with your application, typically controlled through gestures. To take you through working examples for all the different application types and their associated view controllers isn't possible in the constraints of this book. You can explore a number of options independently via the Apple guide, such as `http://developer.apple.com/library/ios/#featuredarticles/ViewControllerPGforiPhoneOS` or comprehensive iOS development books. Here you focus on some specific, useful alternatives that have .NET parallels, and learn how to use them.

Let's take a look at the different application types and their associated view controllers before you delve into the tab bar example.

Utility-Based Applications

In a utility-based application, the user's interaction revolves around a single view. Other views may exist, but they are typically limited to supporting the configuration of the application. A great example is the Stocks application, shown in Figure 6–9, which when invoked displays the stocks you have chosen (or that it defaults to) and their performance. The Compass is another great example, as is the Calculator application.

Figure 6–9. *The Stocks iPhone application is an example of a utility-based application.*

There isn't a specific view-controller class to manage this kind of application; instead, you present views modally in a programmatic fashion. This is exactly what you have done with the Lunar Lander application. In .NET, a utility application might be a console-based application or a Windows Form application with a single window that uses modal dialog boxes to retrieve key information.

Tab Bar–Based Applications

A tab bar application is an application supporting multiple views, whose context is chosen based on the user's interactions and typically shown as tabs. A good example is the Clock application, shown in Figure 6–10, which has many views, accessed through a tab bar at the bottom of the screen. Choosing a tab typically changes the active view controller; a new corresponding view becomes active, thus displaying the new screen.

Figure 6–10. *The Clock iPhone application is a multiview tab bar application.*

It's worth highlighting a common cause of confusion. A toolbar looks very much the same as a tab bar, in that the horizontal bar is used to display icons that can be tapped. The key difference is that the toolbar can contain buttons and other controls, but their selection isn't mutually exclusive. The user can tap more than one, and they don't act as binary switches—instead they simply fire an event for you to capture and process. Conversely, because the tab bar selection determines the view, the tabs are mutually exclusive.

A tab bar application is typically implemented using the tab bar view controller, provided by the `UITabBarController` class. This class is used directly and not subclassed; you use this as the focus for a more detailed example. In .NET, the tab bar is one of the few view-controller type controls that has a comparable direct.NET control in the form of a TabControl in Windows Forms (in the System.Windows.Forms.TabControl namespace).

It's also worth mentioning that the tab bar is usually combined with a tabular type view, which the table view controller, implemented through the `UITableViewController` class, is designed for. It provides support for behavior that you expect when implementing a table, such as editing rows of data and or managing the selection of cells, rows, and columns.

Navigation-Based Applications

A navigation-based application is typically used to present a series of views that have a natural hierarchy. For example, if you consider the Mail application, shown in Figure 6–11, each user interaction builds on the previous one and allows you to drill down into your Mail Account, then your Inbox, then your e-mail messages, and then a specific e-mail. Each step is represented by a view, and you can reverse your way out of the hierarchy by choosing the back button.

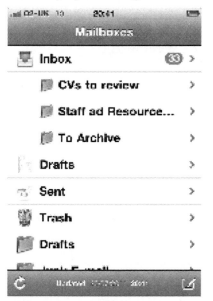

Figure 6–11. *The Mail application is a hierarchical, multiview navigation-based application.*

The navigation controller functionality is contained in the UINavigationController interface. This is very similar to the UITabBarController interface touched on earlier, with the key difference being that the navigation controller works by implementing a stack of views. For example, think of taking a pile of books and placing them on top of each other—you build a stack of books, and when it's complete, the easiest book to take off the stack is the last one you put on. You can then uncover the stack of books, finishing with the first one you put down. This is known as *last-in-first-out* (LIFO).

Implementing a Tab Bar–Based Application

If you cast your mind back to previous chapters, you saw the feature that Xcode provided for project templates, something you'll find very familiar if you've used Visual Studio. Usefully, Xcode provides just such a template for tab bar–based applications, so let's deviate from the Lunar Lander application for the moment and use this template to create another sample application to illustrate the features of a tab bar view controller. Begin by starting Xcode, and follow the procedure to create a new template, this time selecting the Tab Bar template as shown in Figure 6–12.

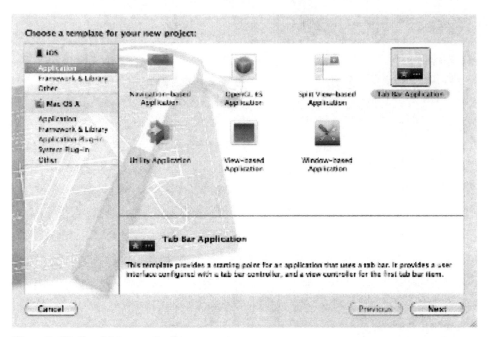

Figure 6–12. *New tab bar application*

Click Next, and provide your application with a name. I've used TabBarExample—not very imaginative, I know! In order for you to understand what Xcode has constructed, let's look at the application when it's running in the simulator straight out of the box. It's also worth reiterating at this point that the .NET platform doesn't have a concept of a view controller or, specifically, a tab bar view controller; but it does have the individual controls that, when combined with your own MVC Pattern implementation, can easily be used to replicate the same functionality. You compare the controls provided in the user interface libraries of the iOS SDK and .NET a little later in the chapter.

First, consider the screens captured from the simulator, in Figure 6–13, showing the two views displayed when you select the tabs provided in the default project implementation.

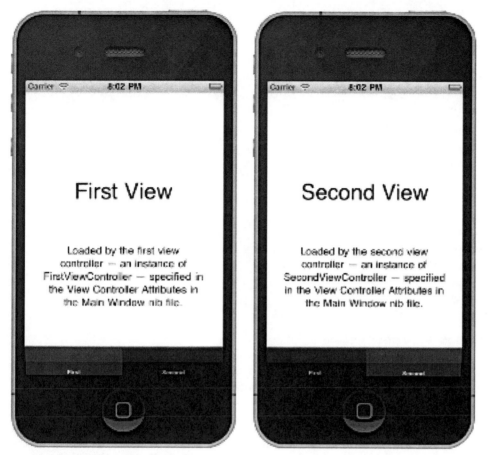

Figure 6–13. *Default tab bar application running*

Let's look at the implementation that results from having created the default application complete with its view/controller switching functionality. Use the project navigator (⌘1) to view the project's structure; you see something similar to Figure 6–14 when each of the three folders (TabBarExample, Frameworks, and Products) is expanded.

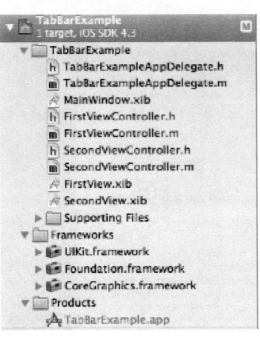

Figure 6–14. *Tab bar default project structure*

Let's start with the easy bits. Products is a single application binary called TabBarExample.app, which uses the UIKit, Foundation, and CoreGraphics frameworks. In Microsoft .NET, as explained in Chapter 4, these are equivalent to libraries of functionality that provide objects and their attributes and methods, all in their representative namespaces.

Working down the list, let's look at the Application Delegate implementation. If you look in both the header and implementation files, they're very similar to those you've seen before but with a few key differences. Consider the TabBarExampleAppDelegate.h file in Listing 6–1.

Listing 6–1. *TabBarExampleAppDelegate.h*

```
#import <UIKit/UIKit.h>

@interface TabBarExampleAppDelegate : NSObject <UIApplicationDelegate,↵
 UITabBarControllerDelegate> {

}

@property (nonatomic, retain) IBOutlet UIWindow *window;

@property (nonatomic, retain) IBOutlet UITabBarController *tabBarController;

@end
```

The key things to notice are that it inherits from NSObject like previous examples, but it implements not only the UIApplicationDelegate protocol but also the UITabControllerDelegate protocol. Among the options available with this protocol's methods, for example, is the capability to perform post-tab selection actions. You see that it also creates a property pointing to a UITabBarController class, which is the instance reference to your tab controller object that is used by the application. Remember that the UITabController class isn't subclassed; you use the class as it is.

I won't go into the details of the TabBarExampleAppDelegate.m file, but it is worth noticing that the rootViewController for the window is set to the tabBarController property as the main view controller to use. This is shown in the following code:

```
self.window.rootViewController = self.tabBarController
```

So far, so good. If you turn your attention to the MainWindow.xib file and double-tap it, it loads in the Interface Builder. Choose the Tab Bar controller view, and you see a screen like the one shown in Figure 6–15 in Interface-Builder.

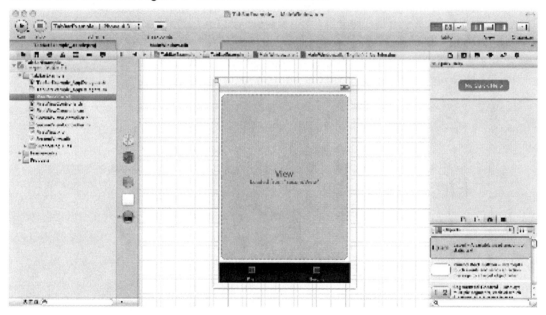

Figure 6–15. *The Tab Bar MainWindow view open in Interface Builder*

In this case, I've clicked the Second button on the tab bar, and you can see that Interface Builder is indicating that SecondView is loaded. If you click the first tab bar button, it predictably says that FirstView is loaded. This control is indicated in the tab bar properties, which you can display using the Attributes Inspector (⌥⌘4), something like that shown in Figure 6–16.

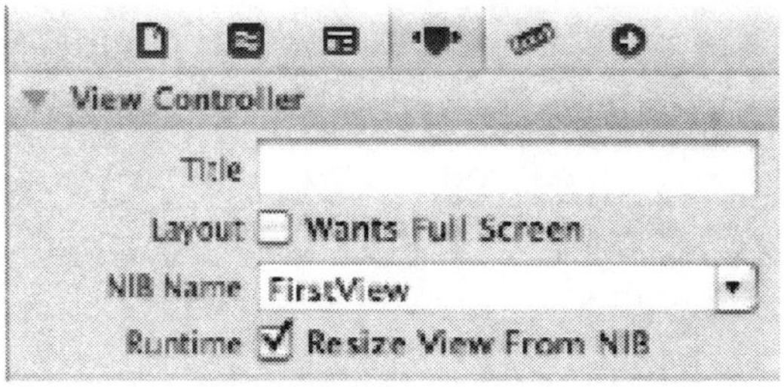

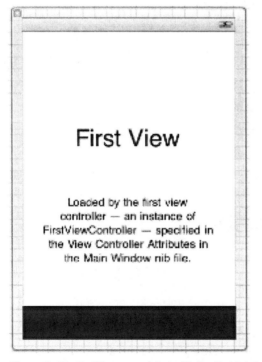

Figure 6–16. *Attributes Inspector for a tab bar control*

Notice the correlation between the tab bar button and the view it selects. This is indicated by the NIB Name property, which points to the NIB file that contains the view to load—in this instance, the first tab bar button displays the view from the FirstView.xib file. If you locate this file in the project and select it, you see a familiar view, shown in Figure 6–17.

Figure 6–17. *FirstView associated with the first tab bar button*

Each of the views associated with each tab creates a class and its associated files, both the header and implementation files. Each view (FirstView and SecondView) provides you with the opportunity to complete custom view-controller code; you can build on the default behavior and implementation, which are pretty vanilla, doing very little other than the typical method implementations you've seen. For example, they return YES or NO depending on whether the orientation is supported (in this case by default only if it's portrait).

However, this demonstrates the ability to have different tab bar items associated with different views and view controllers, and exercise flexibility about how the tab bar items look and behave. For example, you can modify tab bar items by removing the text and adding a logo to the project and to the tab bar item. Figure 6–18 shows an example using the Attribute Inspector for the tab bar item selected.

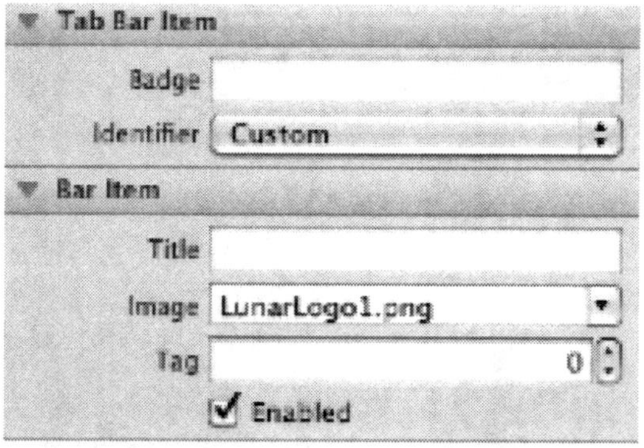

Figure 6–18. *Adding a logo using the tab bar item Attribute Inspector*

If you were to apply this to your game, you could use this mechanism to have a tab for the main game view displaying the actual game, along with a tab for the view used to display the high score. You won't pursue this for your Lunar Lander game because it typically uses modal views until each game session is finished—but you could. You should also now see the correlation between views and their associated view controllers, allowing you to customize these or add additional ones as suits your application's design.

Another useful technique is to use one tab to provide a means of displaying different perspectives of the same data. So your application may present a list of audio files on your device, with tabs relating to views from different perspectives: a tab for albums, a tab for genres, a tab for track names, and so on.

Overview of iPad-specific Controllers

Before you move on from view controllers, let's highlight some view controllers that are provided as part of the iOS SDK but are specific to the iPad device. The iPad form factor differs from the iPhone's in that it's larger and behaves slightly differently when the orientation is changed. For this reason, some specialized view controllers have been created to take advantage of the iPad's form factor; but this book's examples are focused on the iPhone only, so playing with the view controllers is left to those of you with iPad devices.

Popover View Controllers

Although the Popover controller is not strictly speaking a view controller, it does provide a useful mechanism for displaying additional content in your application's window. If you're looking for similar functionality in .NET, I'm afraid you'll be disappointed. Nothing exists currently, but it's possible for you to create your own equivalent using .NET code, or maybe Ajax-based source code. You can see an example in the iPad simulator shown in Figure 6–19. You build this later; let's look at the component parts first.

Figure 6–19. *iPad popover example*

To implement a popover, you need to use the `UIPopoverController` class and have a good idea what condition needs to be met for your popover to be displayed. After all, it's essentially a wrapper for an existing view controller that then displays your floating view over your application. For example, you may have a selection of items the user can choose from, and you wish to use a popover to display the description when a particular option is chosen. It also usefully displays an arrow connecting the popover window with the item to which it relates—in the case of a toolbar button, the button itself. Having made these basic decisions, you're ready to implement your popover.

Let's create a simple popover example to demonstrate these concepts. First, create a view-based application using Xcode 4 for an iPad device. Once created, you notice as before that a view controller is created for the main view. To this view, add a toolbar with a single item, which is the trigger for your popover: do this by editing the associated XIB in Interface Builder and adding the Toolbar object. Your screen in Xcode should look similar to that shown in Figure 6–20.

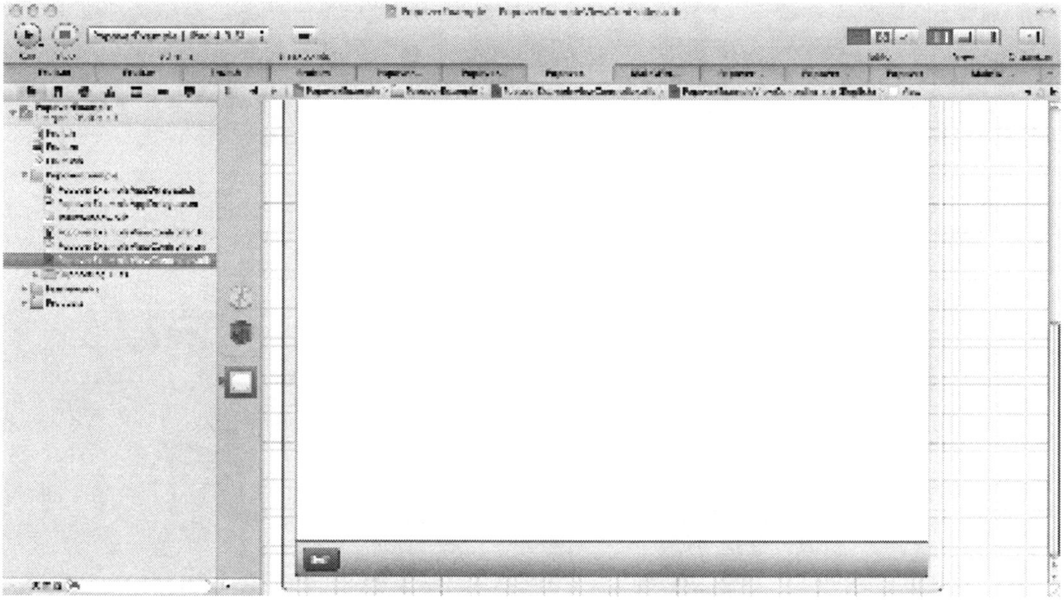

Figure 6–20. *Your example iPad view controller with single toolbar item*

If you were to execute this, you'd have a pretty bland application with the single toolbar item at the bottom. It's blank because in the real world you're more likely to have multiple toolbar items, and it has no functionality behind it yet. Let's create your popover. A popover needs a view controller to manage how the data is displayed; in this case, you provide the opportunity to display data in a tabular format, which is pretty typical for popovers. Add a file to your project (I called it PopoverSelection), ensuring that it's compatible with an iPad and that an XIB is created for it. Critically, it must also inherit from the view controller required to display your data. In this case, the popover displays tabular data, so you use UITableViewController as the subclass. See Figure 6–21.

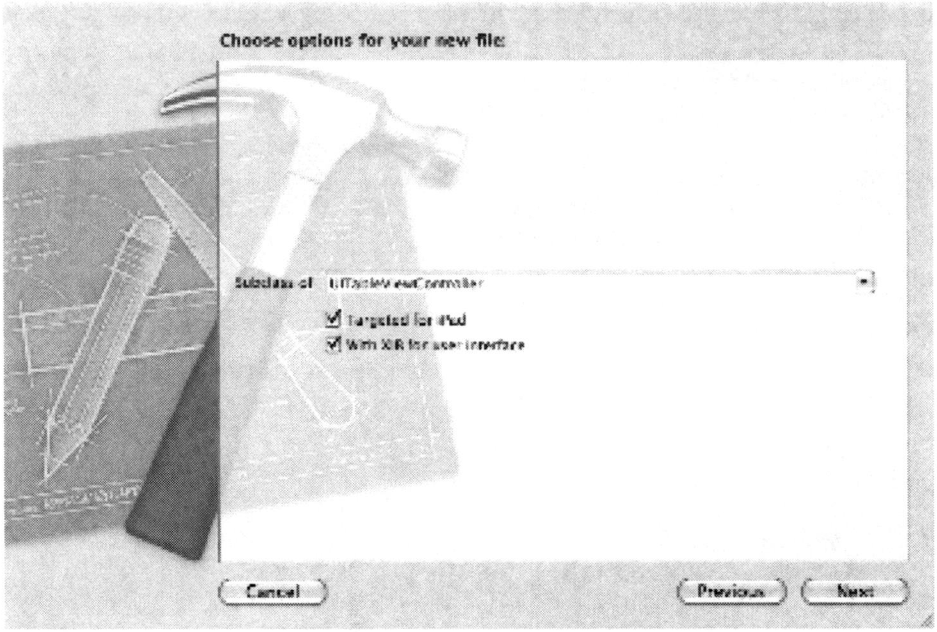

Figure 6–21. *Creating your popover view controller class using the table view base class*

This creates three files in your project: PopOverSelection.h (the header file),
PopOverSelection.m (its implementation), and PopOverSelection.xib (the view). If you
open the associated XIB file in Interface Builder, it should look like the one in Figure 6–22.

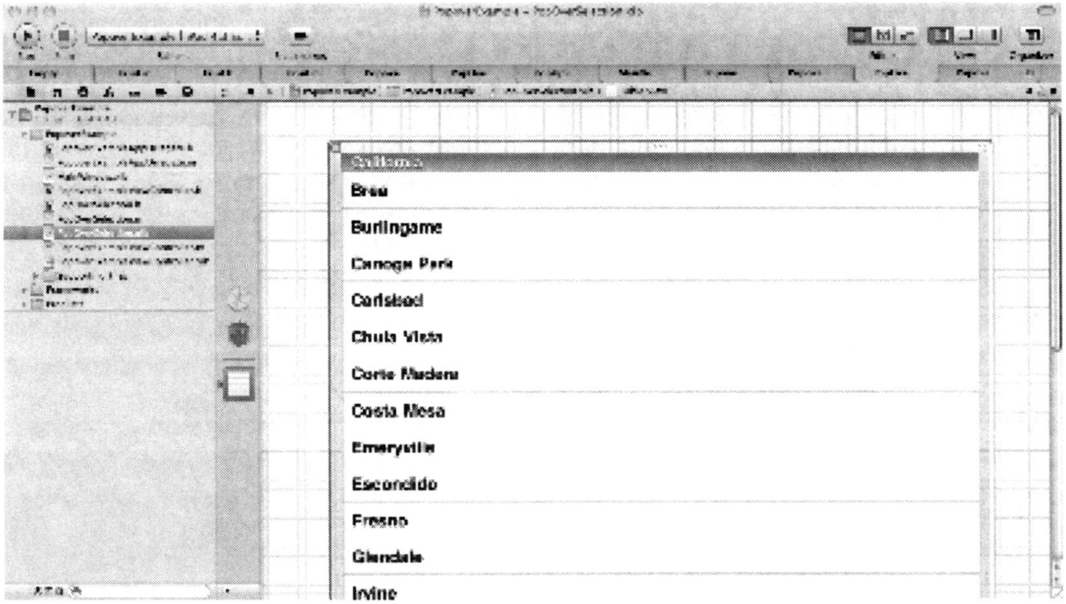

Figure 6–22. *Your tabular popover view controller*

You need to wire this class into your code, so you must define the relevant properties and actions to allow you to both wire up the popover controller action and present the popover. You do this in your main view controller, called PopOverExampleViewController. See Listing 6–2.

Listing 6–2. *PopOverExampleViewController.h*

```
#import <UIKit/UIKit.h>
#include "PopOverSelection.h"

@interface PopoverExampleViewController : UIViewController {
    UIPopoverController *popCtrl;
    PopOverSelection    *selection;
    IBOutlet UIBarButtonItem *bbitem;
}

@property (nonatomic, retain) UIBarButtonItem *bbitem;
@property (nonatomic, retain) UIPopoverController *popCtrl;
@property (nonatomic, retain) PopOverSelection *selection;

- (IBAction)togglePopOverController;

@end
```

If you break this down, the first thing you need is a pointer to your toolbar button item. You do this by defining an IBOutlet property in your class whose name matches the toolbar button on your item. I changed it to bbitem using the Identity inspector:

```
IBOutlet UIBarButtonItem *bbitem;
```

You need a corresponding @property statement, shown next, and of course the @synthesize statement in the implementation file (you see these soon):

```
@property (nonatomic, retain) UIBarButtonItem *bbitem;
```

With your toolbar button exposed via properties, you also need to define an action that your button can be connected to through the Interface Builder—this serves to toggle the popover between being visible or not. This is a simple IBAction like those you've used in previous chapters, the definition for which you can see here:

```
-(IBAction)togglePopOverController;
```

Finally, you need both a property that points to the popover view controller and the UIPopOverController singleton class that provides the required SDK code to implement popover functionality. The following lines define these member variables. Notice that you have to include your PopOverSelection.h file to bring in the popover view controller:

```
UIPopoverController *popCtrl;
PopOverSelection    *selection;
```

And of course you follow these with the appropriate @property and @synthesize statements.

You are now in a good position to connect your action to the toolbar button to invoke the popover selection, and you have the other necessary properties to implement the displaying\hiding of your popover. First you connect the action, as you've done in previous chapters. Using Interface Builder, and with your main view controller open and displaying the toolbar button, open the Connections Inspector for the main file owner. Now drag your togglePopOverController action to the toolbar button and your bbitem IBOUTLET to the same button item. This allows you to reference the button and trap the action when it's clicked. You can see these connections in Figure 6–23.

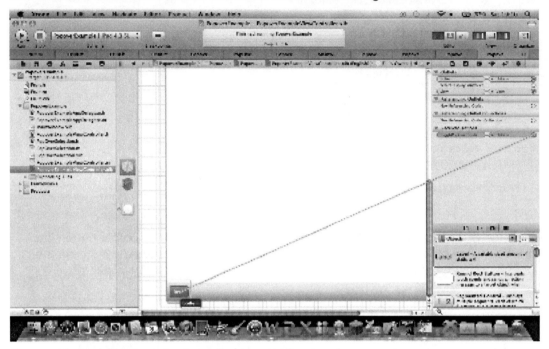

Figure 6–23. *Connecting the toolbar button item to your actions in code*

The only thing remaining is to provide the implementation for the popover functionality. The code in Listing 6–3 shows the core implementation code, and then you walk through it.

Listing 6–3. *Popover's Core Implementation Code*

```
#import "PopoverExampleViewController.h"

@implementation PopoverExampleViewController

@synthesize popCtrl;
@synthesize selection;
@synthesize bbitem;

- (void)dealloc
{
    [super dealloc];
}

- (void)didReceiveMemoryWarning
{
    // Releases the view if it doesn't have a superview.
```

```objc
    [super didReceiveMemoryWarning];

    // Release any cached data, images, etc that aren't in use.
}

#pragma mark - View lifecycle


// Implement viewDidLoad to do additional setup after loading the view, typically from↩
 a nib.
- (void)viewDidLoad
{

    selection = [[PopOverSelection alloc] init];
    popCtrl = [[UIPopoverController alloc] initWithContentViewController:selection];
    popCtrl.popoverContentSize = CGSizeMake(250, 300);

    [super viewDidLoad];
}


- (void)viewDidUnload
{
    [super viewDidUnload];

    // Release any retained subviews of the main view.
    // e.g. self.myOutlet = nil;
    [selection release];
    [popCtrl release];

}

- (BOOL)shouldAutorotateToInterfaceOrientation:(UIInterfaceOrientation)↩
interfaceOrientation
{
    // Return YES for supported orientations
    return YES;
}

-(IBAction)togglePopOverController
{
    if ([popCtrl isPopoverVisible]) {

        [popCtrl dismissPopoverAnimated:YES];

    } else {

        [popCtrl presentPopoverFromBarButtonItem:bbitem permittedArrowDirections:↩
UIPopoverArrowDirectionAny animated:YES];

    }

}

@end
```

Now let's take a look at the various parts of Listing 6–3. First, you need to synthesize your properties with the following code:

```
@synthesize popCtrl;
@synthesize selection;
@synthesize bbitem;
```

You also need to ensure that the view controller for your selection popover window (in this case, the view controller class called PopOverSelection with the property selection) and the UIPopoverController class are allocated and initialized. You do this in the viewDidLoad event as shown here:

```
// Implement viewDidLoad to do additional setup after loading the view, typically from⤸
 a nib.
- (void)viewDidLoad
{

    selection = [[PopOverSelection alloc] init];
    popCtrl = [[UIPopoverController alloc] initWithContentViewController:selection];
    popCtrl.popoverContentSize = CGSizeMake(250, 300);

    [super viewDidLoad];
}
```

First your window's view controller is initialized. Then the UIPopoverController class instance is initialized with your custom view controller object (selection), and you set the default size to 250 × 300 points. The initialization is complete, so let's not forget to release your resources; this is done in the viewDidUnload method, tidying up after yourself:

```
[selection release];
[popCtrl release];
```

Finally, you come to the meat on the bones, as they say. The code associated with the button-click action toggles the popover between being visible or not, depending on its status. If it's visible, you can simply pass the dismissPopoverAnimated message; if not, you use the presentPopoverFromBarButtonItem message, passing the button both its popover and any constraints on the arrow being shown. Simple:

```
if ([popCtrl isPopoverVisible]) {
        [popCtrl dismissPopoverAnimated:YES];

} else {

[popCtrl presentPopoverFromBarButtonItem:bbitem permittedArrowDirections:⤸
UIPopoverArrowDirectionAny animated:YES];

}
```

If you build and execute this code, your main window is shown with the toolbar at the bottom. Clicking the toolbar button displays and then hides the popover. This popover is now ready to use and present the data you require. The presentation depends on what you've used for the view controller. In this case, it's a table view using UITableViewController, which itself is an extensive control. Although the book doesn't cover this in detail, the Apple Developer Program does extensively in the "Table View

Programming Guide for iOS" found in the iOS Developer Library
(http://developer.apple.com/library/ios). If you build and run the application, the
popover is visible, as shown in Figure 6–24.

Figure 6–24. *iPad simulator running the application with the popover visible*

Split-View Controllers

The UISplitView controller allows for two panes: the left pane (here called the *index*
pane) is fixed, and the right pane (the *detail* pane) is resizable. In portrait mode, the
detail pane is the only pane visible, with the index pane replaced by a toolbar button that
displays as a popover. In landscape mode you have more space, so the index and detail
panes are shown alongside each other. You can see them side by side in Figure 6–25.

Figure 6–25. *Split-view controller managing orientation on an iPad*

The UISplitViewController class is used to manage both views in a single view controller, but it must be the root of any interface you create. There is a split view–based application template in Xcode that is a good starting point, and I recommend that you use it as you start to explore. You can see it running in Figure 6–26 in landscape mode, with the two panes clearly visible.

Figure 6–26. *The iPad split-view controller template*

Looking under the hood of the default implementation, when the application has finished launching, you assign the rootViewController to the instance of your UISplitViewController, much the same as any view controller:

```
self.window.rootViewController = self.splitViewController;
```

Now you can use the split-view controller object in Xcode and assign it the view controllers and associated NIB files all in Interface builder, or you can do it programmatically. If you examine the split-view example using the Xcode template, you can see Interface Builder was used to do the hard work—creating a left pane as a table view controller (given the list of data it presents) and the detail view as a standard view controller.

If you were to do this programmatically, you could simply create the two view controllers of your preference and add them to the viewControllers array property of the UISplitViewController class; the first element is the index, and the second is the detail. So, code similar to this should do the trick:

```
// Create your two view controllers as required, giving them the name firstVC and⏎
  secondVC accordingly.
// firstVC and secondVC would be created here

// Create your SplitViewController instance
```

```
UISplitViewController* splitVC = [[UISplitViewController alloc] init];
// Add the view controllers you've created to the viewControllers property as an array↵
 of the two controllers.
splitVC.viewControllers = [NSArray arrayWithObjects:firstVC, secondVC, nil];
 // Add to the rootViewController and make visible.
self.window.rootViewController = splitVC;
[window makeKeyAndVisible];
```

In Microsoft .NET, there are a number of ways you can implement functionality similar to but not exactly the same as a split view, starting with the splitter controls introduced in early implementations of the .NET framework and more recently the SplitContainer class (see http://msdn.microsoft.com/en-you/library/system.windows.forms.splitcontainer.aspx), the replacement for which in WPF is called GridSplitter.

Enough iPad-specific fun. Let's look at what other fun you can have in your user interface.

User Interface Controls

You've covered views and view controllers at length but only touched on some of the elements available to build the user interface for your application. The UIKit framework, provided as part of the iOS SDK, provides an extensive set of UI elements for you to use when designing your application. The same is true of the .NET framework. You likely are familiar with the *user interface controls*, as they are typically called, that are provided for you to drag and drop onto your Windows Forms, or for you to use as part of other Microsoft technologies such as ASP.NET and the Windows Presentation Foundation. This section introduces the Apple UI elements and also refers to their Microsoft counterparts where available.

Controls

An interface element that a user can interact with, or that presents information back to the user, is called a *control*. As in the .NET framework, the iOS toolset provides a large number of controls available for use in your application. For each control, this section provides a brief overview of its purpose and, as space permits, a quick introduction to when to best use it. You also cover similar controls in the .NET framework. Let's start with controls that are used a little less often, followed by those that have a direct .NET counterpart.

Activity and Progress Indicators

These controls are used to indicate to the user that a particular task is progressing. They provide visual feedback that the task is working by showing a spinning gear icon or a progress bar.

For the activity indicator, you use the **UIActivityIndicatorView** class and call the startAnimating method when you being your task and stopAnimating when it's completed. The control looks similar to that in Figure 6–27.

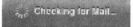

Figure 6–27. *Activity indicator*

The iOS toolset also provides a progress indicator, which is similar to its .NET counterpart the Windows Forms ProgressBar class. The iOS version is shown in Figure 6–28.

Figure 6–28. *Progress bar*

It is implemented through the **UIProgressView** class, and as you'd expect, as progress is made, the bar starts to fill. This control is typically used when the task has a predetermined scope: for example, downloading 50 e-mails. If you cannot measure the progress, you should use the activity indicator instead.

Date, Time, and General Pickers

The date and time picker control, implemented by the **UIDatePicker** class, provides a touch-friendly way of choosing a particular date and/or time by using sliding wheels representing each element of the date or time. You can see this on the control shown in Figure 6–29.

Figure 6–29. *Date and time picker*

You could of course present the date and time in a control that allows you to type in the values, or choose from drop-down boxes, which is the way the .NET framework expects you to enter a date/time. However, on the iPhone, to take full advantage of the touch-based interface, this presents a far more intuitive method. On the iPad, this control is normally presented as a popover.

There is no .NET equivalent that behaves in the same way, although the DateTimePicker class in .NET does provide a good alternative; it presents the date in a calendar-type format, typically with the month displayed and each element as a drop-down box and/or direct input. The iOS **Picker** class uses a similar approach but presents the user with a custom list in a single wheel that the user can then select from.

Detail Disclosure Button

A detail disclosure button, implemented by **UITableViewCellAccessoryDetailDisclosureButton**, allows you to indicate an item of interest on your screen. An arrow in a blue circle indicates that more information is available. When tapped, it displays the additional information as if it were a hyperlink. This control may be familiar from its use as a map annotation on your iPhone or iPad Maps application, as shown in Figure 6–30.

Figure 6–30. *Detail disclosure button*

There is no equivalent in the .NET framework, but as usual, nothing is stopping you from writing your own (although doing so isn't trivial).

Info Button

The info button is used to provide access to a configuration screen for your application. It's implemented using a **UIButton** class and the buttonType property to indicate it's an info button, which thus provides the right image as shown in Figure 6–31.

Figure 6–31. *Info button*

Again, there is no equivalent in the .NET framework, but you could implement similar functionality using the Button class and a suitable image.

Page Indicator

The page indicator, implemented by the UIPageControl class, provides a useful visual indicator of which view is currently open within the bounds of the totals views available, as shown in Figure 6–32.

Figure 6–32. *Page indicator*

As you open a view, a dot is added to represent the active or displayed view's place in the sequence. After 20 dots, the control clips any more dots so they aren't displayed. (I would argue that if you're displaying this many dots, you should rethink your user interface design.)

There is no .NET equivalent.

Search Bar

The search bar control, implemented through the **UISearchBar** class, allows the user to enter a text string and choose to execute a search by tapping the magnifying glass. It also lets you present common information using the bookmark icon. See Figure 6–33.

Figure 6–33. *Search bar control*

There is no direct .NET equivalent control.

Switch

The switch control, implemented through the **UISwitch** class, allows the user to choose between options that are mutually exclusive, such as ON or OFF. See Figure 6–34.

Figure 6–34. *Switch control*

There is no equivalent control in .NET, at least not in look and feel, although a Checkbox performs the same function: it can be checked (ON) or unchecked (OFF).

Segmented Control

A segmented control, implemented through the `UISegmentedControl` class, provides a method for displaying a set of segments, each of which behaves like a button and can display a corresponding view. An example is shown in Figure 6–35.

Figure 6–35. *Segmented control*

The segmented control provides a convenient way to group related buttons and can display either text or an image as the face of each button. The buttons are mutually exclusive, and you can have as many segments as you wish, differentiating it from the switch control.

Again, there is no .NET equivalent control, although the use of mutually exclusive radio buttons in .NET offers similar functionality.

Common Controls

A number of common controls are available in the iOS UIKit framework for which a direct .NET equivalent is available. Their usage and behavior are almost identical to their .NET counterparts, so for brevity I don't describe them in detail. These controls are shown in Table 6–2.

Table 6–2. *Common iOS Controls with Corresponding .NET Classes*

iOS Control	Image	.NET Equivalent Class
Label (UILabel)	Label	Label
Round rect button (UIButton)	Round Button	Button
Text field (UITextField)	Text Field	TextBox
Slider (UISlider)		Slider

Let's take a look at other user interface elements included in the UIKit. Don't forget that you can use the Apple Developer resources to explore the vast array of user interface controls in the UIKit framework of the SDK; and making the correlation (where one exists) to .NET controls is pretty straightforward, as you've seen from the examples in this section.

Navigation and Information Bars

There are a number of user interface elements that are not typically used to define your application but either provide information to the user or manage how you navigate your way around your application. These elements are called *bars,* and they include status bars, toolbars, navigation bars, and tab bars—the latter of which you saw earlier in the chapter.

Status Bar

The status bar is used to display important information to the user and always appears in the upper edge of your device screen, regardless of the orientation of your device. Additionally, although on the iPhone you have some control over the color of your status bar, on the iPad the color is fixed as black. You can see the iPhone status bar in Figure 6–36.

Figure 6–36. *Status Bar*

You implement the status bar by setting the UIStatusBarStyle for your UIApplication or using an Info.plist value (UIStatusBarHidden) to hide it. The Apple Developer usage guidelines are quite specific: if your application is a game or full-screen, then the status bar typically may be hidden; otherwise the recommendation is that it be displayed, especially given the small amount of space it takes.

The StatusBar class in the .NET framework offers similar functionality.

Toolbar

A toolbar, implemented by the UIToolbar class, is pretty well understood in most graphical user interfaces, and the behavior for iOS devices is no different. It's used to provide graphical images that, when tapped, perform actions in your application. You typically place common actions on the toolbar for ease of use. You can see a toolbar in Figure 6–37.

Figure 6–37. *Toolbar*

The toolbar is located on the bottom edge of the screen for iPhone applications and at either edge for iPad applications, depending on the orientation and which edge you snap the control to. The items on the toolbar are context sensitive, which means they reflect actions that are typically performed against the associated view and for that reason may change between views.

The Toolbar class in the .NET framework provides equivalent functionality.

Navigation Bar

The navigation bar, implemented by the UINavigationBar class, is used to manage navigation through a hierarchy of views and is usually associated with the navigation controller. It's shown in Figure 6–38.

Figure 6–38. *Navigation bar*

Navigation bars are common in iOS applications when you're dealing with different views or a tab bar isn't appropriate. However, although their use is relatively straightforward, it's beyond this chapter, and the iOS Developer web site does a good job of describing it. So, the implementation of the navigation bar and associated controller is left to you, armed with the iOS developer web site: http://developer.apple.com/library/ios/#featuredarticles/ViewControllerPGforiPhoneOS/NavigationControllers/.

There is no equivalent to the navigation bar in the .NET framework.

Content Views

The iOS SDK provides a number of user interface elements intended to present custom content back to the user from your application. You've seen two iPad-specific views, the split view and the popover, but a number exist for the iPhone too.

You walk through these in turn; they are commonly used in iPhone applications because of the useful capabilities they provide.

Table View

The table view element, implemented through the UITableView class, is used as its name suggests, to present data in tabular format (rows and columns of information). An example is shown in Figure 6–39.

Figure 6–39. *Table view*

The table view control is highly configurable and used extensively in many iPhone applications. For example, the Contacts List is a table view implementation, as is the Language selection screen when choosing your device's international settings. Such diverse examples show the flexibility of the control. Remember the table view, because you'll use it to display your Lunar Lander game's High Score table.

The DataView control, when bound to a data source, provides similar functionality in the .NET framework. In the Windows Presentation Foundation, the DataView control has been replaced with a table view capability that offers similar functionality to the iOS table view element.

Text View

The text view control, implemented by the UITextView class, is used to present and allow the input of several lines of text in your application. An example is shown in Figure 6–40.

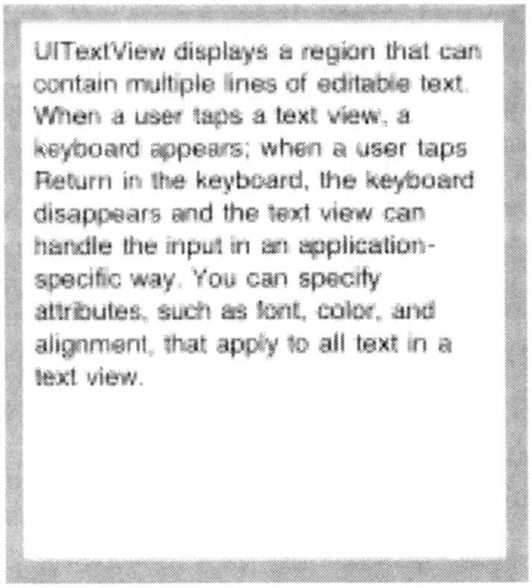

UITextView displays a region that can contain multiple lines of editable text. When a user taps a text view, a keyboard appears; when a user taps Return in the keyboard, the keyboard disappears and the text view can handle the input in an application-specific way. You can specify attributes, such as font, color, and alignment, that apply to all text in a text view.

Figure 6–40. *Text view*

The equivalent in the .NET framework is the TextBox control.

Web View

The web view control, implemented by the UIWebView class, allows your application to display rich HTML content. It isn't recommended that you create an iOS application that behaves like a web page—that's what the Safari browser is for—but if you need to wrap a web page of any description in your iOS application, this is the control to use. An example loading the www.bbc.co.uk home page is shown in Figure 6–41.

This example can be easily created using a view-based template in Xcode 4 and adding a web view control along with an associated property. You then simply add the code snippet in Listing 6–4 to the viewDidLoad event for the view that loads the home page using the loadRequest WebView message. As you can see, the web view control is acting as a wrapper to the existing web-based content, in this case the BBC's home page.

Figure 6–41. *A web view example showing the BBC home page*

Listing 6–4. *Web View Example*

```
// Load the WWW.BBC.CO.UK homepage within the WebView
NSString *urlString = @"http://www.bbc.co.uk";
[wvBrowser loadRequest:[NSURLRequest requestWithURL:[NSURL URLWithString:urlString]]];
```

The equivalent in the .NET framework is the WebBrowser class, using the Navigate()
method as an equivalent loadRequest message.

Other Elements

Although the last few pages have introduced quite a few UI elements, there are still more
left for you to discover. However, I didn't want to leave a few other useful UI elements
untouched, specifically alerts and action sheets.

Alerts

Alerts are designed to provide important information to the user of your application. When invoked, the alert presents a pop-up window over your existing views, and you cannot continue with your application until it is closed.

In .NET it is very similar to a MessageBox, invoked by a method of the same name. In iOS, you use the UIAlertView class to implement an alert and to display the short alerting text along with one or two buttons.

An alert is typically used to inform the user that something of significance has happened and may not be associated with their most recent actions. For example, if you kicked off a background task as part of your application and then moved on to do something else, you could use an alert to signify its completion. An example is shown in Figure 6–42.

Figure 6–42. *Alert view example*

You can easily create this alert view example using the code snippet in Listing 6–5. The parameters are pretty self-explanatory.

Listing 6–5. *Alert View Example*

```
UIAlertView *alert = [[ UIAlertView alloc]
                        initWithTitle: @"Important Fact"
                        message: @"Something important has happened"
                        delegate: nil
                        cancelButtonTitle :@"OK"
                        otherButtonTitles: nil];
[alert show];
[alert release];
```

Action Sheets

The final UI element introduced here is the action sheet, implemented by the
UIActionSheet class and providing a mechanism for presenting a set of choices in
relation to a particular user action. For example, the Safari browser provides an action
button that, when chosen, presents a number of choices based on the web page
being displayed—for example, you can add it as a bookmark, make it your home
screen, and so on. This window with multiple choices is called an *alert sheet* and is
shown in Figure 6–43.

Figure 6–43. *Alert sheet example*

On the iPhone, the alert sheet appears from the bottom of the screen, and on the iPad it
appears as a popover. There is no direct equivalent in .NET, although you could argue
that a ContextMenu provides similar functionality.

Apple's User Interface Resources

Apple provides a number of resources that are essential reading when designing your
own user interface. Some of these are listed here:

- *iOS Human Interface Guidelines:* Provides guidelines and describes principles
  for designing that superlative user experience.
  http://developer.apple.com/library/ios/#documentation/userexperience/con
  ceptual/mobilehig/Introduction/Introduction.html.

- *View Controller Programming Guide for iOS:* Provides guidance about
  structuring and managing your application's user interface.
  http://developer.apple.com/library/ios/#featuredarticles/ViewContr
  ollerPGforiPhoneOS/Introduction/Introduction.html.

■ *View Programming Guide for iOS:* Provides guidance for presenting and animating your user interface.
`http://developer.apple.com/library/ios/#documentation/WindowsVi`
`ews/Conceptual/ViewPG_iPhoneOS/Introduction/Introduction.html.`

■ *Drawing and Printing Guide for iOS:* Provides guidance on drawing custom content and printing information.
`http://developer.apple.com/library/ios/#documentation/iPhone/Conceptual/`
`iPhoneOSProgrammingGuide/Introduction/Introduction.html.`

Summary

This chapter started by taking a look at the different device types and their capabilities from a user interface perspective. You should always be cognizant of the device or devices to which you are targeting your application when designing its user interface.

You then examined the different application types, and specifically the view controller and view combinations possible. You already looked at presenting single views, including one modal-based view, using the Lunar Lander example, but many other options exist. There are too many options to cover in a single chapter, so you looked at a tab bar example (which might be appropriate for your game) and then some of the other view controller types.

After you saw the different view controllers and the mechanisms for managing the presentation of different views, you looked at the user interface elements available with which you can design your actual view. In the Lunar Lander game, you are painting a number of graphics in real time. But if you have developed .NET applications using Window Forms, or even ASP.NET, the use of UI controls to design your user interface will be familiar—and some of the iOS controls should be well-known to you. The chapter provided examples of how you might use some of the controls that are slightly more unusual.

You should now be armed with enough knowledge to navigate view controllers, views, and user interface controls, and map your .NET knowledge onto the iOS equivalents where they exist. This chapter has reiterated a number of times the importance of the user experience when building an iOS mobile device application, and it's no surprise that Apple provides numerous resources you can use to support the knowledge you've built so far, to help understand the examples in this chapter, and to provide a reference for your own exploration. Enjoy!

Chapter 7

Get the Data: Storing and Retrieving Data and Configuring your Applications

So far, we've covered a number of topics, all designed to introduce how to create iOS-based mobile applications running on iOS-based mobile devices, using the iOS SDK and supporting languages and tools. However, while we have walked through how to build an application, one key thing has been missing: the application's ability to hold what is known as *state*.

State can be thought of as the equivalent to a human's memory. If we didn't have a memory, doing the simplest of tasks would require us to discover how to do it every time. Since we do have a memory and can remember how to perform a particular action, doing it again is far easier, faster, and arguably enjoyable—skiing is a good example.

Computers have memory in the form of volatile memory (RAM), which is lost when you switch off the computer, and a mobile device is no different. But if you want to persist state between application instances—that is, you want the application to remember where it left off—you're going to need to store state somewhere else, like a hard disk.

In this chapter, we'll look at how you can store information as data either on your mobile device or other sources, and how you can use this data to configure your application. Specifically we'll take a look at the following:

- An overview of the options for storing data
- Guidance on how to store information
- Guidance on how to retrieve information
- How to use data to configure your application between instances

What Are Our Options for Storing Data?

You may want to store various types of data, such as dynamic data that is entered by the application user, or parameterized data that the user does not influence but may want some flexibility in configuring (kind of like the Registry in Microsoft Windows). The following options are available for storing data:

- Filesystem storage
- Property lists
- Internet storage
- Database storage

Let's look at each of these options in turn.

Using the Sandbox to Provide Filesystem-Based Storage

In Chapter 4, we touched on the concept of the application's sandbox. Recall that one of its primary purposes is to provide security mechanisms for both your application and your device. Let's revisit the sandbox briefly, focusing on how it can help you store data.

When your application is installed on a mobile device, by default, it establishes a number of folders that have constraints on how they are used. The Apple developer documentation provides some guidance on these folders, and it is important to understand the guidelines before you proceed to use any of these folders. The folders, their typical purpose, and relevant notes are listed in Table 7–1.

Table 7–1. *Default Application Folders*

Folder	Purpose	Notes
/tmp	Used to write temporary files that are not required between different instances of your application	The system may purge files in this directory if it requires space.
/Library	Top-level directory used for files that are *not* user files	You should not use this folder for user files.
/Library/Preferences	Used to contain application-specific files	The contents of this directory are backed up by iTunes.
/Library/Caches	Used to contain application-specific support files that are required to persist between application instances	The contents of this directory are *not* backed up by iTunes. Note that the NSCachesDirectory constant points to this path.

Folder	Purpose	Notes
/Documents	Use this directory to store user-specific documents and application data files	The contents of this directory are backed up by iTunes. Note that the NSDocumentDirectory constant points to this path.

Even when using the simulator you can see these folders. Using Finder, you can navigate to this folder, as it exists on the simulator, by going to \Library\Application Support\iPhone Simulator\4.3.2 (or whatever version of the simulator you are using) and look in the Applications folder. You will see folders with the application IDs we touched on in Chapter 4, with the structure shown in Table 7–1.

> **NOTE:** The folder names may change depending on what your application has specified it will use. Also, different SDKs will have their own folder roots.

You can use the folders listed in Table 7–1 to store persistent data (or state) for your application, although you will need to take into account the constraints highlighted. Given it is a filesystem, you will need to store the data in one or more files, and your application must be able to interpret them.

Although adding a simple file to act as your data store may seem like the easiest approach, the job of storing and retrieving the data you want from it may actually make your application's data-handling code more complex than it needs to be. Therefore, it's worth checking out the other options before you decide to use a simple file for all your application's data storage needs. For example, you may want to investigate using the embedded database approach discussed later in this chapter if your data storage and retrieval needs are not that simple and require more than one file.

Managing the Data Within Your Application

The first hurdle is that you need to store the data in the application itself. You could use a lot of individual variables, but that wouldn't be particularly elegant, and the result would be very messy code when it comes to reading and writing the data to storage. Fortunately, the iOS SDK, much like the .NET Framework, makes provisions for simplifying this task. After all, working with data in your application is commonplace, and therefore expected in most modern programming languages and frameworks. Several mechanisms are available for storing data within your application.

Chapter 4 introduced the concepts of serialization and deserialization. The iOS SDK—and the .NET Framework, for that matter—provides the ability for objects to be serializable. This means that the object's structure and the data, or state information, it holds within it can be persisted (or written) to a storage medium that will survive the application being terminated and the mobile device being switched off. When the application is restarted, you can deserialize this data from your storage medium back into an object instance that has exactly the same structure and data as it did when it was serialized, therefore persisting state.

In Objective-C, it is possible to serialize any object, converting it into a series of bytes that can be written to storage. However, Objective-C also provides what are called *collection classes*, which enable you to store multiple objects and then serialize the whole collection—and in doing so, serializing all the data within it.

In .NET—specifically, C#—you mark an object as [serializable], which means it can be converted into binary, Simple Object Access Protocol (SOAP), or XML within .NET. The .NET Framework separates the representation of the data from mechanisms for transporting it, such as by tagging your class in .NET with the [serializable()] attribute and ensuring your class derives from the ISerializable class. You can then use the appropriate method for writing your class to the destination. This may be a file using the System.IO namespace, or you may be using formatters such as System.Runtime.Serialization.Formatters.Binary to write to a binary stream.

The default serializable objects in Objective-C are shown in Table 7–2 with commentary.

Table 7–1. *Serializable Objective-C Objects*

Objective-C	.NET Commentary
NSArray	Use an object[] for nontype-specific objects, or use type-specific arrays. For example, use string[] for an array of strings. This is also very similar to a variety of classes in System.Collections, including ArrayList.
NSDictionary	This is similar to the System.Collections.Generic.Dictionary class.
NSData	This provides support for a byte stream, which in .NET could use a byte[] array or one the more specific classes, such as MemoryStream.
NSNumber	This provides the equivalent of boxing in C#, where any number can be contained within NSNumber and referenced. In C#, you can assign the number to an Object class instance, such as: int I = 50; Object o = i;
NSString	This is similar to the System.String class.
NSDate	This is similar to the System.Date class.

To bring this to life, let's look at a working example that allows us to use one of these types to create an array of values that we can use to hold our data, and then we'll serialize this array as a property list.

First, let's set up a dynamic array using the NSMutableMutable class:

```
NSMutableArray *highscores = [[NSMutableArray alloc] init];
// High score 1
[highscores addObject:@"Mark"];
```

```
[highscores addObject:@"200"];
// High score 2
[highscores addObject:@"Rachel"];
[highscores addObject:@"300"];
// .. others could be added
```

At this point. we can write this to the persistent storage of our choice (as we'll do next), and then finally release the array with the following command:

```
[highscores release];
```

Using Property Lists As Storage

Earlier in the book we touched on property lists within iOS and their existence in the filesystem as files with the `.plist` extension, known as *plist files*. Property lists offer a way to persist application data. Within Objective-C, the `NSArray` and `NSDictionary` collection classes provide a method that serializes their content to plist files. These collection classes also provide an easy mechanism to store and retrieve values from plist files.

Using the `NSMutableArray` we just set up (or indeed, any serializable collection), we can then use the `writeToFile` method to serialize this string to a plist file for later reading and interpretation. Simply execute the method with the destination of your file, as in this example:

```
[myArray writeToFile:@"/some/file/location/output.plist" atomically:YES];
```

If you execute an application with this snippet of code in place and then examine the file produced, you'll find it looks like this:

```
<?xml version="1.0" encoding="UTF-8"?>
<!DOCTYPE plist PUBLIC "-//Apple//DTD PLIST 1.0//EN"
"httpfhighscor://www.apple.com/DTDs/PropertyList-1.0.dtd">
<plist version="1.0">
<array>
        <string>Mark</string>
        <string>200</string>
        <string>Rachel</string>
        <string>300</string>
</array>
</plist>
```

Notice that it is serialized as an XML file, against the property list schema and using strings.

This file can then be read back into an array for manipulation or use using the `initWithContentsOfFile` method. The following deserializes the file we just created into a new `NSMutableArray` with the same values:

```
NSMutableArray *highscores = [[NSMutableArray alloc] initWithContentsOfFile:↵
 @"/some/file/location/output.plist"];
```

Using the Internet to Store Data

For persisting data, we've looked at property lists and using methods available as part of some of the serializable Objective-C types. However, what if you want to use the Internet in some form to serialize your data? What if you want to store this information in some kind of central location, rather than locally on the device?

The first and most obvious solution is to still use the property list method, except that the path to the file is the fully qualified URL of a file that exists on some internal-based storage—one of the many digital-storage platforms, such as Dropbox and Digital Vault.

But there is an alternative. The serializable collections such as NSMutableArray have a method called writeToURL, which instead of taking an NSString argument takes an NSUrl argument. However, if when writing to a file your argument is a file:// reference, then there is no real difference to the behavior of these methods. Therefore the following:

```
[myArray writeToURL: @"file://www.mamone.org/highscore.plist" atomically:YES];
```

is exactly the same as this:

```
NSURL *url = [NSURL URLWithString:@"http://www.mamone.org/highscore.plist"];
[myArray writeToURL:url atomically:YES];
```

Using the iOS-Embedded Database

Our previous examples, while perfectly adequate, have been restricted to creating data using objects that are serializable to either locally held or Internet-based filesystems. You may want to persist data using a more comprehensive mechanism, especially if you want to manipulate the data without needing to resort to complex file or object manipulation in code, which would be a by-product of storing data using a simple filesystem-based storage mechanism. In these cases, you can use the iPhone's embedded database, which is called SQLite.

SQLite is an embedded relational database management system (RDBMS), which is similar in many ways to the more traditional server-based database servers you may be familiar with, such as Oracle and Microsoft SQL Server, in that you can use the Structured Query Language (SQL) to access and manipulate the data held within the database. However, there is no application you need to run. You simply use the API code provided within your application to invoke the SQLite functionality provided as part of the iOS.

Let's take a look at how you might use the SQLite capability within your mobile iOS device to access database functionality.

> **NOTE:** If you're not familiar with the SQL language, many resources are available on this topic. For example, see *Beginning SQL Server 2008 for Developers* and other titles from Apress.

Before we get started, you need to add support to your application for SQLite by referencing the library with the supporting library code, and then including the relevant header file. So, first add the library called `libsqlite3.dylib` to your project using the Build Phases tab of your project summary and choosing the + button. The dialog box should look similar to that shown in Figure 7–1.

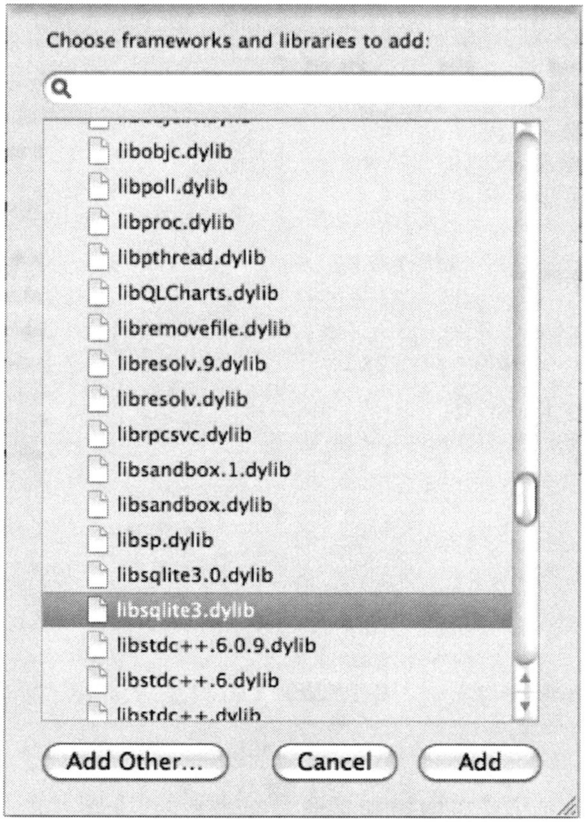

Figure 7–1. *Adding the SQLite library to the build phase of a project*

Then you'll need to include a reference to the supporting header file with the following #import directive in the source code file containing your SQLite code:

```
#import "/usr/include/sqlite3.h"
```

What are the iOS SDK Options?

Using the SQLite API isn't the only option for accessing the iOS device database. Core Data is a framework that is confusingly described as a "Schema-driven object graph management and persistence framework." This essentially means that not only does the Core Data API manage where data is stored, how it is stored, and how management of that data for performance reasons is handled, but it also allows developers to create and use a relational database under SQL-less conditions. It allows you to interact with

SQLite in Objective-C and not need to worry about connections or managing the database schema. Most of these features will be familiar to ADO.NET developers as a .NET Framework that abstracts access to the database.

However, we won't cover both SQLite and Core Data in this chapter. My goal is to take you through the principles with a working example using the SQLite API. This will provide a good foundation for you to apply this knowledge to whichever approach you take: SQLite or Core Data.

I recommend that you explore Core Data using the online resources available, specifically the *Core Data Programming Guide* at `http://developer.apple.com/library/mac/#documentation/Cocoa/Conceptual/CoreData/cdProgrammingGuide.html`.

Creating or Opening Your Database

SQLite is written in portable C, not Objective-C. Therefore, we'll need to write in the C language and use conversion between types where necessary.

Let's start by opening the database using the `sqlite_open()` method, and using the provided constants to look for success (`SQLITE_OK`) and log an error if it fails. The following code achieves this:

```
sqlite3 *db;
int result = sqlite3_open("/documents/file", &db);
if (result == SQLITE_OK)
{

} else NSLog(@"Failed to open database");
```

In this example, if the database exists, it will be opened. If it doesn't exist, it will be created.

> **NOTE:** The `sqlite_open()` method expects a UTF-* string as an argument—that is, an 8-bit encoded string. This isn't the same as an `NSString`, but you can use the `UTF8String` method to convert from an `NSString` to a UTF-8 string.

Note that at some point when trying to open a database—especially when it's not located locally on your machine—you will almost certainly encounter the problem of your database connection timing out. This is usually because of the delay (or latency) involved in accessing a resource that is not local, especially when you are connecting over the Internet. Therefore you should always intercept any error messages and deal with them as appropriate. For example, you might want to retry if the request has timed out.

Creating a Table in the Database

With our database open and ready for use, the next step is to create a table in which we will store our data. The SQL command CREATE TABLE can be used with the optional condition to create the table only it if doesn't already exist. The following code executes the CREATE TABLE command and creates a table with two columns called NAME and SCORE, both of type text.

```
char *errMsg;
const char *sql = "CREATE TABLE IF NOT EXISTS HIGHSCORE (NAME TEXT, SCORE TEXT)";
if (sqlite3_exec(db, sql, NULL, NULL, &errMsg) == SQLITE_OK)
{
    // code to write here
} else NSLog(@"Failed to create table");
```

Now the table will be created (if it didn't already exist), and we can begin to populate it with data from our array.

Writing Data to the Database

To write data to the database, you have two options:

- Construct an INSERT SQL statement from your string and traverse the array you have created.

- Bind your variables to your SQL statement, which has each of the parameters replaced with a ? symbol. This approach has the added advantage of ensuring that the data you insert matches the format of the data expected in the table.

So, first we need to loop through our array extracting the values held within it. This is simply done in our example by using a loop and an integer-based index, which starts at 0 (the first element) and continues while it is less than the count of all items in the array, determined by the count attribute.

```
int count = [highscore count];
int idx = 0;
while (idx < count)
{
        // loop through the array, increasing idx
}
```

Extending this to cycle through the array, accessing its elements and using the SQL binding feature to replace the ? parameter indicators with values from the array and then finalizing the statement, has the effect of writing the row to the database. Here is the extended code:

```
sqlite3 *db;
int result = sqlite3_open("/documents/file", &db);
if (result == SQLITE_OK)
{
    int count=[highscore count];
    int idx = 0;
```

```
        char *insert_sql = "INSERT INTO HIGHSCORE VALUES(?, ?);";
        sqlite3_stmt *stmt;
        while (idx < count)
        {
            // Prepare our statement for binding
            if (sqlite3_prepare_v2(db, insert_sql, -1, &stmt, nil) == SQLITE_OK) {
                // Bind the name
                sqlite3_bind_text(stmt, 1, [[highscore objectAtIndex: idx++] UTF8String],↵
    -1, NULL);    // NAME
                // Bind the score
                sqlite3_bind_text(stmt, 2, [[highscore objectAtIndex: idx++] UTF8String],↵
    -1, NULL);    // SCORE
                // Step and finalize the write
                sqlite3_step(stmt);
                sqlite3_finalize(stmt);
            }
        }
    } else NSLog(@"Failed to open database");
```

In this example, we prepare the SQL statement with the parameters using the
sqlite3_prepare() statement. Then while within the loop, we use the
sqlite3_bind_text() method to mind a variable's value—in this instance, the array
index to the parameter in the SQL statement referenced by its index position, starting at
0.

After each pair of array entries completes, we finalize the statement, which writes the
row to the database. We continue until all array entries have been covered.

Reading Data from the Database

To check that our code works, we can now use a simple SQL SELECT statement to read
back the rows we've just written to our database. For simplicity, we will use the NSLog()
method to write the data to the debug output view within Xcode.

Just as in the previous example, we need to prepare a SQL statement and execute it,
using the sqlite3_step() method to cycle through the rows until no more are found,
and using the NSLog() method to output each row's data. This is shown in the following
example:

```
// READ FROM TABLE
sqlite3_stmt *readstmt;
const char *readSQL = "SELECT NAME, SCORE FROM HIGHSCORE";
sqlite3_prepare_v2(db, readSQL, -1, &readstmt, NULL);
while (sqlite3_step(readstmt) == SQLITE_ROW)
{
        NSString *name = [[NSString alloc] initWithUTF8String:(const char↵
 *)sqlite3_column_text(readstmt,0)];
        NSString *score = [[NSString alloc] initWithUTF8String:(const char↵
 *)sqlite3_column_text(readstmt,1)];
        NSLog (@"NAME: %@ SCORE: %@", name, score );
}
```

If you execute the complete set of code and examine the output in the debug window of your Xcode application, it should resemble something similar to the following (excluding all of the other debug output associated with the running application):

```
2011-08-15 22:19:05.251 DataStorage[953:207] NAME: Mark SCORE: 200
2011-08-15 22:19:05.253 DataStorage[953:207] NAME: Rachel SCORE: 300
```

This example should have given you some insight into using the embedded database as a more comprehensive way of persisting data to a database represented as a local file.

Connecting to Other Databases

We've explored the use of the embedded database found in the iOS, SQLite, but what if you have a different database and it's held remotely? For example, what if you want to access a remote MySQL or Microsoft SQL Server database from your device? You have several options:

- You can use a third-party client for your database. For example, Flipper (found at http://www.driventree.com/flipper) is a MySQL client for the iPhone that allows you to connect to MySQL databases.

- If you have a Microsoft SQL Server database, you might want to access it by using a database-agnostic API, such as an Open Database Connectivity (ODBC) driver.

- You can access the database by sourcing a similar local client API, or exposing a services layer from SQL Server and using an XML-based API over HTTP, like SOAP.

Creating the High-Score Example

So far, we've looked at persisting our application's data using a number of different techniques. Now let's explore how we can put this to use in our example application, the Lunar Lander game we started in Chapter 5. The one thing that jumps out in a game like ours is the need to persist our scores in a high score table, providing the players with another competitive dimension to the game. So, we'll apply our data persistence knowledge and look at creating an internal high-score structure that is available to be displayed on the start screen and persists between application instances.

Creating a Persistent High-Score Class

Our high-score feature is pretty straightforward. It will hold five entries, each with the name of the person who attained the high score and the score itself. We could carry on as in the previous example, and use standard Objective-C object types like NSString. This would have the advantage of being written to a plist file, but would incur complexity in how we interpret the file. Instead, we'll use a custom object that inherits from NSObject to store the actual high-score entries.

To build on our Objective-C foundation, let's create a class that holds an individual high-score entry with properties that reference its values. This will then be contained within an NSMutableArray, which we will use to write the storage of our local high score to the local device using SQL Server. However, this does present a problem when trying to serialize the object to a plist file, as the writeToFile method doesn't support serializing custom objects. In our example, we'll look at how to solve this problem.

First, let's create our high-score entry class, called HighScoreEntry. Listing 7–1 shows the code for the header file.

Listing 7–1. *HighScoreEntry Class Header*

```
// HighScoreEntry class
//
@interface HighScoreEntry : NSObject {
    NSString * name;
    int score;
}
-(id)initWithParameters:(NSString*)aName:(int)Score;
@property (readwrite, retain) NSString* name;
@property (readwrite) int score;

@end
```

> **NOTE:** Remember that the readwrite attribute of a property means you can both access the property's value and set the property's value. Additionally, retain ensures that a strong reference is created, meaning as a resource, it will not be released until you explicitly release it.

This is pretty straightforward, and with the material we've covered, it should be familiar. The code simply implements a class that contains a string and an integer using the class member names of name and score, respectively. We have two properties of the same name that will reference these class member variables, and we've implemented an initialization method that takes two parameters of type NSString and int, which are used to initialize the class. Listing 7–2 shows the source code for its implementation.

Listing 7–2. *HighScoreEntry Class Implementation*

```
// HighScoreEntry class
//
@implementation HighScoreEntry

-(id)initWithParameters:(NSString*)aName:(int)aScore
{
    self = [super init];
    if (self)
    {
        name = [aName copy];
        score = aScore;
    }
    return self;
}

@synthesize name;
```

```
@synthesize score;

@end
```

Again, this is pretty straightforward. Our implementation provides the `initWithParameters` method to initialize the class member variables with values passed, and, of course, we synthesize our two properties.

Now let's take a look at the actual collection. We'll call this our `HighScore` class. Again, we'll start with the source code for the header file, as shown in Listing 7–3.

Listing 7–3. *HighScore Class Header*

```
// HighScore class
//
@interface HighScore : NSObject {
    NSMutableArray *scores;
}
-(void)addHighScoreEntry:(HighScoreEntry *)score;
-(void)persist;
@end
```

This contains a single member variable for our scores, held in a member variable of the same name and using the `NSMutableArray` type to allow flexibility. We also declare two class methods: one that will add a high-score entry to the list called addHighScoreEntry, and the other to persist the high score to storage—in our case, a local database. The implementation for the class is a little more complex, as shown in Listing 7–4.

Listing 7–4. *HighScore Class Implementation*

```
// HighScore class
//
@implementation HighScore
-(void)addHighScoreEntry:(HighScoreEntry *)score
{
    if (scores == nil)
        scores = [[NSMutableArray alloc] init];

    [scores addObject:(score)];
}

-(void)persist
{
    // Open our database
    sqlite3 *db;
    int result = sqlite3_open("mydb.sqlite3", &db);
    if (result == SQLITE_OK)
    {
        // CREATE TABLE
        char *errMsg;
        const char *sql = "CREATE TABLE IF NOT EXISTS HIGHSCORE (NAME TEXT, SCORE↵
INTEGER)";
        if (sqlite3_exec(db, sql, NULL, NULL, &errMsg) == SQLITE_OK)
        {
            // WRITE ARRAY TO TABLE
            int idx = 0;
            char *insert_sql = "INSERT INTO HIGHSCORE VALUES(?, ?);";
            sqlite3_stmt *stmt;
```

```
                    while (idx < [scores count])
                    {
                        // Prepare our statement for binding
                        if (sqlite3_prepare_v2(db, insert_sql, -1, &stmt, nil) == SQLITE_OK) {
                            // Get entry
                            HighScoreEntry *hse = [scores objectAtIndex:(idx)];

                            // Bind the name
                            sqlite3_bind_text(stmt, 1, [hse.name UTF8String], -1, NULL);   //↩
        NAME

                            // Bind the score
                            sqlite3_bind_int(stmt, 2, hse.score);   // SCORE
                            // Step and finalize the write
                            sqlite3_step(stmt);
                            sqlite3_finalize(stmt);
                            // Next item
                            idx++;
                        }
                    }
                    // READ FROM TABLE
                    sqlite3_stmt *readstmt;
                    const char *readSQL = "SELECT NAME, SCORE FROM HIGHSCORE ORDER BY SCORE";
                    sqlite3_prepare_v2(db, readSQL, -1, &readstmt, NULL);
                    while (sqlite3_step(readstmt) == SQLITE_ROW)
                    {
                        NSString *name = [[NSString alloc] initWithUTF8String:(const char↩
        *)sqlite3_column_text(readstmt,0)];
                        NSString *score = [[NSString alloc] initWithUTF8String:(const char↩
        *)sqlite3_column_text(readstmt,1)];
                        NSLog (@"NAME: %@ SCORE: %@", name, score );

                    }
                } else NSLog(@"Failed to create table");

            } else NSLog(@"Failed to open database");
    }
    @end
```

First, let's consider the addHighScoreEntry method, which should be pretty self-explanatory. If the scores array is null, we create it. We then add the object passed to the array using its addObject method.

The persist method, although lengthy, should again be familiar. We walked through the code earlier. However, I will point out some of the key differences:

■ **Using an integer for the score**: In our table, we now use an integer type rather than a string to store the actual score value.

■ **Counting array count**: When looping around the array, we use the count attribute of NSMutableArray to return how many objects are in the array, and when we reach the maximum, we exit the loop.

■ **Extracting an object**: We extract the high-score entry object from the class using its index, and we can then use this to reference the object's values through the properties provided—specifically, name and score.

■ **Binding**: We bind the name as text and the score as an integer to the parameters in our SQL statement. This is virtually identical to our previous example, except we are using the sqlite3_bind_int method for our integer.

■ **Moving along the array:** As we are looping through the array's members, we must remember to increase the index that not only selects the next object in the list, but is also used when determining whether to exit the loop.

Also notice that the same code exists to reread the data and output it to the log file, which, in the case of Xcode 4, is the debug window. This obviously isn't required for the actual implementation and is left in only for testing purposes. For clarity, here's the code that does this:

```
// READ FROM TABLE
sqlite3_stmt *readstmt;
const char *readSQL = "SELECT NAME, SCORE FROM HIGHSCORE";
sqlite3_prepare_v2(db, readSQL, -1, &readstmt, NULL);
while (sqlite3_step(readstmt) == SQLITE_ROW)
{
        NSString *name = [[NSString alloc] initWithUTF8String:(const char↵
 *)sqlite3_column_text(readstmt,0)];
        NSString *score = [[NSString alloc] initWithUTF8String:(const char↵
 *)sqlite3_column_text(readstmt,1)];
        NSLog (@"NAME: %@ SCORE: %@", name, score );
}
```

Testing the High-Score Class

Doesn't our class look lovely? Well, at least it's better than holding a sequence of strings that you then need to interpret. Now let's see if it works.

The code in Listing 7–5 represents a test harness to execute our high-score code and see if it works. Where you place it in your project is pretty much up to you, but you would see something like this in the initialization of your game—for example, to preload the default high scores if none exist in a table.

Listing 7–5. *Test Harness for the High-Score Code*

```
// Initialize our high score
HighScore *hs = [[HighScore alloc]init];
// Create 5 default entries
HighScoreEntry *e1 = [[HighScoreEntry alloc]initWithParameters:@"Mark":900];
    [hs addHighScoreEntry:(e1)];

HighScoreEntry *e2 = [[HighScoreEntry alloc]initWithParameters:@"Rachel":700];
    [hs addHighScoreEntry:(e2)];

HighScoreEntry *e3 = [[HighScoreEntry alloc]initWithParameters:@"Oliver":500];
    [hs addHighScoreEntry:(e3)];

HighScoreEntry *e4 = [[HighScoreEntry alloc]initWithParameters:@"Harry":300];
    [hs addHighScoreEntry:(e4)];

HighScoreEntry *e5 = [[HighScoreEntry alloc]initWithParameters:@"Tanya":100];
```

```
[hs addHighScoreEntry:(e5)];
```

```
// Persist our initial high score to the database
[hs persist];
```

If you execute the code in Listing 7–5 with the debug code that rereads the data after persisting it, you should see debug output similar to the following:

```
2011-08-17 19:59:37.237 DataStorage[676:207] NAME: Mark SCORE: 900
2011-08-17 19:59:37.237 DataStorage[676:207] NAME: Rachel SCORE: 700
2011-08-17 19:59:37.238 DataStorage[676:207] NAME: Oliver SCORE: 500
2011-08-17 19:59:37.238 DataStorage[676:207] NAME: Harry SCORE: 300
2011-08-17 19:59:37.239 DataStorage[676:207] NAME: Tanya SCORE: 100
```

In your game, you would hold the instance variable for the high scores with a class that has suitable visibility, and you would initialize it with the default values only if the table didn't exist. You would also want to release the high-score class variable at a suitable point when your application terminates.

But what about reading the high-score data if your application isn't being run for the first time? This requires a few changes. First, when persisting the data, we need to clear the table's contents so the table is ready to receive the new data. This is easily done by adding the following code between the table being created (if it needs to be created) and before we start writing any content:

```
// DELETE from the table
const char *sqldelete = "DELETE FROM HIGHSCORE";
sqlite3_exec(db, sqldelete, NULL, NULL, &errMsg);
```

We can also use the code we wrote to read the table and dump it to the log file to help us implement a method that reads the data from the table to initialize the high score. We'll call this method readHighScores, and its implementation is shown in Listing 7–6.

Listing 7–6. *Reading the High-Score Data from the Table*

```objc
#import "MainViewController.h"
#import "HighScore.h"


// readHighScores method
-(void)readHighScores
{
    // Open our database
    sqlite3 *db;
    int result = sqlite3_open("mydb.sqlite3", &db);
    if (result == SQLITE_OK)
    {
        // We've opened the database, so let's clear our array
        [scores removeAllObjects];

        // READ FROM TABLE
        sqlite3_stmt *readstmt;
        const char *readSQL = "SELECT NAME, SCORE FROM HIGHSCORE";
        sqlite3_prepare_v2(db, readSQL, -1, &readstmt, NULL);
        while (sqlite3_step(readstmt) == SQLITE_ROW)
        {
            NSString *name = [[NSString alloc] initWithUTF8String:(const char↵
```

```
*)sqlite3_column_text(readstmt,0)];
            int score = (const int)sqlite3_column_int(readstmt,1);
            HighScoreEntry *e = [[HighScoreEntry alloc]initWithParameters:name:score];
            [self addHighScoreEntry:(e)];
            [e release];
        }
    } else NSLog(@"Failed to open database");
}
```

This should be pretty easy to follow, as it uses a lot of the code we've used previously. We use a SELECT statement to read the data from the table and cycle through the data while rows of data still exist. In doing so, we then extract the data—in this case, the name as text (converting to UTF-8 to comply with the NSString class) and the score as an integer. We then use these as parameters in creating a HighScoreEntry class instance, which is added to our high-scores array and then released.

Completing the Class

Almost complete, our class can now be initialized with a default high-score table. We can persist this to a local database on our iOS mobile device using SQLite, and we can reread this data back into our high-score display. The presentation of this high score is left to you, but you might consider using a Table view, something we'll touch on in Chapter 10, as we'll be looking at impressive user interface transformations there.

At the moment, there is nothing to limit your number of high-score entries. This is by design, as you can decide what a suitable limit is and use the knowledge gained so far to create a method that implements that constraint when it adds a high-score entry. Also, you will want to sort your high scores, typically in order of score, with the highest first, assuming a bigger score is better.

As this chapter's focus is on persistence, not sorting arrays, we won't go over the complete implementation. But to help you get started, I will provide some pointers on how to approach sorting.

First, to sort an NSMutableArray that contains custom objects (that is, a class that inherits from NSObject), you use the sortArrayUsingSelector method, which performs the sort, but asks that you provide as a parameter the method to use as the comparator, called the *selector*.

Next, you to need to implement your own comparator that can make sense of the objects in your array. In our case, we would compare the score member variable and sort with the highest first. The beginning of such a method is shown here for you to experiment with and complete.

```
(NSComparisonResult)compare(HighScoreEntry* otherObject
{
  return ( // DO YOUR COMPARISON HERE between self and otherObject)
}
```

Comparing the Serialization Example with .NET

In this chapter, we've taken a look at the options for basic data persistence using Objective-C and the iOS SDK, and even looked at some of the persistency properties of .NET. But how would this example compare with a .NET implementation?

Well, the use of a custom class to hold the high-score names and scores would still be valid in .NET. We would use a very similar mechanism, with the exception of syntax differences, and hold the name as a String and the score as an int. We could even have the same method names and approach.

NSMutableArray could be implemented in .NET as an ArrayList, allowing you to Insert() or Remove() items using methods. It also has a Sort() method, similar to our sortArrayUsingSelector method, which takes a comparator as an argument.

Finally, serializing could be done using a similar method to our example, cycling through the entries and writing to some persistency storage, such as a database using an ODBC driver or a similar database API. Alternatively, you could use the XMLSerializer class to serialize the class using a StreamWriter if you wanted to write to a file. Consider the C# example in Listing 7–7, which assumes we have a HighScoreClass that behaves as in our example, but also defines the [Serializable()] attribute surrounding those members we want to serialize.

Listing 7–7. *Serializing a Class in C#*

```
// Create our High Score class (note that this won't compile, as we've excluded
// the definition of this for brevity)
HighScoreClass hs = new HighScoreClass()
// Create a new XmlSerializer instance with the type of our high score class
XmlSerializer so = new XmlSerializer(typeof(HighScoreClass));

// Create a new file stream to write the serialized object to
TextWriter WriteFileStream = new StreamWriter(@"C:\output.xml");
so.Serialize(WriteFileStream, hs);

// Clean up
WriteFileStream.Close();
```

The example in Listing 7–7 is very similar to our earlier plist example using Objective-C, in that it serializes a class's content to an XML file. This is the most common method within the .NET Framework for serializing a class. The use of embedded SQL statements executed against the database is also very similar in .NET.

Summary

In this chapter, we've taken a tour of the options for persisting data to storage other than the mobile device's memory, which is volatile; that is, when the device is switched off or the application is closed, the memory and any data associated with it is lost.

We've looked at the techniques for persisting data to a file, to a database, and to the Internet. We've also explored the features provided by the iOS to help with this, such as the application's sandbox. We then took a look at the language and SDK support for storing data and writing it to different storage types, including to a plist file and to the embedded database.

We concluded by implementing a couple of simple classes to test the theory, providing support for a table of high scores that could be persisted to storage for our Lunar Lander game. Now between application instances, we can retain a list of the highest scores, thus increasing the competitive enjoyment of our game.

Chapter 8

Extend Your Apps: Extending Your iOS Application with Libraries

The ability to extend your application's functionality beyond that provided through the iOS itself and the iOS SDK is fairly typical of most operating systems. The Microsoft Windows operating system was built with the ability to extend its functionality through the provision of both static and dynamically linked libraries. And this isn't limited to the Windows operating system. Unix, Linux, and many other operating systems offer the same abilities, and Apple's iOS is no different.

Building on some of the examples of using other options discussed in Chapter 3, this chapter provides some guidance on how to build your own libraries and how to use other libraries that complement the iOS operating system. Specifically, we'll look at the following:

■ An overview of how libraries work and the different types of libraries

■ How libraries are used by the iOS

■ How you can use libraries within your applications

■ Third-party libraries and their benefits

Overview of Libraries

We'll start by providing some context around the different types of libraries, their purpose, and how they work within the context of the iOS. We'll discuss what a library is, what types exist, and why you may use one rather than the other–or both!

What Is a Library?

A *library* is a set of routines and variables that may exist locally, or remotely, to realize a prescribed set of functionality—at least in the computer-science sense (just in case you were thinking of a place to go to read books!). These routines and variables are realized in code, irrespective of the programming language used. The way you reference them and the way they are used may differ, and this is what identifies the different types of libraries.

What Types of Libraries Exist?

The types of libraries can essentially be categorized as follows, regardless of whether they are local or remote.

- Static library
- Dynamic library

Let's look at these in turn.

Static Library

A *static library* is a collection of routines and variables that are held in a single file and are referenced within your code. An associated header file provides the method signatures and sometimes variables. At compile time, your library is referenced, which enables the code that implements the required functionality to be included in your executable. This is usually handled by a program called the *linker*, which is why they are sometimes called *statically linked libraries*.

On iOS devices, static libraries have an extension of .a. On Windows, the extension is typically .lib.

Dynamic Library

A *dynamic library*, as its name suggests, is dynamic in the way it works. The library is still referenced through the use of a header file, but it isn't included into the executable during compilation; it is referenced at runtime. This means that the library is loaded on first use, or before, to resolve the call and execute the referenced functionality.

On iOS, dynamic libraries have an extension of .dynlib. On Windows, they have an extension of .dll.

Use of dynamic libraries has the added advantages of making your executables smaller and allowing common functionality to be more efficiently shared. However, it does introduce some penalties, some of which caused big problems in the early days for Microsoft Windows. These problems were related to version control of different libraries with the same methods but whose implementation was different. In Windows, this was called *DLL hell*.

While the iPhone and the iPad are quite capable of producing and using dynamic libraries, the Apple Developer Agreement specifically prohibits the use of dynamic libraries other than those provided by the system or official SDKs. This is why the embedded SQLite library is supported. However, if you try to create your own and submit your application to the App Store, it will be rejected.

Why has Apple done this? This has been the source of much debate for many years. Indeed, the Developer Agreement was only recently updated to list some of the restrictions around interpreted code, but it is still quite rigid, and I highly recommend you read it carefully. We'll talk more about the Apple Developer Agreement later in the chapter. For now, either use system-provided dynamic libraries or stick to static libraries, especially if you want your application to be approved upon submission to the App Store.

Comparing iOS Libraries with .NET Equivalents

Before we move on to creating your own libraries and taking advantage of third-party options, let's take a look at some of the more common iOS libraries. Not surprisingly, the iOS SDK, like most SDKs, provides a set of libraries as part of its installation. I won't list all the iOS libraries, as you'll quickly find that iOS frameworks are a suite of libraries, with associated header files and supporting documentation. Instead, I'll note several particularly useful libraries available as part of the iOS SDK but not published as iOS frameworks. Table 8–1 lists those libraries, along with brief descriptions and comments about how they compare with .NET.

Table 8–1. *Comparing iOS and .NET Libraries*

iOS Library	Description and .NET Commentary
Sqlite3 (libsqlite3.dylib)	Provides access to the embedded iOS database, which we covered in more detail within Chapter 7. In .NET the framework provides for a number of data providers, including SQL Server, ODBC, and Oracle. The nearest comparison for the iOS SQLite in .NET is SQL Server Compact edition and ADO.NET (Active Data Object for .NET).
Archiving (libarchive.dylib)	Provides the ability to compress and uncompress files, including support for a number of different compression formats. The .NET equivalent is the System.io.compression namespace, or either Libarchive on SourceForge (http://gnuwin32.sourceforge.net/packages/libarchive.htm), or the DotNetZip library (http://dotnetzip.codeplex.com/).
XML (libxml2.dylib) XSLT (libxslt.dylib)	Provides access to functionality for managing eXtended Markup Language (XML) files and performing transformations using Extensible Stylesheet Language Transformations. The .NET equivalent is the System.XML namespace, which provides functionality for both

Many more libraries than those listed in Table 8–1 are available, but with the iOS frameworks and those listed, you should have most of the capability required. Then you always have the option of using third-party libraries or your own custom libraries to extend your application's capability further.

Creating Your Own Static Libraries

You can create your own static libraries for iOS. In this section, we'll cover how to create one using Xcode 4, and then we'll look at creating a comparable library, or assembly, in .NET.

Creating a Static Library with Xcode 4

Xcode 4 makes it easy to create your own static libraries. Start by choosing the Cocoa Touch Static Library template from the Framework & Library iOS category, as shown in Figure 8–1, and then click Next.

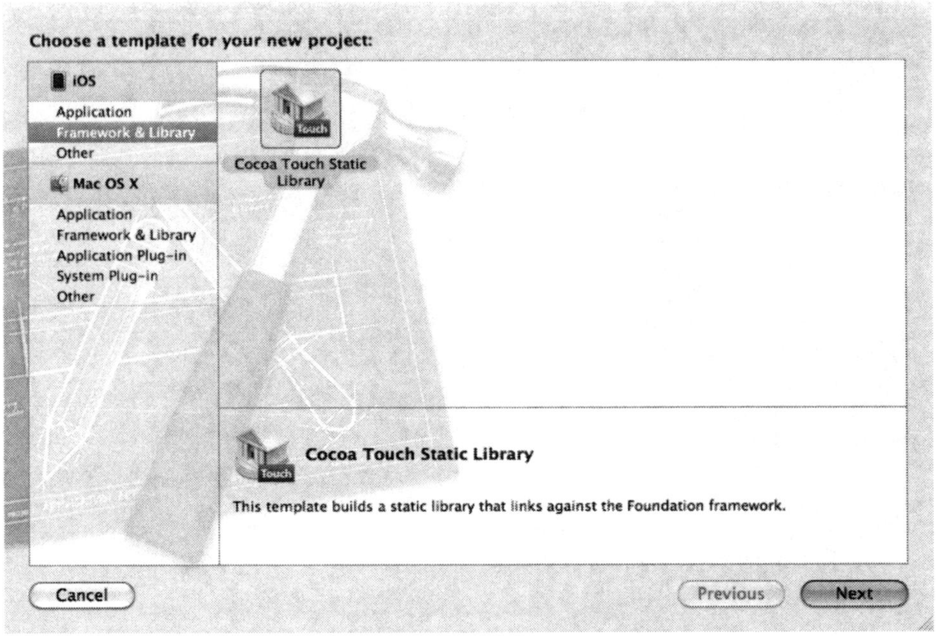

Figure 8–1. *Selecting a static library template*

On the following screen, choose the product name for your project, as shown in Figure 8–2. At this point, you may want to introduce a version number in your file name to help manage different versions of the same library, or you could be really clever and start to use the snapshot feature and source code control within Xcode (see http://developer. apple.com/library/mac/#documentation/ToolsLanguages/Conceptual/Xcode4UserGuide/ SCM/SCM.html). Once you've decided on the file name, hit the Next button again.

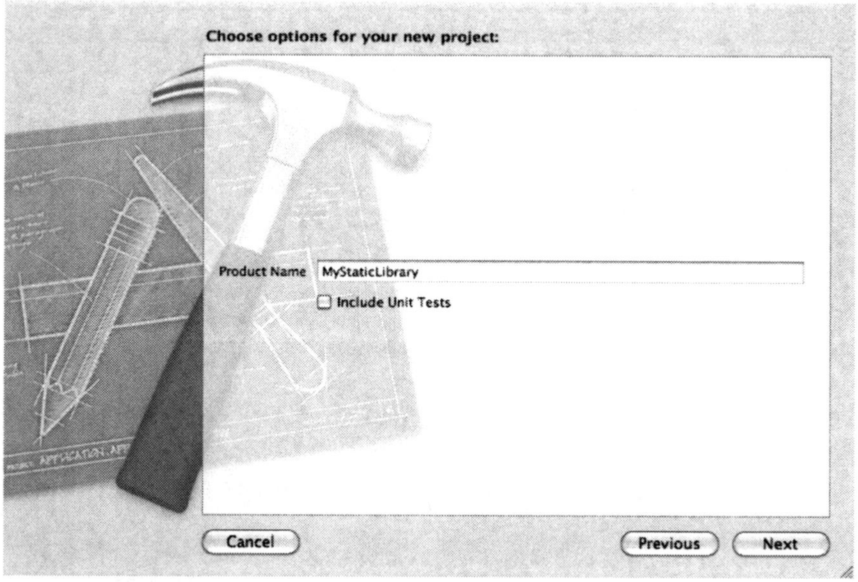

Figure 8–2. *Choosing your static library's product name*

Finally, choose the location for your project (see Figure 8–3), and then click Create.

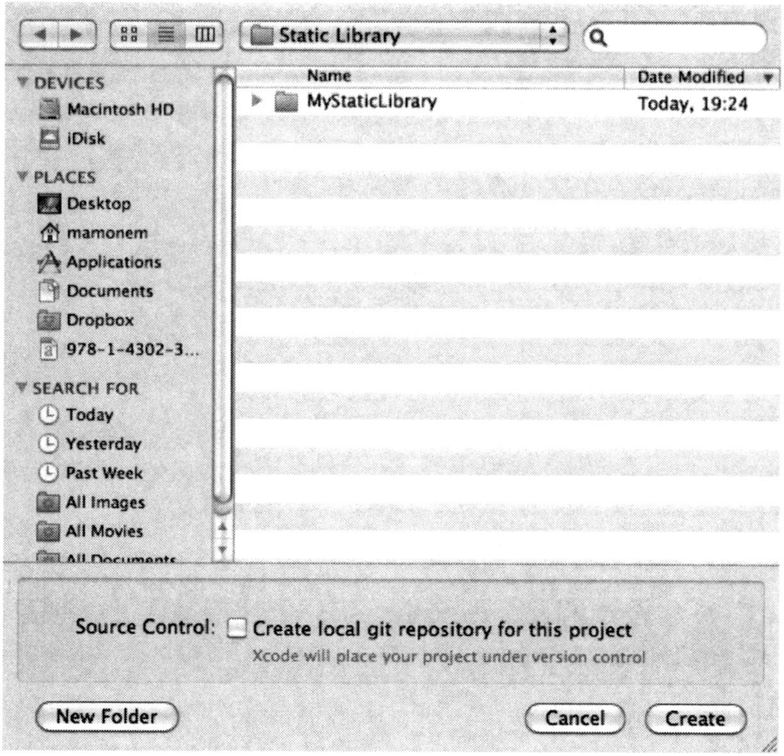

Figure 8–3. *Choosing your project location*

This will create your project structure in a manner similar to the other projects we've built, except the number of predefined files created is reduced. This is because the functionality is for you to define. This framework will simply create an empty static library under the name defined in your Products structure—MyStaticLibrary.a in this example.

Now we need to add some functionality to our library. You could go ahead and create classes and constants for your library. But to keep things simple for our example, let's just add the files we created to support our high-score functionality in Chapter 7 to create our static library.

In Xcode, choose File ➤ Add Files and navigate to where you stored your high-score source code. In our example, the header code is in a file called HighScore.h, and the implementation is in HighScore.m.

Highlight the two files and select the "Copy items into destination group's folder (if needed)" checkbox, as shown in Figure 8–4. Then click the Add button.

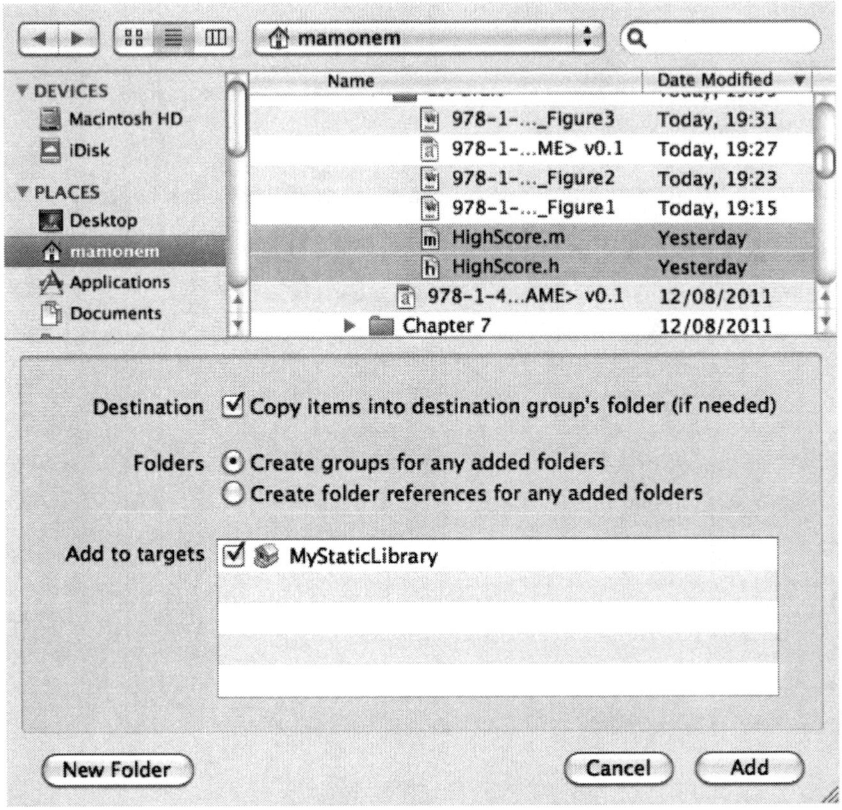

Figure 8–4. *Adding files to the static library project*

This will add the files to your static library and create a static library with this functionality contained within it. To locate the library produced, assuming you have not changed the default target destination, you can select the library under the Products folder and choose File ➤ Show in Finder. The Xcode default is to place it in the

`/Library/Developer/Xcode/DerivedData` folder, and then in subfolders beneath that per project, as shown in Figure 8–5.

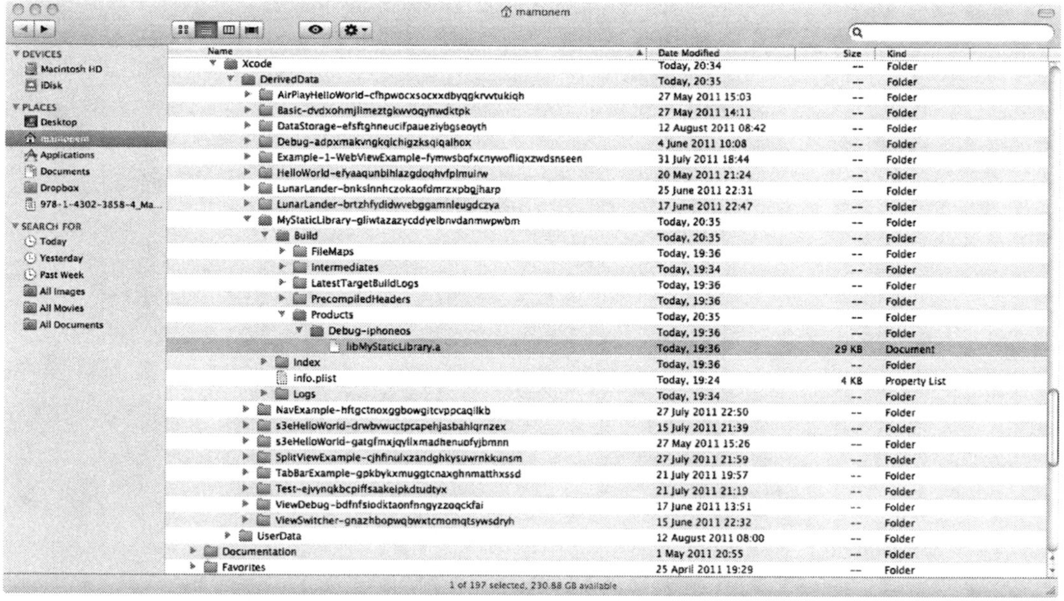

Figure 8–5. *Locating your static library*

NOTE: In our example, you'll notice the folder name is `Debug-iphoneos`. This is deliberate to highlight the fact that when building a static library, it defaults to the iPhone operating system, which has an ARM-based CPU. You will need to ensure you change your build settings to compile for the iPhone simulator theme; otherwise, it won't compile, as the simulator runs on the i386 CPU. You can tell if you have it right because the director will change to `Debug-iphonesimulator`, and it is from here that you should reference your static library.

Let's test the library by creating a very simple application. For my test, I created a utility application. Once you've created a test application, select the top-level project entry in the Build Phases tab, as shown in Figure 8–6.

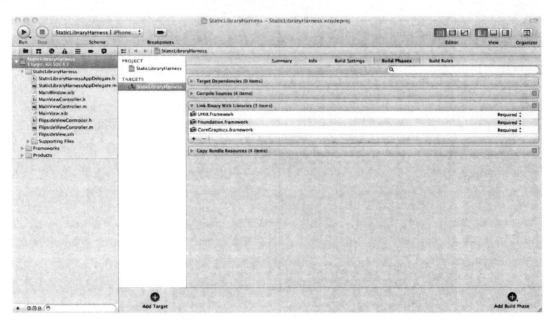

Figure 8–6. *Configuring the build phases of your project*

Under the expanded Link Binary with Libraries selection, you will notice that three libraries are already referenced by default: UIKit.framework, Foundation.framework, and CoreGraphic.framework. Choosing the + icon will display a dialog box allowing you to choose another library. As shown in Figure 8–7, you can select from the default iOS SDK list or click Add Other.

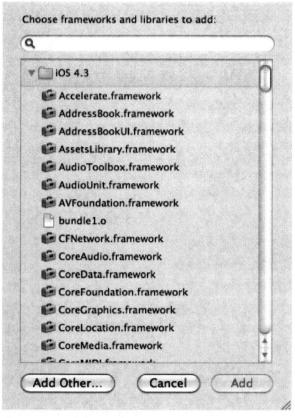

Figure 8–7. *Adding a library to your build phase*

Choose Add Other, and you'll see a dialog box that allows you to navigate to the location of the library you wish to include. As shown in Figure 8–8, navigate to the library built by the previous static library project.

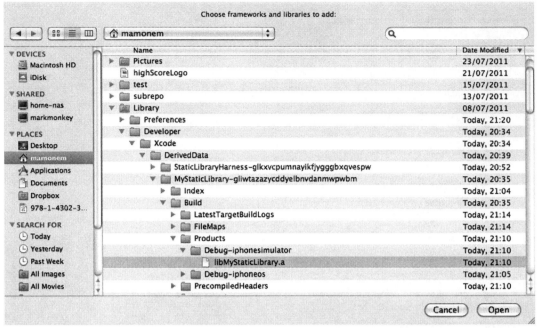

Figure 8–8. *Choosing the library to add*

Select the library and choose Open. This will add the library to the list of libraries linked with the build of your application, as shown in Figure 8–9.

Figure 8–9. *List of libraries to be linked to your project build*

Now we can complete the project in order to test our library. First, add the `HighScore.h` header file to your project. Next, we can add some test harness code. For this, copy the code we used in the previous example and place it in the `viewDidLoad` event method of our main view controller (in `MainViewController.m`). This means when the application is started and the view loaded, our test harness code will execute. You'll need to uncomment the event code and ensure it looks similar to that shown in Listing 8–1.

Listing 8–1. *Test Harness Code*

```
// Implement viewDidLoad to do additional setup after loading the view, typically from
 a nib.
- (void)viewDidLoad
{
    [super viewDidLoad];
    HighScore *hs = [[HighScore alloc]init];

    HighScoreEntry *e1 = [[HighScoreEntry alloc]initWithParameters:@"Mark":900];
```

```
[hs addHighScoreEntry:(e1)];

HighScoreEntry *e2 = [[HighScoreEntry alloc]initWithParameters:@"Rachel":700];
[hs addHighScoreEntry:(e2)];

HighScoreEntry *e3 = [[HighScoreEntry alloc]initWithParameters:@"Oliver":500];
[hs addHighScoreEntry:(e3)];

HighScoreEntry *e4 = [[HighScoreEntry alloc]initWithParameters:@"Harry":300];
[hs addHighScoreEntry:(e4)];

HighScoreEntry *e5 = [[HighScoreEntry alloc]initWithParameters:@"Tanya": ];
[hs addHighScoreEntry:(e5)];

[hs persist];

[hs readHighScores];

[hs release];

}
```

Don't forget to also add a reference to the libsqlite3.dylib for our database support, and then build and execute your application. You should see the same output in the debug window as before, because we didn't remove this test code. It should look similar to the following:

```
2011-08-18 21:29:39.639 StaticLibraryHarness[1034:207] NAME: Mark SCORE: 900
2011-08-18 21:29:39.641 StaticLibraryHarness[1034:207] NAME: Rachel SCORE: 700
2011-08-18 21:29:39.641 StaticLibraryHarness[1034:207] NAME: Oliver SCORE: 500
2011-08-18 21:29:39.642 StaticLibraryHarness[1034:207] NAME: Harry SCORE: 300
```

You have now created your first static library and referenced it from another application. If your static library contained some "must-have" functionality, simply distributing this library and the header file is all that would be required for another person to use it. It's this mechanism that third-party library makers use to share and deploy their libraries, usually in a provisioning profile.

Creating an Assembly in .NET

Creating an assembly in .NET is straightforward and similar to the method shown for Xcode 4. You can simply start by creating a blank Visual Studio C# solution and adding your library code that defines a class and its functionality within a given namespace, as follows:

```
Using System;
Using System.Text;
Using System.Windows.Forms;
Namespace TestLibrary
{
        public static class Test
{

        public static void TestMethod()
        {
                MessageBox.Show("You are in my library");
```

```
        }
    }
}
}
```

Building this simple example will result in a `.dll` file, which is a dynamic library that you can reference in another project, and then call the `TestMethod()` from a class instance of `Test`. Make sure you reference the library in your project references.

Note that this is a private assembly and is linked to your application, a bit like a static library. If you wanted this to be shared among many programs (stored in the Global Assembly Cache of your .NET environment), then you would need to do a little more work and make it a strong-named assembly. This allows it to be versioned and authenticated. We won't go into the details here, but here's a hint: look at the command-line utility called `sn.exe`.

The Apple Developer Agreement

When registering and paying for your subscription to be part of the Apple Developer Program, you will be provided with a copy of the Apple Developer Agreement, a document that describes what is permissible by Apple when using their tools and technologies. The document is protected by a nondisclosure agreement (NDA), which means you are not allowed to know what's in it before you join. And when you have joined, you're not allowed to share its content! However, copies have been leaked to the Internet through Freedom of Information Act requests.

Around the use of libraries more broadly, the Agreement in its more relaxed form (which was put into effect in 2010), defines certain conditions under paragraph 3.3 (Program Requirements for Applications), which describes some restrictions to consider when writing your application. These conditions are as follows:

- Applications made with the iOS SDK can be distributed only through the App Store, essentially meaning that black-market application distribution networks such as Cydia are in breach of the agreement.

- Reverse-engineering is not permitted. Also, enabling others to do reverse-engineering is not permitted.

- Apple may revoke your application's membership from the App Store at any time, even after it has already been approved.

- You may use only document APIs and in the manner prescribed. You must not call any private APIs.

> **NOTE:** It wasn't until much later in 2010 that the requirements summarized here went into effect. Previously, Apple was specific about the languages supported, which meant third-party frameworks such as MonoTouch were in danger of being noncompliant.

If you don't follow these restrictions, you'll be in breach of the Agreement, and Apple may choose to reject any application submitted to Apple's App Store. But as long as the resulting application does not download any code and conforms to API usage, it should be permissible.

We'll talk more about the Apple Developer Agreement in Chapter 9, which covers deployment.

Third-Party Libraries

We've established that Apple finally saw sense and lifted previous restrictions, which means that third-party libraries are more broadly supported. We've also established which kinds of libraries exist and how you can use them under the Apple Developer Agreement.

In Chapter 3, we looked at third-party solutions for writing applications. These third-party frameworks come with a suite of libraries that provide the required functionality, so they are always an option. But what if you want a smaller, more specific library to provide functionality that will extend your application? Well, you'll be pleased to hear that they exist. Indeed, using the information you garnered about writing libraries, you could even publish and make money from your own third-party libraries.

First, we'll look at the two categories of third-party libraries, and then we'll review some of the more useful libraries currently available.

Categories of Third-Party Libraries

Third-party libraries fall into two general categories: commercial and open source.

As its name suggests, a *commercial library* is one that is owned by an organization that places restrictions on its use and typically charges a fee for obtaining it, using it, or both. For example, in the .NET world, it is common for developers to buy extensions to the .NET library in the form of assemblies that do things like draw fancy graphics or compress files. The same is true of Apple, and many commercial organizations sell libraries for use on the iOS platform. But be sure to check the license agreements associated with any libraries and their use of such licenses.

An *open source library* is a library whose use is restricted to a degree, for example, under the GNU General Public License (GPL), but it is free to use.

Apple does, however, have its Developer Agreement, and your library must be conformant. It also still reserves the right to refuse or to revoke any application in the App Store. Again, this hasn't won any favors in the community, but as you can see from the App Store, it certainly has not put off people from writing applications with libraries, free or otherwise.

Useful Third-Party Libraries

So we've touched on writing your own library, and consider the different types of libraries you might find on the Internet. Let's take a look at some example third party libraries that exist and provide both a brief synopsis and an Internet URL for you to access them.

> **NOTE:** I do not recommend or imply any warranty on the use of these libraries. If you choose to use them, this is your choice, and I cannot guarantee their functionality, performance, or that they will be accepted by Apple for the App Store.

- **ZBar–Barcode Reader:** This can be found at `http://zbar.sourceforge.net/iphone/index.html` and is both a Library and Example Application (available from the App Store) that enables you to write software to read a variety of different bar codes using the iPhone's camera and even link them to stores such as Amazon or search engines such as Google.

- **GData - Google Data:** This can be found at `http://code.google.com/p/gdata-objectivec-client/` and provides an API as an Objective-C based static library that allows access to a variety of Google-based services and for you to read and write data. For example, Google Analytics, Google Books, Blogger, and Google Docs are all supported.

- **Three20 – Facebook API:** This can be found at `http://three20.info/`, and while known as the Facebook API, this isn't strictly accurate. However, it is used by the Facebook Application and many others to provide powerful view controllers, a photo browser, and an Internet-aware table.

- **iPhone Analyzer:** This can be found at `http://sourceforge.net/projects/iphoneanalyzer/` and allows you to analyze the contents of your iPhone device in great detail, including plists, databases, and the internal file structure of your device. However, at present iOS 4 is not supported.

- **Leaves:** This can be found at `https://github.com/brow/leaves` and is a library for both the iPhone and iPad that provides page-turning functionality like iBooks.

- **Core-plot:** This can be found at `http://code.google.com/p/core-plot/` and provides a plotting framework for the 2D visualization of data on both the iOS and Max OSX.

Looking Elsewhere for Libraries

While I've highlighted some third-party libraries, many more exist in common repositories for not just iPhone- or iPad-based libraries and source code, but also to support other platforms, such as Mac OS X, Windows, and Linux. Here are two popular sites:

- SourceForge: This is a library for sharing free open source software. It supports many different platforms, including mobile iOS devices like the iPhone and iPad. It can be found at `http://sourceforge.net/`.

- Github: Using the Git repository, GitHub is the home of many libraries, including a lot of useful mobile iOS-based libraries. It can be found at `https://github.com/`.

Summary

In this chapter, we've explored the concept of libraries, including iOS-provided libraries, third-party libraries, and your own creations. We looked at the different types of libraries and similarities to the .NET Framework and how to create your own static library, either for use within your application or for distribution.

The different types of third-party libraries were then introduced, and we've provided some examples of both the libraries, as well as popular repositories for libraries and source code for iOS-based devices. Now we clearly didn't list every library available. There are far too many to list, and the number is growing by the day. However, this introduction should help you to explore and discover libraries that suit your needs.

If you wish to write your own libraries, you can share these with others across the Internet. However, as per the Apple Developer Agreement, please do be cognizant of the restrictions applied to any application you write for a mobile device, and be conscious of the powers that Apple has when submitting your application to the App Store.

Chapter 9

Get Published: Testing, Deploying and Distributing Your Applications

The chapters thus far have taken you through everything from introducing the devices, the software development kits, the language, and the tools to a series of chapters on how to write your first iOS mobile device-based application. This knowledge culminates with you having an application, or even a library, that you will want to test, deploy, and publish—typically in that order. In this chapter you'll use the features of Xcode 4 and the iOS Simulator to thoroughly test your application. You'll also test it on a real device before you learn how to deploy and publish your application through the App Store. Specifically, you'll be looking at the following:

■ Introduction to the testing features available to you.

■ Overview of Xcode 4 and the iOS Simulator's testing capabilities.

■ How to deploy your application.

■ Preparing to publish your application.

■ Publishing via the App Store.

Available Test Features

There are a number of tools and techniques available to you for testing your application, some with very advanced features. At a high level, you typically use a combination of discrete unit based tests plus broader system-wide testing on both virtual (the simulator) and physical (a real one) devices to ensure that your applications work. You'll look at these in turn.

Unit Testing

While creating your example projects and source code files, you may have noticed a checkbox titled "Include Unit Tests." An example is shown in Figure 9–1 when creating a simple utility-based application called Calculator.

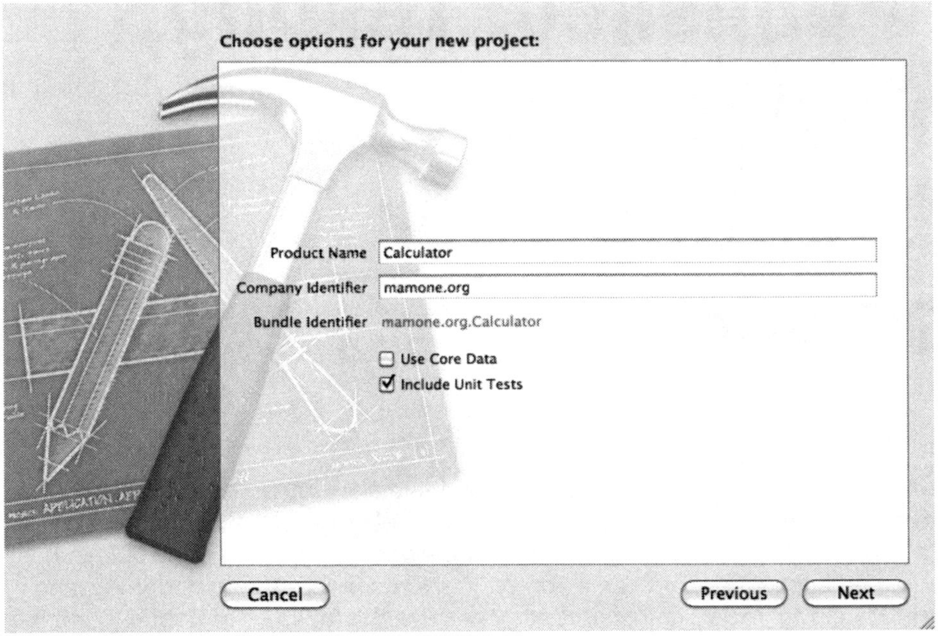

Figure 9–1. *Creating a project with unit tests*

After your project has been created, you'll notice a folder (in addition to those that are typically created) with the format of <project name>Tests. In this case, that folder is called CalculatorTests; exploring this folder will display a header and implementation file of the same name, which is provided for you to implement your unit tests.

Defining Your Testing Approach

As you're already a seasoned .NET professional, the concept of unit testing will be familiar to you. However, how Xcode embraces this will not, and perhaps other testing concepts such as integration testing or even Test Driven Development may be new to you also. Let's take a brief tour through these terms before you look at Xcode's support.

Unit Testing

To ensure a baseline of understanding, let's briefly recap the term *unit test*. A unit test is code written specifically to test a particular part of your application's code. In the world of testing you'll have a series of test cases that assert that the module you are running is behaving as expected. For example, if a method was written to add two numbers, you may have test cases that check if the addition is performed correctly and that if you pass invalid parameters it handles such a circumstance elegantly.

This is no different in any other language, certainly not when writing .NET based applications. In the days before Visual Studio supported unit testing or before it even existed, it was common practice to use tools such as NUnit to implement unit tests (Java uses JUnit). Thankfully, Visual Studio has caught up and has a plethora of testing capability including a Unit Test framework with unit tests much like Xcode 4 (but I would argue even more advanced).

Integration Testing

Unit testing is, of course, only the start of your testing journey. It helps to test discrete units of code, but when your application starts to link these together, you're into the realm of integration testing. The key distinction between integration and unit testing is that unit testing usually supposes the quite simplistic stand-alone testing of single "units" and does not require more complex test environments or tools. Xcode doesn't make any specific provision for integration testing, other than writing your own unit tests that integrate other unit tests, but other options are available to you. For example, iCuke allows you to write integration tests without any changes to your application. iCuke uses Cucumber, a behavior-driven test environment (see more in the "Test Driven Development" section) to implement its functionality. Both are fairly complex products and not the core scope of this book, but I recommend you take a look at them. You can find more information on iCuke at `https://github.com/unboxed/icuke`, and Cucumber at `http://cukes.info/`.

Test Driven Development

You've now looked at tools that support concepts such as integration testing but rather than focus on testing the code's implementation, an alternative is to look at the functionality or behavior expected. In this example, you start by writing the test case in the first instance, articulating its behavior. Specialist products such as iCuke and Cucumber do this, but you can achieve a more limited Test Driven Development approach using Xcode.

Again, Test Driven Development (TDD) involves writing test cases before any production code. In Xcode, you'd achieve this by generating your class with unit testing support included, but focus on writing your unit tests in the first instance by calling your empty class implementations. These tests will fail initially, but as you implement your class, these should pass if they demonstrate the required behavior.

Given the importance of using unit tests as building blocks for a number of test strategies, let's take a look at how to implement them using Xcode.

Writing and Running Your Unit Tests

So, having created your project with unit tests, you need to perform a series of steps to implement your tests. If you examine the example implementation file provided, you'll notice two methods for processing code before the test begins (setup) and then after the test has concluded (teardown). It also provides an example method for you to change as its default implementation— the method STFail(), indicating that tests have yet to be implemented.

At this point, rather than creating unit tests for the Lunary Lander game, let's focus on a much simpler example to convey the methods and tools. For this simple example, you create a very simple Calculator class with a Header and Implementation file and a single method called add() that returns the addition of the two numbers passed. First you'll define your class declaration as shown in Listing 9–1.

Listing 9–1. *Calc.h*

```
#import <Foundation/Foundation.h>


@interface Calc : NSObject {
}
- (int) add:(int)num1 to:(int)num2;

@end
```

Next you'll add your implementation of the class, as shown in Listing 9–2.

Listing 9–2. *Calc.m*

```
#import "Calc.h"


@implementation Calc

- (int) Add:(int)num1:(int)num2
{
    return (num1+num2);
}

@end
```

You then implement your unit tests by providing an implementation for the test cases, changing the testExample() method to test the add() method. You can see the example implementation in Listing 9–3.

Listing 9–3. *UnitTest Implementation*

```
#import "CalculatorTests.h"


@implementation CalculatorTests
```

```objc
- (void)setUp
{

    [super setUp];

    // Set-up code here.
}

- (void)tearDown
{
    // Tear-down code here.

    [super tearDown];
}

- (void)testExample
{
    Calc *calculator = [[Calc alloc] init];
    int v = [calculator add:5 to:5];
    if (v != 10)
        NSLog(@"add is not working");
    else
        NSLog(@"add is working");
    [calculator release];
}
```

So, ensuring that you're building against the iOS Simulator, you can now choose to test your product by choosing "Build for Testing" from the Product menu or using the shortcut key combination (⇧⌘U). This will build your application and include the necessary debug information, which when executed for testing using the Test option or shortcut combination of (⌘U) will execute your application and the unit test cases selected (more on this in a minute), outputting a whole bunch of diagnostic information to your debug log from the unit test code. In the example, using the Log navigator (⌘7), you can jump to the log file for your executed tests. The log should display something similar to the following output. Your testExample method's specific output is in **bold**.

```
Test Suite 'All tests' started at 2011-08-20 11:06:32 +0000
Test Suite '/Developer/Platforms/iPhoneSimulator.platform/Developer/SDKs/↩
iPhoneSimulator4.3.sdk/Developer/Library/Frameworks/SenTestingKit.framework(Tests)'↩
 started at 2011-08-20 11:06:32 +0000
Test Suite 'SenInterfaceTestCase' started at 2011-08-20 11:06:32 +0000
Test Suite 'SenInterfaceTestCase' finished at 2011-08-20 11:06:32 +0000.
Executed 0 tests, with 0 failures (0 unexpected) in 0.000 (0.000) seconds

Test Suite '/Developer/Platforms/iPhoneSimulator.platform/Developer/SDKs/↩
iPhoneSimulator4.3.sdk/Developer/Library/Frameworks/SenTestingKit.framework(Tests)'↩
 finished at 2011-08-20 11:06:32 +0000.
Executed 0 tests, with 0 failures (0 unexpected) in 0.000 (0.001) seconds

Test Suite '/Users/mamonem/Library/Developer/Xcode/DerivedData/↩
Calculator-ecegbkyjngnxqjgpddxmtkxtvkzp/Build/Products/Debug-iphonesimulator/↩
CalculatorTests.octest(Tests)' started at 2011-08-20 11:06:32 +0000
Test Suite 'CalculatorTests' started at 2011-08-20 11:06:32 +0000
Test Case '-[CalculatorTests testExample]' started.
2011-08-20 12:06:32.581 Calculator[791:207] Add is working
```

```
Test Case '-[CalculatorTests testExample]' passed (0.001 seconds).
Test Suite 'CalculatorTests' finished at 2011-08-20 11:06:32 +0000.
Executed 1 test, with 0 failures (0 unexpected) in 0.001 (0.001) seconds

Test Suite '/Users/mamonem/Library/Developer/Xcode/DerivedData/↵
Calculator-ecegbkyjngnxqjgpddxmtkxtvkzp/Build/Products/Debug-iphonesimulator/↵
CalculatorTests.octest(Tests)' finished at 2011-08-20 11:06:32 +0000.
Executed 1 test, with 0 failures (0 unexpected) in 0.001 (0.003) seconds

Test Suite 'All tests' finished at 2011-08-20 11:06:32 +0000.
Executed 1 test, with 0 failures (0 unexpected) in 0.001 (0.006) seconds
```

You can see from the diagnostic information there are many performance-related timings, allowing you to see how performant your methods are. Additionally, you can implement many test cases within your code and are not limited to the single testExample() method. Just go ahead add more methods, each representing a particular test case.

But what if you don't want to execute ALL the test cases every time you test your application? What if you want to test only one or two? This is expected and easily provided for within Xcode. Simply edit your project scheme using the Scheme editor (⌘<), which will display the dialog box that allows you to manage a number of aspects of your application, including the tests performed. Choose the test item in the left-hand panel, and you'll see the tests you can choose from (see Figure 9–2).

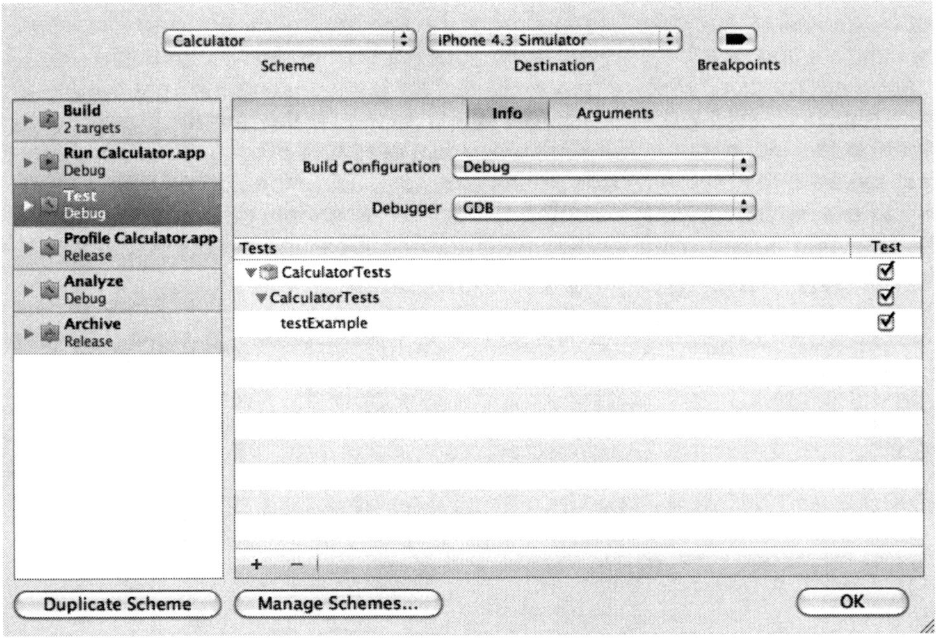

Figure 9–2. *Choosing which tests to execute from the Scheme editor*

Using this dialogue box, you can choose which of the unit tests are executed when you test your application. Select those that you wish to run using the checkbox provided against each test. When you've selected those tests you wish to take place, select the

OK button; this will save your scheme, meaning that when executing your application, these unit tests will be executed. You can then use the Log navigator to examine the output and the test results.

Using the Xcode 4 Debugger

So now you know some of the debugging capabilities of Xcode 4 through the generation and use of unit tests. However, it can do much, much more. The really advanced features such as profiling will be covered a little further into the chapter, so let's take a look at some other slightly less advanced features that are incredibly useful when testing your application.

Xcode 4 features a debugger with very similar capabilities to that of Visual Studio or other integrated development environments. It allows you to place breakpoints in your code—specific points at which execution stops for you to examine your application's state. Breakpoints allow you to walk through your code line by line and examine all aspects of your application's execution including variables, their values, etc. This works when running your application or testing it.

> **NOTE:** When debugging your application, you must compile it for debug output. This lets the compiler add additional information to your code that allows you to perform the debugging features. It also adds a considerable size to your compiled code, so remember to switch it off by compiling your application for Release when you deploy your application.

So, let's use the previous example and ensure that you are building for debug. In the CalculatorTest.m implementation file, let's add a breakpoint. This can be done by simply clicking in the gutter to the left of your source code window. Doing so will place a dark blue breakpoint indicator in the gutter, indicating that your code will stop here when debugging. In Figure 9–3 you can see a breakpoint in the gutter; you can also see other breakpoints that were previously been added but are switched off and inactive. These are indicated by a lighter blue breakpoint indicator and can be re-activated simply by clicking them.

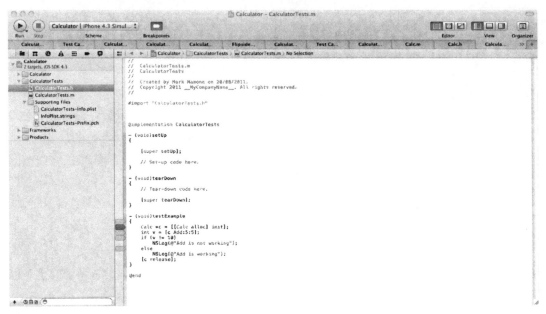

Figure 9–3. *Breakpoints, both active and inactive, in the code window gutter*

Once breakpoints have been added, you can build your application for testing (⇧⌘U) as before and then test your application (⌘U). Your application will launch in the simulator as before. Your unit tests will start to output debug text to the log file, but your application will stop at the breakpoint. When it does this, it will also display the Debug window automatically at the bottom of your screen. This is shown in Figure 9–4.

Figure 9–4. *Application stopping at a breakpoint and showing the Debug window*

The left-most pane shows the navigator windows, which when debugging default to the Thread pane, showing threads (that is parallel units of code execution) of your application and their call stack, with the Debug window below the code pane. The Debug window shows the local variables in the Local pane, which can be explored simply by navigating through them. The application's output is sent to the Console window, stored in a log file, but shown in the Output pane, which can be unfiltered (All Output), of filtered by Debugger output or the Target output.

The header bar for the debug window allows you control how you navigate through your code. Having hit the breakpoint, the icons have the meanings defined in Table 9–1.

Table 9–1. *Debug Shortcut Icons*

	Minimize debug window
	Continue program execution
	Step over the breakpoint
	Step into the code at the breakpoint
	Step out of the code at the breakpoint

You can also use the search box to look for/filter the variables you may wish to examine.

Using the debugger, defining strategic breakpoints, and examining variable values, you can quickly decide whether the path of execution your application takes is as expected; more importantly, you can also look how variables are being initialized and whether this is as you intended.

Finally, if you wish to remove all breakpoints, active or inactive, use the Breakpoint Navigator (⌘6) to see all breakpoints defined in one place and remove them or activate them. This can be seen in Figure 9–5.

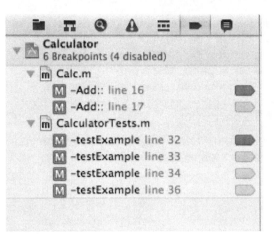

Figure 9–5. *Breakpoint Navigator*

Other Debugging Options

There are other options available to you when debugging your application—not just traditional techniques such as using the console to output debug text, but advanced features such as Profiling. Let's look at them next.

Using NSLog to Capture Diagnostics

Using the Xcode 4 tool to debug your application is easy and feature rich—much the same as using tools in the .NET environment, such as in Visual Studio. Before such tools were available, you were far more limited, but some of the older tools can still be useful. For example, you may still find it convenient to add some debug code to your application that simply outputs some diagnostic information to the Debug window. This might be appropriate if you don't want to go to the extent of creating unit tests and simply want some detail diagnostics in real time.

In Objective-C, you can use the NSLog command to send diagnostic text to the Debug window (also known as the Console window) and include variable values through parameter substitution.

NSLog works like sprintf() works in C/C++ languages, or like Debug.WriteLine in .NET within the System.Diagnostics namespace. This method takes a string, within which "specifiers" are defined and substituted by the parameters you pass to the method following the string declaration. Substitution of the specifiers occurs in the order you pass them. The specifiers are show in Table 9–2.

Table 9–2. *NSLog Specifiers*

%@	Object
%d, %i	Signed int
%u	Unsigned int
%f	Float/double
%x, %X	Hexadecimal int
%o	Octal int
%zu	Size_t
%p	Pointer
%e	Float/double (in scientific notation)
%g	Float/double (as %f or %e, depending on value)
%s	C string (bytes)
%S	C string (unichar)
%.*s	Pascal string (requires two arguments, pass `pstr[0]` as the first, `pstr+1` as the second)
%c	Character
%C	Unichar
%lld	Long long
%llu	Unsigned long long
%Lf	Long double

Profiling Your Application

Profiling goes beyond simple testing and allows you to use the advanced features of Xcode 4 to find detailed code errors such as memory leaks or why a particular piece of code may be running slowly. A full explanation of the Profiler is beyond the scope of this chapter as it's a complex topic and feature-rich tool. However, it's worth considering it at a high level. You can refer to a more advanced reference guide or the iOS Developer Library if you choose to implement profiling in your applications.

Your application should be built for profiling (⇧⌘I) beforehand to ensure that all the necessary instrumentation is available. To launch the profile, you can choose Profile from the Product menu or use the ⌘I shortcut with the application open in Xcode. Once launched, the Profiler will look like that shown in Figure 9–6.

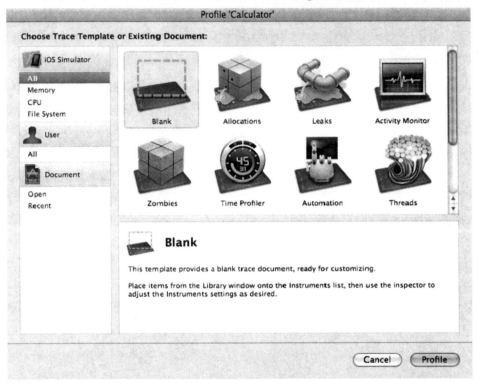

Figure 9–6. *Profiling with all its options visible*

The tool provides a number of templates that are tailored to understanding your application in a specific manner, whether looking for memory leaks, timing the execution of your code, or looking at how memory is allocated. The amount of data it collects and makes available is immense—comparable with the many .NET-based profiling tools on the market—and it's free in Xcode 4.

Let's take a quick look at one profile template as an example; the most obvious would be the Leaks profile, a common one to use. Select this template for a simple project (see Figure 9–6), such as the Calculator application, and select Profile (the screen in Figure 9–7). The application is running in the Profiler and all allocations are displayed.

NOTE: While profiling provides a number of useful templated instruments such as Memory Leaks, if you're using Automatic Reference Counting (ARC), memory leaks will be a thing of the past.

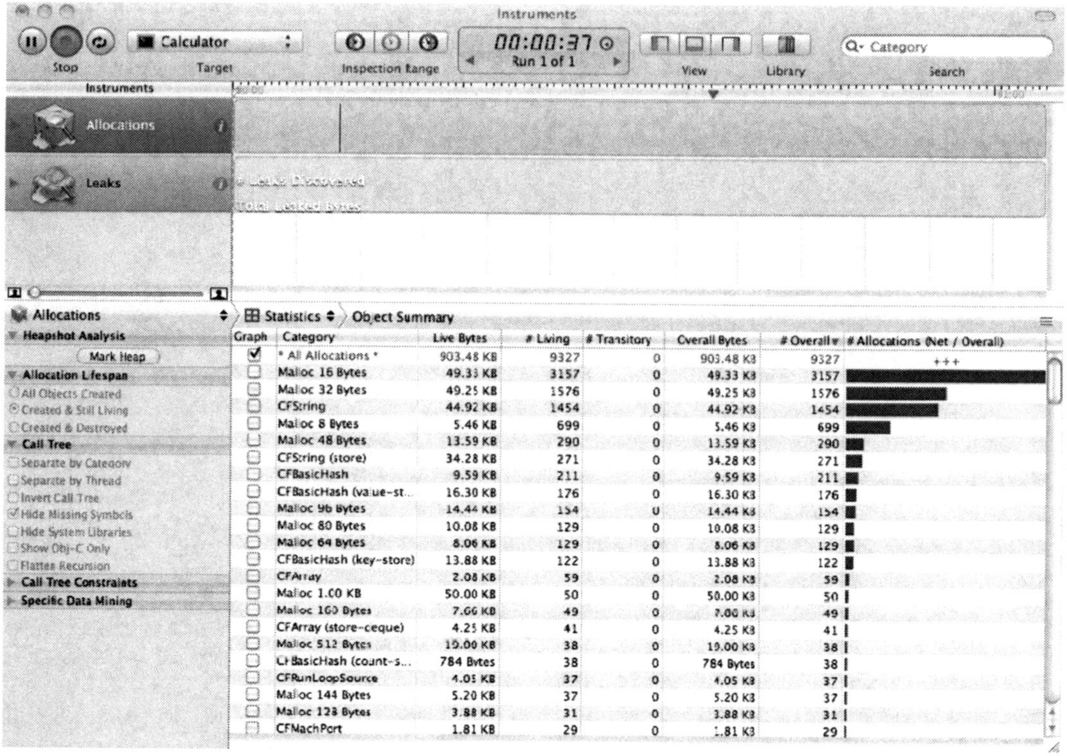

Figure 9–7. *Profiler with All Allocations displayed*

If you switch to the Leaks view, you will be presented with a specific view of where memory leaks have been detected. In Figure 9–8, you'll see that the default Calculator application has no leaks, as a good program shouldn't.

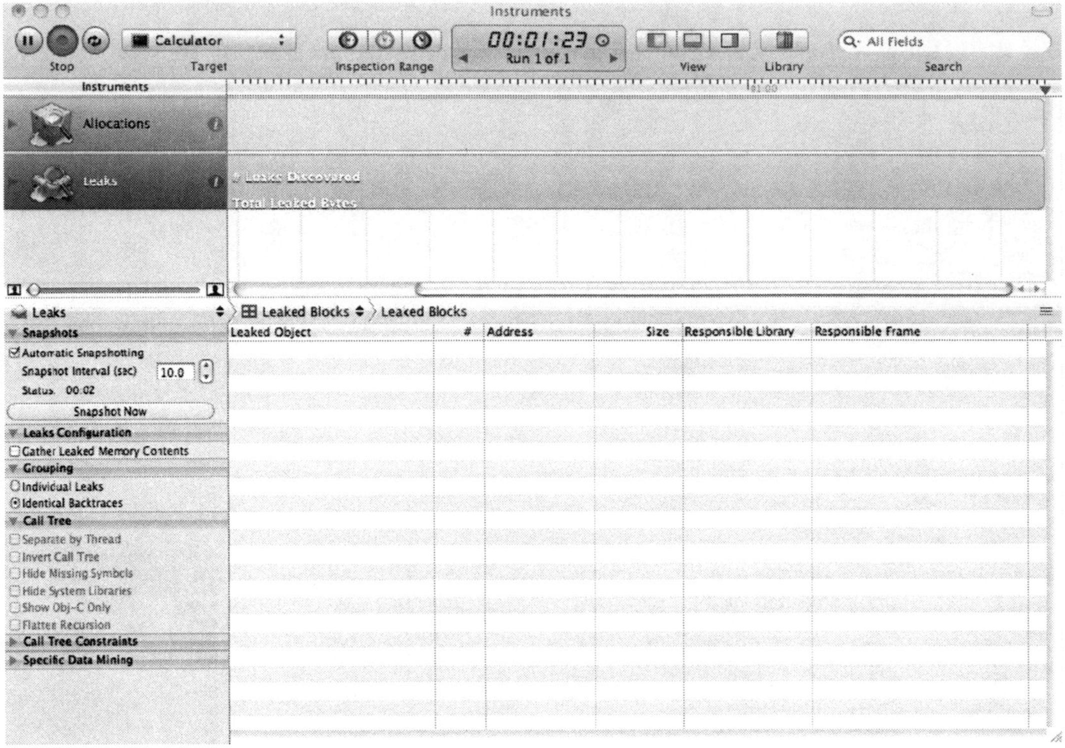

Figure 9–8. *Leaks view within the Profiler with no leaks*

Not much of a test, so let's be naughty! Let's declare a simple UIImage member variable, allocate memory, and initialize the object with this line:

```
UIImage *img = [[UIImage alloc] init ];
```

But don't add the corresponding release statement. Now rebuild your application for profiling and view the Profiler. It should present a screen similar to that in Figure 9–9 when you select the same Leaks view.

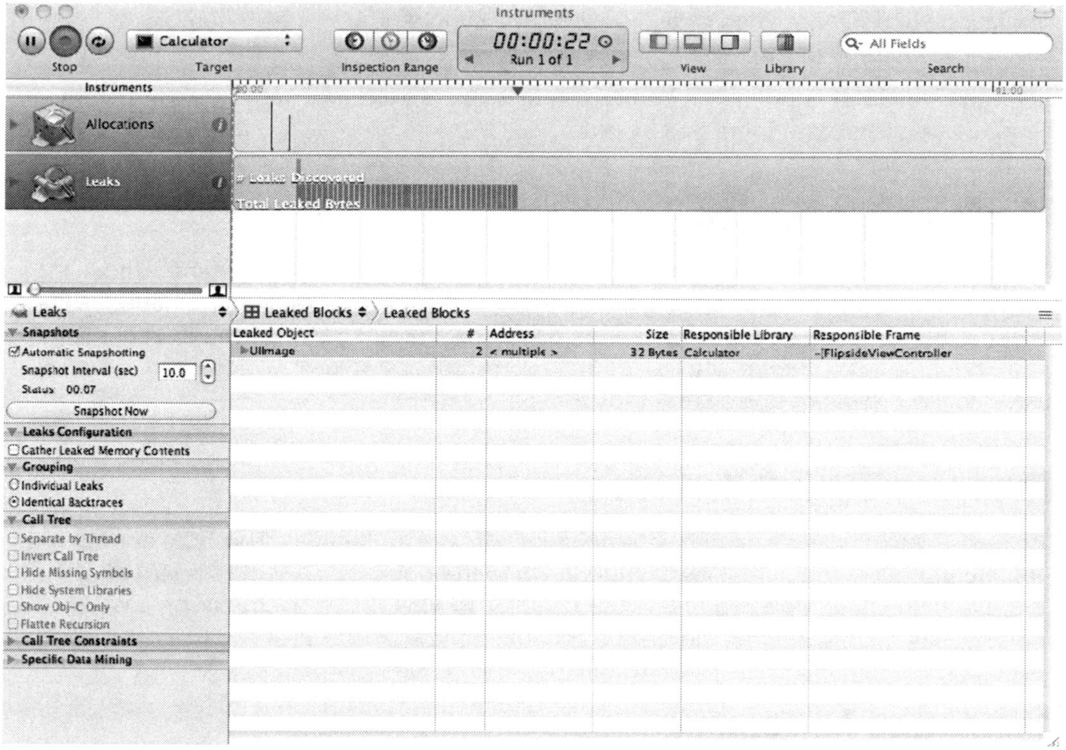

Figure 9–9. *Profiler displaying memory leaks*

You can clearly see that memory leaks have been detected, as expected; it highlights what type of object is leaking, how much is being leaked, and which library and which view is leaking it. All of this information is invaluable in tracing the fault.

The Profiler and its other templates provide similar detailed information allowing you to fine tune or just understand how your application is executing in minute detail.

Play around some more. This is a great tool for learning the inners of your code, the iOS, and its SDK.

> **NOTE:** You may find profiling useful if you choose to complete your Lunar Lander application. See Appendix A for a discussion on how to complete the game.

Using the Simulator's Debug Features

So, you can do quite a lot with Xcode 4 around debugging, but there are some things that are not possible, especially if they are specific to the device. For example, how do you test how your application behaves to a change in orientation, or how your application scopes with lack of memory? The features of Xcode 4 don't help you with simulating such things. Thankfully, however, the simulator itself has a number of debugging features of its own.

When the simulator is open, the debugging features are located under the Hardware menu. Let's go through them one by one.

Changing the Device

An obvious but useful feature is the ability to change the actual device type. Under the Device menu are options to simulate the iPad and the iPhone, including iPhone 4 Retina versions and other iOS versions provided as part of the iOS SDK, although excluding the iPod Touch. Simply choose the device type you want and the simulator will respond by displaying the relevant device and simulating it.

Changing the iOS Version

The next useful feature is to simulate different versions of the iOS. The SDK comes with the different supported versions of the iOS up to the point the SDK was released, so SDK 4.3 includes all versions of the iOS from 3.2 to 4.3. This is useful for backward compatibility testing against the device and iOS combinations your application targets.

Simulating Movement

Clearly, if you had the physical device, then you could test rotating it and shaking it. This is not so easy with a simulated device. You can rotate your Mac and shake it all you want—it won't help. However, the simulator provides menu options to both rotate the device to the left and right, and to simulate a shake gesture, all so that you can cope with such events in your application and test them in the simulator.

Triggering Low Memory

Your mobile device has a finite amount of memory, and every time you open an application, it will consume some of that memory. Unless you specifically choose to close the application down using the double-click of the Home button, that memory will remain used if you're using iOS 4.0 or above. On the older versions of the iOS, the applications did not retain memory as multitasking wasn't supported. So at some point your application might hit low memory, and it knows this because the iOS sends a low memory event (the didReceivedMemoryWarning event) to your application for it to handle. On receiving this event, you may choose to cope with it by releasing resources you no longer need or can afford to reload, for example.

To trigger such an event in the simulator, you can select the Simulate Memory Warning menu item to fire the event into your application so you can test its response.

Other Features

There are some additional features that aren't really related to debugging your application but act as shortcuts or assistants to the whole testing process. For this reason, I'll mention them for completeness.

- **Home** simulates pressing the home button.

- **Lock** simulates locking your device.

- **Toggle In-Call Status Bar** switches on the in-call status bar, thus reducing the user interface space.

- **Simulate Hardware Keyboard** switches your Mac keyboard to the keyboard for your iPhone device. It's good for entering text into your application.

- **TV Out** sends the output to the TV Out port of your Mac using the resolution chosen under this option.

Testing on Real Devices

The iOS Simulator is an amazingly useful tool, especially for quickly testing your applications on a number of different devices and iOS versions. But it's important to understand that testing on the simulator alone is insufficient. For example, if you want to test the real-world performance of a device with multiple applications running and varying external conditions such as poor signal strength (whether it be Wi-Fi, GPRS, 3G or GSM), then there really is no substitute for testing on a real device.

So, while I encourage you to use the simulator, be sure to test your applications on all devices you intend to target and under a variety of real-world scenarios. You can do this by following the instructions that follow on application deployment, but this does require you to be a signed up and paid member of the Apple Developer Program.

Some of the real-world considerations you might consider when testing your application are as follows:

- *Signal Strength*: I've touched on this but your wireless network connection (Wi-Fi) or your mobile signal, whatever you might be using, will not always be at full strength, and if your application relies on this kind of network connectivity, you should test different signal-strength scenarios.

- *User Interface*: Consider what your application's user interface looks and feels like, especially when using gestures, and consider the different characteristics of the human tester. For example, get different people to use it (sometimes called usability testing).

▪ *Speed*: Try your application out, not just running on its own, but with other applications running. You can trigger low memory within the simulator, but you can proactively restrict device memory above this. Real-world performance testing is important for this very reason.

Also consider testing your application beyond your own individual testing. For example, it's not unusual to offer a beta program where you offer a limited distribution of your application to beta testers who get the application for free but provide you with feedback.

Deploying Your Application

To deploy your application to a device, any device, you need to sign it; that is, you need to add a digital certificate to your application that proves its authenticity. The iOS on your device will check all applications' authenticity before they are executed. This is a security measure to make sure that no applications make their way onto your device that might cause harm.

So, you need to sign your application, but it's not quite as straightforward as that. As explained earlier in the book, Apple requires that you are a registered and paid-up member of its iOS Developer Program in order for you to sign and submit your application. Thus, in order for you to deploy your application to your iOS device and submit it to Apple's App Store, you will need to join the program at a cost of $99. This will allow you to test your applications directly on the iPhone device and also enables support for ad hoc distribution and for you to publish to Apple's App Store.

> **NOTE:** You will probably know that you can jailbreak your iPhone device; this removes such restrictions and allows you to install applications directly onto your device using a variety of different tools. However, since Apple frowns on such activity, we are not going to promote it in this book. We will leave this for you to investigate if it's something you are interested in. Be warned: requiring a jailbroken iOS device will limit your distribution options.

Let's go ahead and complete some of the remaining tasks in order to allow you to provision applications to both your mobile device and the App Store. Most of this can be done from the Provisioning page, which you access by selecting the iOS Provisioning Portal in the Member Center, shown in Figure 9–10.

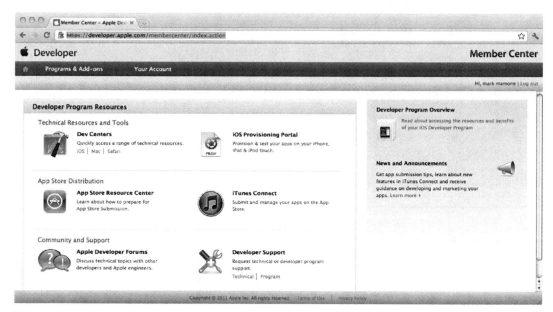

Figure 9–10. *Apple Member Center*

The Member Center also provides a number of useful resources, including technical support.

Creating a Certificate to Sign Your Application

The provisioning page allows you to upload a certificate request from your computer for it to authorize. You can subsequently use this certificate to sign your applications. To create this request, open the Keychain application from the Utilities folder within your Applications. Once launched, select the "Request a Certificate from a Certificate Authority" option from the menu, as shown in Figure 9–11.

Follow the on-screen instructions and enter your name and e-mail address, choosing to save the request to disk. You'll need this file for the Provisioning page.

Once saved, go back to the Certificates section of the Provisioning Portal. Under the Development tab, you'll notice instructions on how to complete the process and an option to upload your request complete with a Choose File button. Select this, and then point it at the file you just saved from the Keychain request. This will upload the request to Apple for processing. Initially it will show as Pending, but in a relatively short space of time, it will be processed and its status changed to Issued, as shown in Figure 9–12.

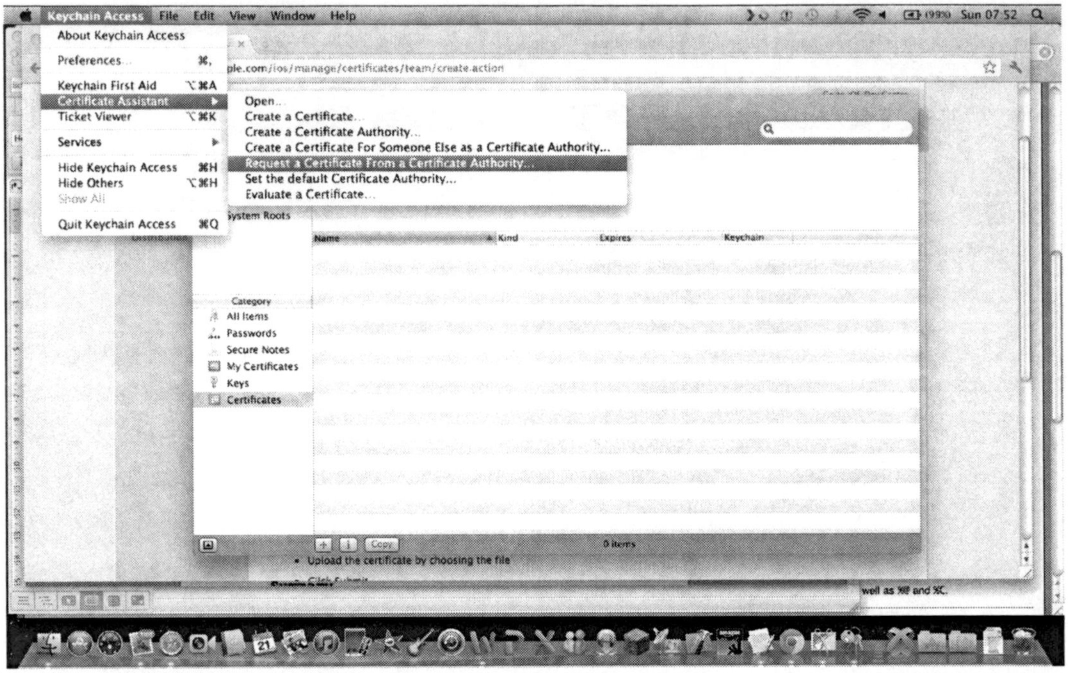

Figure 9–11. *Requesting a certificate using Keychain*

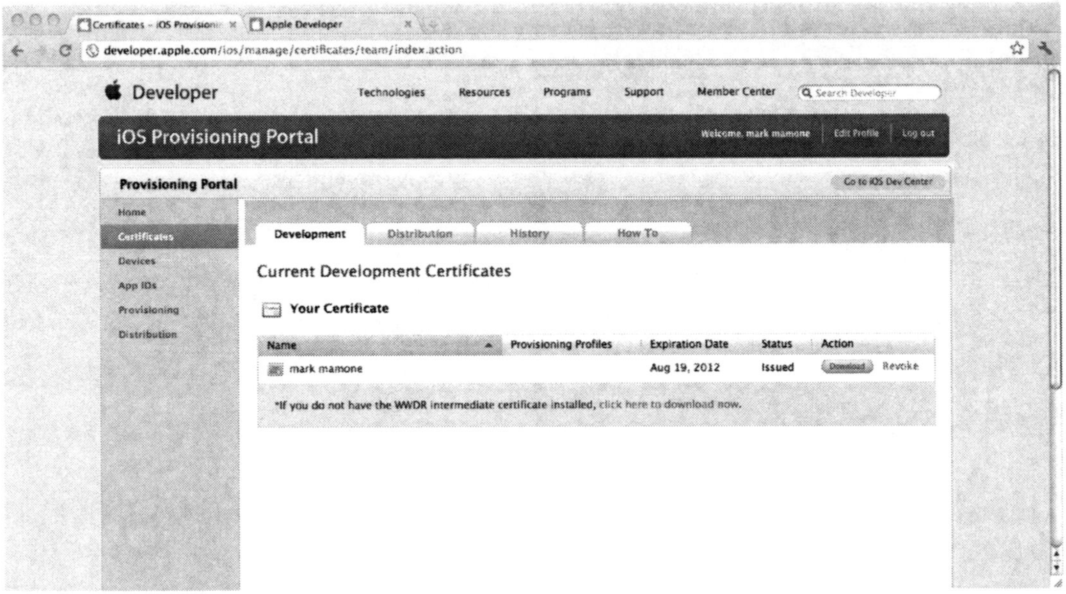

Figure 9–12. *Issued Certificate on the provisioning page*

You can now download this certificate and install it within your Keychain by simply double-clicking it and following the on-screen instructions.

Registering Your Device

Next, you will need to register your mobile device for development. Again, this can be done through the Provisioning Portal. First, you'll need the Unique ID of your device. You can use the Devices section in Xcode 4's Organizer to retrieve this ID. With your device connected to your computer, launch Xcode 4 and it will automatically take you to this page, showing the Unique ID that you need. You can see this in Figure 9–13.

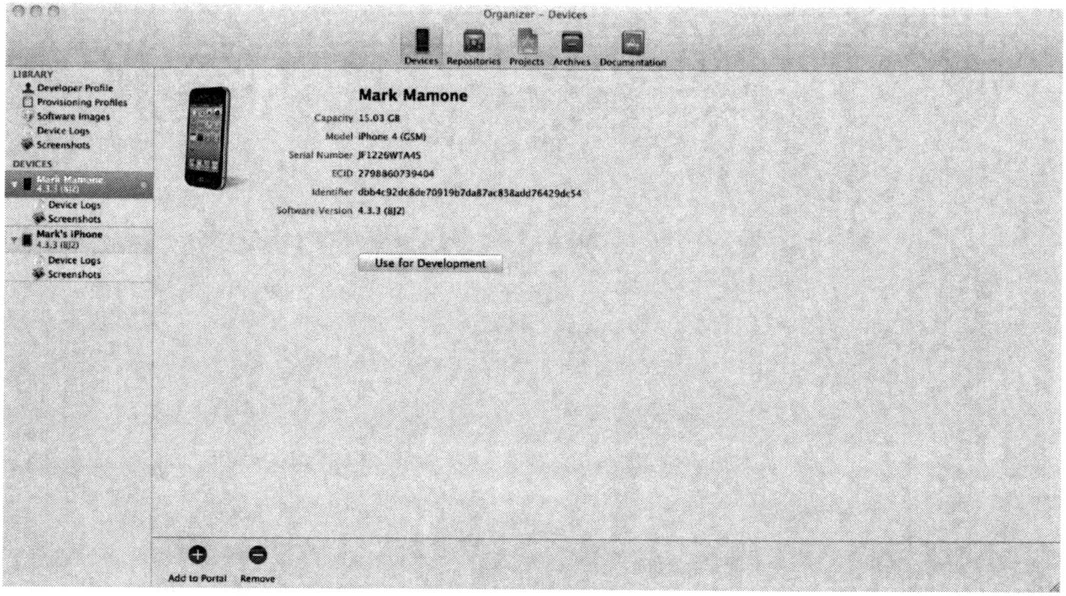

Figure 9–13. *Using Xcode's Organizer to retrieve your device's Unique ID*

Make a note of this device ID, and then go back to the Provisioning Portal and the Devices page. Here you can choose the Add Devices button, shown in Figure 9–14, and enter a name for the device (which can be whatever you want) and the Unique ID, taken from the Xcode screen. Complete this screen and your device will be registered within the Provisioning Portal.

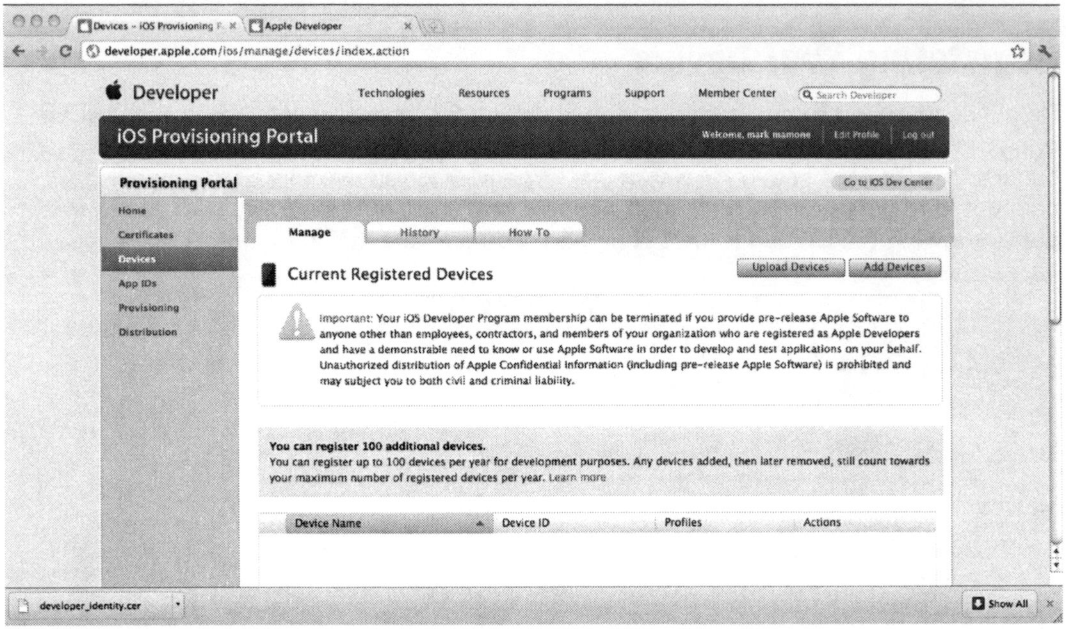

Figure 9–14. *Registering a device*

You may have noticed the Use for Development button on the Xcode Organizer screen, suggesting it will allow you to use the device for development. Xcode has the ability to create, download, and install on your behalf a Developer Certificate, Distribution Certificate, and a basic Developer Provisioning Profile (known as the Team Provisioning Profile), all with the click of a button.

So, go back to the Organizer screen and choose this option by selecting this button and following the simple on-screen instructions, which simply prompt you for passwords at certain stages. Once complete, your device will be registered under Xcode for development.

Using the Provisioning Portal to Get Started

The Provisioning Portal also provides a Launch Assistant to help you to install the necessary certificates and create the required provisioning profiles, allowing you to start to build applications. It's pretty straightforward and accessed from the Provisioning Portals home page, but I'll take you through it for completeness and to explain some points. First, select Home on the Provisioning Portal and choose the Development Provisioning Assistant. You'll be presented with the screen shown in Figure 9–15 where you will create an App ID.

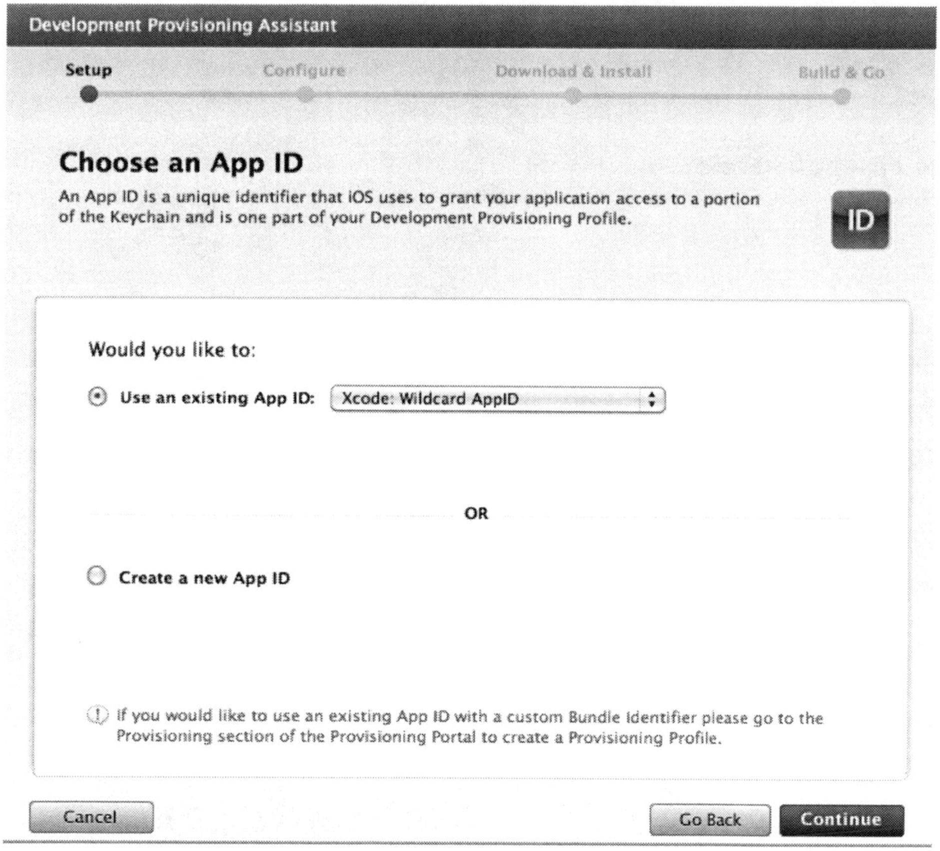

Figure 9–15. *Creating an App ID*

The first step is to create an App ID, a unique ID associated with your application. You can choose to create an App ID here manually or select the wildcard option from the list that automatically chooses an App ID for any app you deploy. Unless you specifically want to associate a single App ID with multiple apps, I suggest you choose this option.

Pressing Continue will take you to the next stage, shown in Figure 9–16.

Figure 9–16. *Choosing an Apple Device*

This stage involves choosing the device you wish to use. Because I've already registered mine, it appears in the Use an existing Apple device list. If it's your only registered device, it is automatically selected. So leave it as is and move on using the Continue button.

The Development Certificate screen in Figure 9–17 opens.

Figure 9–17. *Choosing a Development Certificate*

This step involves choosing your iOS Development Certificate, which again should already exist from the previous steps. Leave this screen with your existing Development Certificate selected and again move on using the Continue button. The Provisioning Profile page will be displayed next, seen in Figure 9–18.

Development Provisioning Assistant

Setup   Configure   Download & Install   Build & Go

Name your Provisioning Profile

A Provisioning Profile is a collection of your App ID, Apple device UDID, and iOS
Development Certificate that allows you to install your application on your device.

PROV

Enter a common name or description for your Provisioning Profile using
alphanumeric characters. The description you specify will be used throughout the
Provisioning Portal to identify this Provisioning Profile.

Profile Description: development profile

You cannot use special characters such as @, &, *, " in your
description.

App ID: **Xcode: Wildcard AppID**
6Q27HJ4429.*

Device: **Mark Mamone**
dbb4c92dc8de70919b7da87ac838add76429dc54

Certificate Name: **mark mamone**

Cancel   Go Back   Generate

Figure 9–18. *Provisioning Profile page*

A Provisioning Profile is a collection of data collected under a named profile and
required for you to install applications on your device. On this screen, give your profile a
name and the rest is auto-populated. Then choose the Generate button, which will
generate the profile. When complete, you'll see a screen similar to that in Figure 9–19.

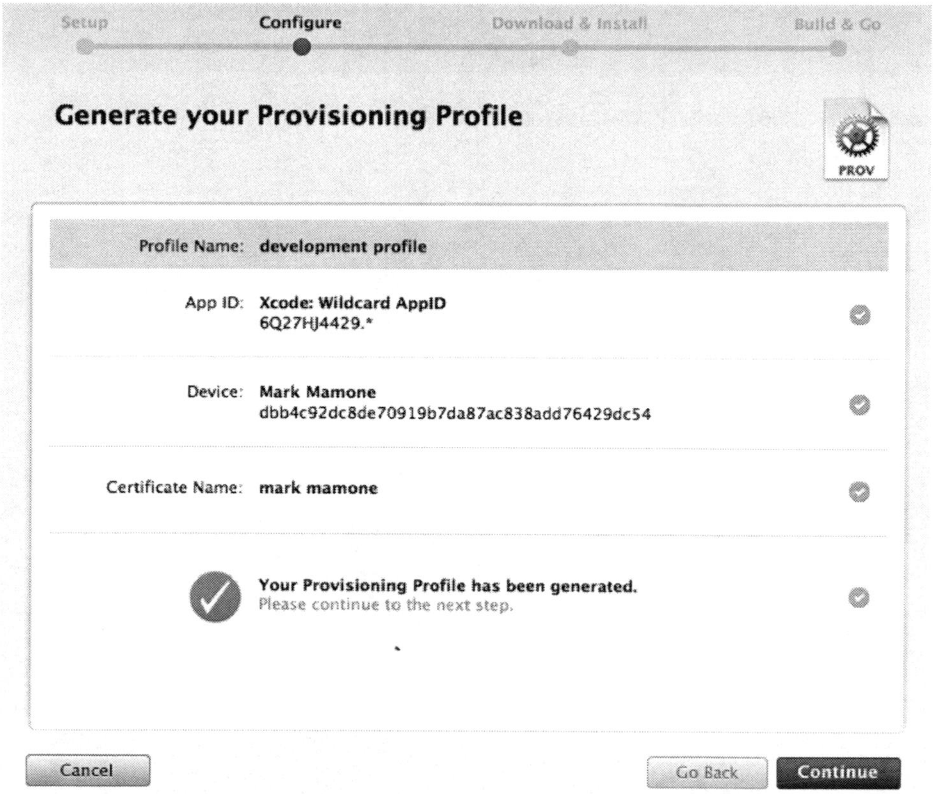

Figure 9–19. *Provisioning Profile generated*

You can then continue. You'll be presented with instructions on how to install the Provisioning Profile, shown in Figure 9–20.

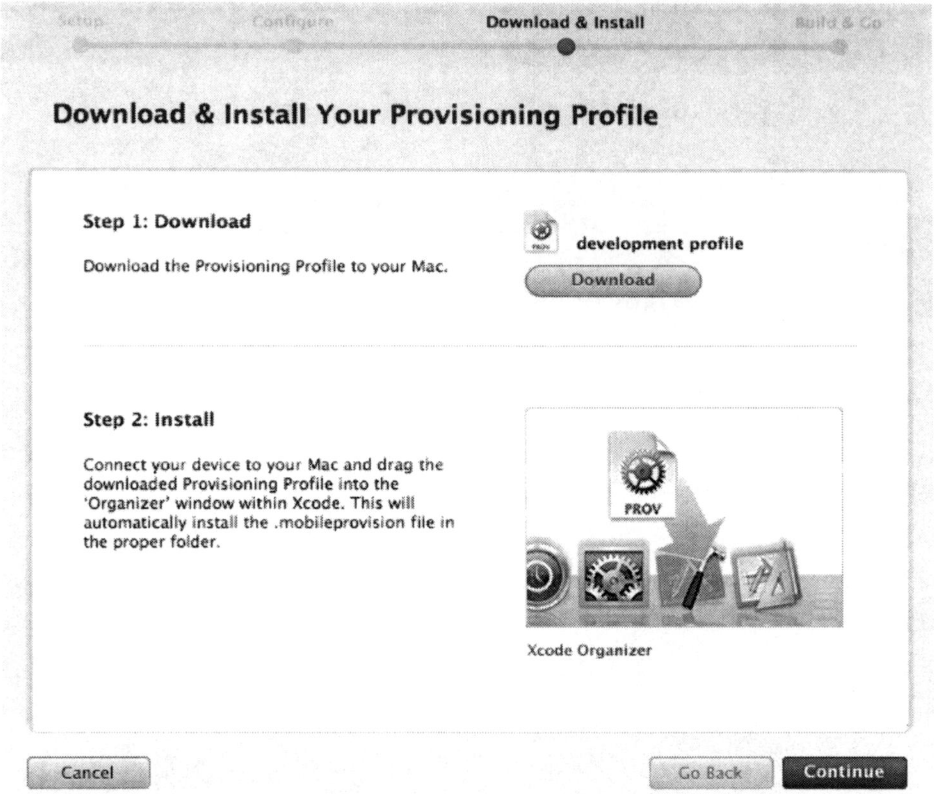

Figure 9–20. *Installing your Provisioning Profile*

Follow these instructions and your Provisioning Profile will be installed. Finally, check that the installation has completed by looking in Xcode's Organizer to see that the profile is present. It should be from the work Xcode has already done anyway.

Build and Deploy Your Application

So you've done all the preparatory work. Now let's build an application and deploy it on your device. Open up an application you wish to deploy in Xcode. I started with the initial Hello World program, but in your case it will be the application you wish to deploy. In Xcode, the main thing you need to do is to sign the application. Remember all the steps you went through to create the certificates and Provisioning Profile?

So, open up your application and select Build Settings in the main pane (see Figure 9–21). In the Code Signing section, choose an appropriate profile; given I'm still developing, I chose my development profile but if you were targeting the App Store or Adhoc provisioning (more on these later), then you would choose profiles that reflect this.

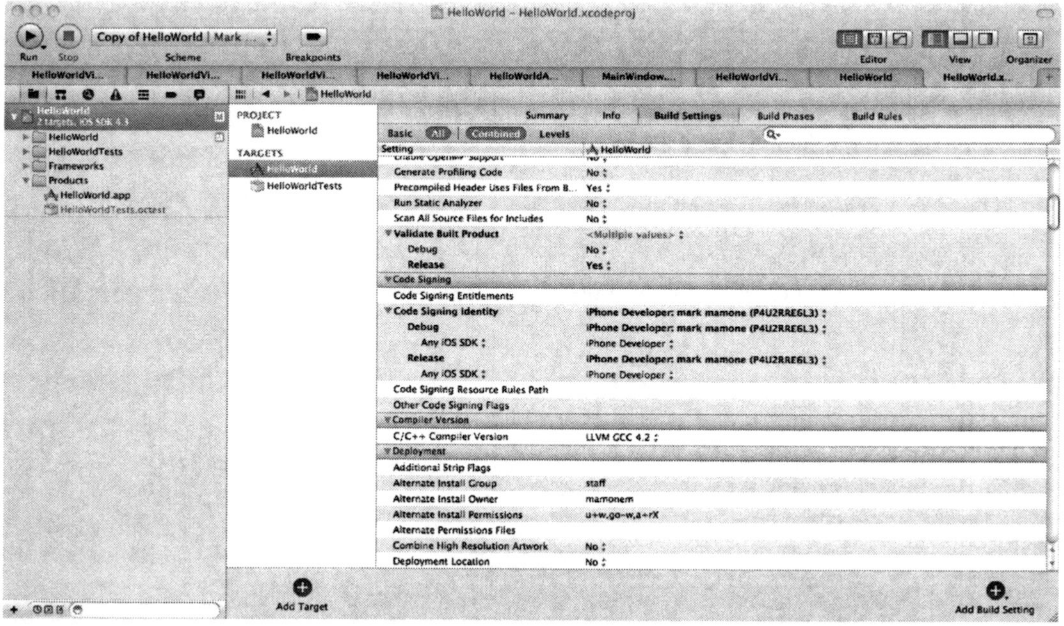

Figure 9–21. *Signing your application in Xcode*

At this point, before you build your application, check that your application identifier is correct under Summary. This identifies the application on your device. In Figure 9–22 you can see I've added one that includes my domain and the application's title.

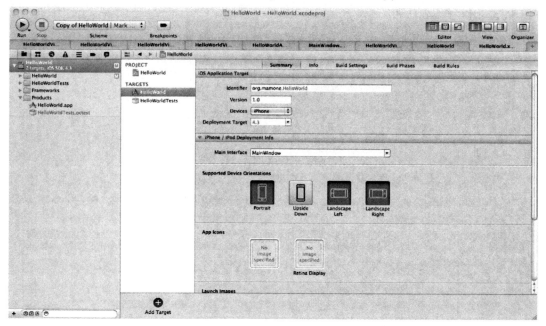

Figure 9–22. *Adding your Application's Identifier*

Now go ahead and build your application, ensuring that your target scheme in Xcode is for your target device and not left on the simulator. Also check that your application icon is included as an `icon.png` file and the filename is included within your `info.plist` file by using the Icon file setting under the Info tab. When you start to build your application, you will be prompted to accept its request to sign the application using your Keychain certificate. Accept this request, and allow the build to complete and the signing of your application to happen. You now have an application built and ready for deployment.

To deploy your application on your device, open up the Xcode Organizer and select your device in the left hand pane; you'll notice that an Applications option exists. You can see this and the installed application in Figure 9–23.

Figure 9–23. *Xcode's Organizer with Device and Applications*

At the bottom of the Applications pane you will notice two options, Add and Delete. These allow you to add or delete an application from your device. Choose Add. At the dialogue that requests you locate application to add, point it at the Hello World application binary that you just built in Xcode. Alternatively, you can drag the executable onto this page. In either case, this will install the application to your device. Take a look at your mobile device when complete and you should see your application there, ready to test!

You have now built and deployed your first Apple mobile device application. You can use this to do some real-world testing and when happy with it, move to the next stage, which is deployment to either the App Store or via another mechanism called Adhoc deployment.

Publishing Your Application

Once you've tested your application on your local device, you are ready to publish it to other devices. Here you have two options: Adhoc deployment or deployment via the App Store. The first thing to note is you'll need Provisioning Profiles for each, and these are easily set up through the Provisioning Profile page, as shown in Figure 9–24.

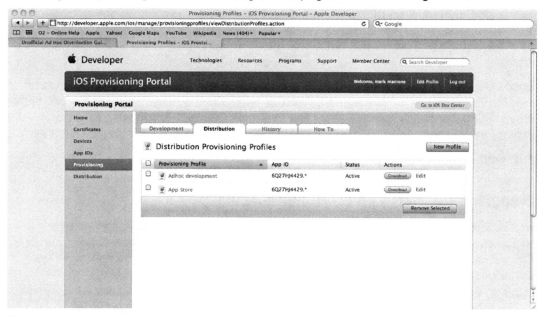

Figure 9–24. *Distribution profiles on the Provisioning Profile page*

As you can see, I've created one distribution profile for both Adhoc and App Store deployment. I'll use these later in Xcode.

Publishing via the Adhoc Mechanism

The Adhoc mechanism allows you to distribute your application to up to 100 other iPad, iPhone, or iPod Touch users using e-mail or the Internet as a distribution mechanism. From there the user can download and install the application.

The first thing to note is that your application must be built against a profile that is configured for Adhoc deployment. You do this through the Provisioning Profile page. In the Build configuration for your application under Code Signing, choose the Adhoc profile for your build and build the application as before.

Once built, you will need to distribute both the application (usually archived) and the Adhoc Distribution profile (.mobileprovision file) to allow the other users to install it.

The installing user drags these onto The Library ➤ Applications folder in iTunes. If the application has been archived, they will need to unarchive the file to leave the .app binary, and drag this across.

The application can then be synced as normal with the device using the iTunes sync feature. The application should be then ready to run on the device.

Publishing via the App Store

To publish your application to the App Store, you have to follow a similar routine in that your application must be built and signed against an App Store Provisioning Profile. To do this, you follow the same instructions and change your build settings in Xcode to sign your application on compilation but in this instance, choose the App Store Provisioning Profile.

Once built, you're ready to submit your application to the App Store. To do this, go to the Member Center from the Apple Developer page. On the home page, just beneath the Provisioning Portal link, you will see a link to iTunes Connect. If you wish to jump straight there, navigate to `https://itunesconnect.apple.com` in your favorite browser.

But wait!

Preparing for Your App Store Submission

Just before you submit your application, to ensure the best possible chances of a successful acceptance, I recommend you review the App Store Review Guidelines for iOS just one last time. It's not a small resource, but Apple reserves the right to refuse any application that doesn't comply. You can find a copy at `https://developer.apple.com/appstore/resources/approval/guidelines.html` or via the Member Center. In fact, there is a very good resource center that provides all manner of information to help you submit your application to the App Store, which can found at `https://developer.apple.com/appstore/`.

In addition to your application binary, you will need to complete information for a number of attributes that accompany your application. You might as well get these ready, because you're going to need them. They are

- Application name
- Application description
- Primary and secondary category
- Subcategories
- Copyright
- App rating
- Keywords
- SKU number
- Application URL
- Screenshots
- Support URL
- Support e-mail address
- End user license agreement
- Pricing, available date, territories
- OS binaries: Includes 57px and an optional 114px hi-res icon for iPhone and iPod touch or a 50px and 72px icon for iPad using iTunes Connect

iTunes Connect is a suite of web-based tools created for you to submit and manage apps via the App Store. In iTunes Connect you will be able to check the status of your contracts, manage iTunes Connect and test users, obtain sales and finance reports, view app crash logs, request promotional codes, and much more.

It's a pretty comprehensive suite so I'm not going to cover the whole suite in fine detail. There is a very good developer guide that does that for you at `https://itunesconnect.apple.com/docs/iTunesConnect_DeveloperGuide.pdf`.

However, I will take you through the basics of submitting an application to the App Store, assuming that you've already completed all of the preparatory work mentioned earlier.

So, once again, visit `https://itunesconnect.apple.com` and log in. Once you've done this, you will be presented with the iTunes Connect Home Page, as shown in Figure 9–25.

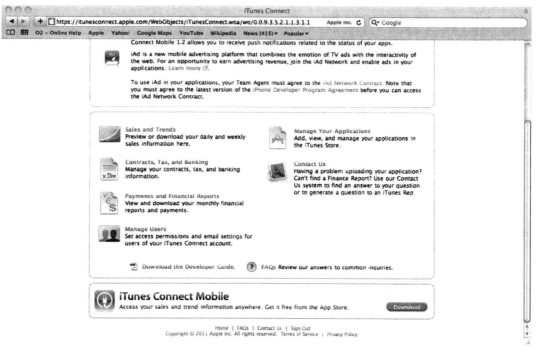

Figure 9–25. *iTunes Connect home page*

Once you're at the home page, choose the Manage Your Applications link. This allows you to manage your applications within the App Store and add new applications. The first time you enter this page, the list will be empty. That's because you haven't uploaded any apps yet. You can see this in Figure 9–26.

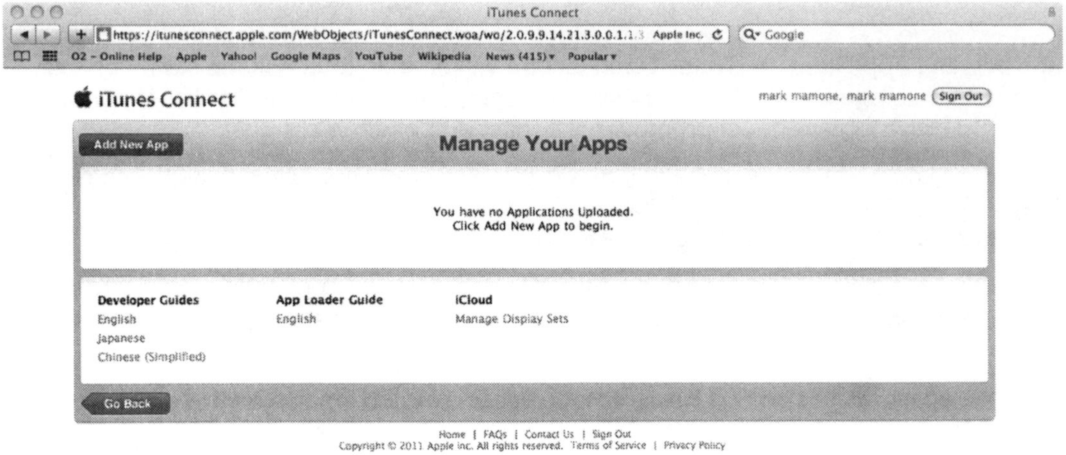

Figure 9–26. *Empty Application list*

Choose the Add New App button. This will prompt you to enter information relating to your application. Be warned; they require a lot of information, hence my recommendation for you to get it ready before you commence your upload.

I'm not going to list all the fields and their meanings. There are many, and as mentioned, the iTunes Connect Developer Guide does a great job of describing this information and its purpose.

Once you've entered the information required, you will be asked to upload some binaries. These include the various images to accompany your application, including icons for the application and screenshots. Once all of this information is entered and the image resources are uploaded, you will be taken to the App Summary page. On this page are additional buttons to the right of the page that allow you to manage further information about your app, such as localization and pricing.

Uploading Your Application Binary

On the Version Details page, click the Ready to Upload Binary button. You'll have to answer some final questions about Export Compliance. Then, depending on whether you are adding a new application or updating one already uploaded, you'll be taken to the Application Loader Instruction page or the Version Release Control page accordingly.

If you are using iOS SDK 3.2 or later, you already have Application Loader stored on your computer in your Utilities folder at `/Developer/Applications/Utilities/Application Loader.app`.

You also have the option of delivering from Xcode, which also happens to utilize the same Application Loader technology. See the Using Application Loader section in the developer guide to learn more about how to deliver your binary using this mechanism.

Once the Application Loader has been started, you be presented with a screen like the one in Figure 9–27.

Figure 9–27. *Application Loader start screen*

Once you hit Next, you'll be asked to enter your login details, and then the application will provide you with a list of applications it is expecting an upload for. If you didn't successfully complete the process of adding your application via the iTunes Connect page, you'll see a screen similar to that in Figure 9–28.

Figure 9–28. *No eligible applications were found.*

This indicates that you've not added your application through iTunes Connect, or if you thought you had, it failed. If you did upload the list correctly, you will be prompted to choose an application from the drop-down list, which contains all the applications you've uploaded. Choose the appropriate application from the list, as shown in Figure 9–29.

Figure 9–29. *Choosing your App Store application binary to upload*

Once you've chosen the application you're adding to the App Store and click Next, you'll be asked to complete a series of questions. These include confirmation that you've tested and qualified the binary on iOS, and then you will be asked to choose the binary for the application to upload. Using the Choose button, select your application package (this is your application compressed into a single .zip file), as shown in Figure 9–30.

Application Information

Application	TheHelloWorld
Version Number	1.0
SKU Number	1.mamone.org
Primary Language	English
Copyright	Mark Mamone
Type	iOS App

Figure 9–30. *Choosing your application package to upload*

Once chosen, you will be presented with the summary screen shown in Figure 9–31. You'll have the option to submit the application by selecting the Send button or cancel the whole process. Select the Send button.

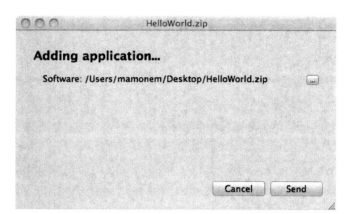

Figure 9–31. *Summary Application submission screen*

This will then submit your application to the App Store, showing a screen similar to that in Figure 9–32.

Figure 9–32. *Submitting your application to the App Store*

Once uploaded successfully, you will see a screen confirming this and reminding you that you will receive an e-mail confirming the upload and at any point, you can use iTunes Connect to track its process through the Apple approval process.

Additional Resources

The process of submitting your application is now complete. You have tested your application using Xcode features such as unit testing, the iOS Simulator, and real-world device testing. You have also submitted your application to the App Store. However, the themes of testing and iPhone marketing\submission are significant topics, so I've highlighted some additional reading material that explores these topics in much more detail.

- *Design Driven Testing: Test Smarter, Not harder* (ISBN13: 978-1-4302-2943-8) brings sanity back to software development by restoring the concept of using testing to verify a design instead of pretending that unit tests are a replacement for design.

- *The Business of iPhone and iPad App Development: Making and Marketing Apps that Succeed* (ISBN13: 978-1-4302-3300-8) shows you how to incorporate marketing and business savvy into every aspect of your iPhone and iPad apps design and development process.

These resources are in addition to those included as part of the Apple Developer Program and iOS Development Centre (see `http://developer.apple.com`).

Summary

In this chapter you learned how to test your application using features found in both Xcode and the Simulator. You also learned how to get your machine, including your Xcode installation, ready for provisioning applications to your own device as well as provisioning using the two mechanisms recognized by Apple: Adhoc and the App Store.

You looked at how to set up local certificates and Provisioning Profiles to make this possible and how to use both the Provisioning Portal and iTunes Connect on the home page of the Member Center. After successfully deploying to your local device, you briefly looked at how to provision using the Adhoc method and then you looked in detail at using iTunes Connect to provision an application to the App Store.

You are now ready to make millions of dollars (hopefully!) using the guidance provided in this book to both create your iOS-based application and submit it to the App Store for others to purchase.

Chapter 10

Extend Your Skills: Advanced Features

In this chapter you take a look at some of the more advanced features available through the SDK and as part of the associated Apple tools. These features build on the experience you've gained so far but look at capabilities specific to certain devices and, in some cases, how you can target more than one iOS-based device with a single code base. You also consider the future for iOS development technologies.

Specifically in this chapter you look at the following:

- Using your device's Global Positioning System (GPS)
- Exploiting your device's camera
- Using the accelerometer
- Detecting gestures
- Writing multidevice-compatible code
- What's on the horizon for iOS development

Using the Global Positioning System

Your iOS device, when fitted with a Global Positioning System (GPS), has the ability to determine its location anywhere in the world. There are other methods available for determining your location, but GPS is by far the most accurate. The iOS SDK exposes a variety of location-based services and determines which mechanisms to use under the hood. This means you don't have to concern yourself with the different technologies; you simply state some characteristics such as desired accuracy, and the device does its best.

Overview of Location Services

The SDK provides a class called the LocationManager, which through a simple API exposes location-based services while hiding which technologies it uses. However, you should still carefully consider the way you use these services. For example, you should not allow your application to constantly poll for your location, because this affects not only application performance but also battery performance. Your application's implementation should therefore poll for location updates as required; but if you do not need continuous updates, you can simply wait for the location update event to be fired and then stop updates until you are ready to start and determine the location again.

As you may have guess by now, you can control whether the location manager sends updates about location changes. You do so by calling startUpdatingLocation when you want updates to start and stopUpdatingLocation when you want the event updates to stop.

Once you've created an instance of the class and started the location-event polling, one of two events is fired: either didUpdateToLocation or, if an error is encountered, didFailWithError.

When a new location event is fired, it passes two variables, each of type CLLocation—one for the old position and one for the new position. This provides you with the current location and has the added benefit of giving you the ability to calculate the distance travelled by using the old position.

Each CLLocation parameter contains the location coordinates, the altitude, and the speed of travel. It also provides the methods necessary to calculate distance.

Let's look at how to use this class.

Implementing Location-Based Services

Start by creating an instance of the LocationManager class. This class encapsulates some of the location-based services provided by the SDK. The syntax is shown here:

```
CLLocationManager *lm = [[CLLocationManager alloc]init];
```

To provide a hook for notification events, you also need to provide a delegate to receive key location-based events, such as a location change. You essentially use the delegate to host callback methods to receive the event and process it. In order for this to work, you use CLLocationManagerDelegate, ensuring that it conforms to the protocol signature that defines two optional methods (more on these later). So, the easiest mechanism is to create a container class for this purpose, as shown in Listing 10–1 (the header file) and Listing 10–2 (implementation).

Listing 10–1. *LocationManager.h*

```
#import <Foundation/Foundation.h>
#import <CoreLocation/CoreLocation.h>

@interface LocationManager : NSObject <CLLocationManagerDelegate> {
    CLLocationManager* lm;
        CLLocation* l;
}

@property (nonatomic, retain) CLLocationManager* lm;
@property (nonatomic, retain) CLLocation* l;

@end
```

Listing 10–2. *LocationManager.m*

```
#import "LocationManager.h"

@implementation LocationManager
@synthesize lm,l;

// Default Constructor which allocates the CLLocationManager instance
// assigns the delegate to itself and sets maximum accuracy
//
- (id)init
{
    self = [super init];
    if (self != nil) {
        self.lm = [[[CLLocationManager alloc] init] autorelease];
        self.lm.delegate = self;
        self.lm.desiredAccuracy = kCLLocationAccuracyBest;
    }
    return self;
}

// Event : didUpdateToLocation
//
- (void)locationManager:(CLLocationManager*)manager
didUpdateToLocation:(CLLocation*)newLocation
fromLocation:(CLLocation*)oldLocation
{
    // Handle your events as required here
}

// Event: didFailWithError
// TODO: This is left for you to implement in this example

@end
```

You can therefore change your class instantiation to use this class instead of
CLLocationManager, as follows:

```
LocationManager*        lm = [[LocationManager init] alloc];
```

In your constructor you not only set up the delegate to point to itself but also set the
accuracy for the services by using the desiredAccuracy property with one of the
predefined constants that indicates the level of accuracy you desire. Setting this to a

value of kCLLocationAccuracyBest gives you the best location within 10 meters; additional settings are available to an accuracy of 100 meters, 1 kilometer, and 3 kilometers. Although you have the option of setting a desired accuracy, the accuracy is not guaranteed; and the higher the accuracy setting, the more battery power and device performance are impacted.

What's in a Location?

The location-update event is fired with the new and old locations passed as instances of the CLLocation class. This class contains a number of properties of interest. Suppose that, in your application, you declare an instance of the LocationManager class called lm, and then at a suitable point you create an instance of the object and start updating the location as shown:

```
LocationManager* lm =[[LocationManager alloc] init];
[lm.lm startUpdatingLocation ];
```

You can then provide an implementation for this event in your code. For example, let's output the location to the log file using the following example code:

```
// Handle your events as required here
NSLog(@"Long %f Lat %f",newLocation.coordinate.longitude,
 newLocation.coordinate.latitude);
```

If you execute your application in the simulator, after a short delay you should see output like this:

```
2011-08-24 15:50:51.133 locationExample[607:207]
```

```
Long 115.848930 Lat -31.952769
```

It updates every time your location changes. My simulator isn't fitted with a GPS, but if you have access to a network, then the simulator determines the location where you are. I used Google Maps to test this functionality, entering the latitude and longitude as a search string as follows:

```
-31.952769, 115.848930
```

This correctly returned my current location in Australia, as shown in Figure 10–1.

Figure 10–1. *Using Google Maps to test the simulated GPS*

You can do other things when the event is fired, using the CLLocation class. For example, you can calculate speed:

```
double gpsSpeed = newLocation.speed;
```

You can also look up the timestamp at which the coordinate was taken, or view the altitude in meters above (positive) or below (negative) sea level.

The .NET framework provides for similar capabilities as part of its System.Device.Location namespace, although as you'd expect, its implementation differs slightly. For example, you use the GeoCoordinateWatcher object to acquire data from the .NET location service, similar to your delegate class. The CLLocation class is replicated by the GeoCoordinate class in .NET, providing similar properties relating to location. Finally, the GeoPositionAccuracy property in .NET controls accuracy with the same effect on device performance, but it has two options: default (optimized for accuracy and device performance) and high accuracy.

As you can see, both SDKs have comparable features, and converting the code semantics from one to the other is relatively straightforward. You can find the .NET documentation at http://msdn.microsoft.com/en-you/library/system.device.location.aspx.

The iOS SDK's equivalent is at http://developer.apple.com/library/ios/#documentation/UserExperience/Conceptual/LocationAwarenessPG/Introduction/Introduction.html.

These are SDK-based capabilities, but other options always exist. If you are developing a web-based application, you can also consider HTML 5's GeoLocation capabilities.

Using the Camera

Another much-used capability in the iPhone and iPad is the device camera. In the case of more recent devices, there are two cameras—one front facing and one rear facing to support videoconferencing. Thankfully, as with the location-based services you've seen, the SDK provides methods for accessing these features. It is very easy to create an application to take advantage of the camera; the SDK provides a class called UIImagePickerController that provides access to the camera and the ability to take a photo and preview the results.

Let's take a look at the basics of implementing the camera and then walk through an example application.

Camera Basics

Create a simple project that employs a view controller, and then, in the didLoad method, enter the following code:

```
if (([UIImagePickerController isSourceTypeAvailable:
    UIImagePickerControllerSourceTypeCamera] == YES))
{
    UIImagePickerController *cameraUI = [[UIImagePickerController alloc] init];
    cameraUI.delegate = self;
    cameraUI.sourceType = UIImagePickerControllerSourceTypeCamera;
    cameraUI.allowsEditing = NO;


    [self presentModalViewController: cameraUI animated: YES];

} else NSLog(@"Camera not available");
```

This presents the camera, assuming one is available, and allows you to use the dialog to take photos—or video, if you switch to video using the picker. The mediatypes property controls which options the picker presents to you, and this can be set to kUTTypeMovie for movies, kUTTypeImage for camera, or as follows for a choice of both (where supported):

```
cameraUI.mediaTypes = [UIImagePickerController
 availableMediaTypesForSourceType:
UIImagePickerControllerSourceTypeCamera];
```

> **NOTE:** On the iPad 2, you can also use a popover as the view controller.

The controller provides you with basic editing features such as scaling and cropping. Also, you can pass back to the delegate an image the user takes or selects from the library. It is then the responsibility of the delegate to dismiss the controller and process the image.

The following example provides a delegate method that retrieves the original image as passed back from the picker:

```
-    (void)imagePickerController:(UIImagePickerController *)
 didFinishPickingImage:(UIImage *)image
editingInfo:(NSDictionary *)editingInfo
{
        // Your processing code goes here
        // processing code

        // Dismiss the picker
         [p dismissModalViewControllerAnimated:YES];
}
```

You manage the same functionality on a camera-enabled Windows Mobile device in a similar way using the `Microsoft.Devices.PhotoCamera` class, along with a `MediaLibrary` object to hold the video/images captured from the camera. It's more complex than it is on the iPhone because a single class isn't provided, but you can argue that it gives you more flexibility.

Writing an Example Camera Application

You can easily piece together the example code fragments for a camera application. Start by creating a new project that uses the view-based template. This creates a project with the standard view controller and interface as you've done before many times in this book.

You need to add the appropriate framework to use your camera, so again as you've done before, go to the project's Build Phases tab (accessed from the root project settings) and add `MobileCoreServices.framework` to the Link Binary with Libraries setting. This provides access to the library that contains your camera code. Before you create your user interface, include the `UTCoreTypes.h` file in your header, ensure that two delegates are implemented for your image picker and navigation, and add the `IBActions` and `IBOutlets` for your Image property and the Camera and Roll buttons. Your code should resemble Listing 10–3, all of which should be familiar to you.

Listing 10–3. *Camera Example* `ViewController.h` *File*

```
#import <UIKit/UIKit.h>
#import <MobileCoreServices/UTCoreTypes.h>

@interface CameraExampleViewController : UIViewController
            <UIImagePickerControllerDelegate, UINavigationControllerDelegate>
{

    UIImageView *imageView;
    BOOL newMediaAvailable;
}
@property (nonatomic, retain) IBOutlet UIImageView *imageView;
- (IBAction)useCamera;
- (IBAction)useCameraRoll;
@end
```

Open the view controller's Interface Builder file, and add your `UIImageView` control along with a toolbar that has two items: Camera and Roll. After you open the Connections Inspector in Xcode and connect the image and the Camera and Roll buttons, it should resemble the screen shown in Figure 10.2.

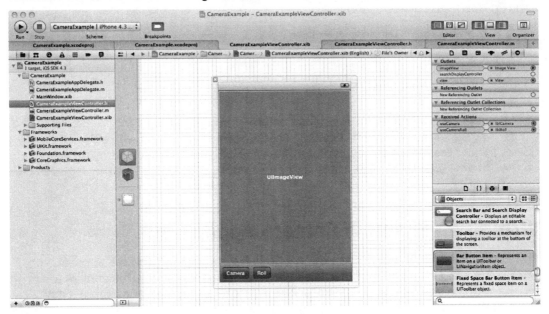

Figure 10–2. *The camera example user interface with connections made*

You can now implement the code against both your Camera and Roll buttons, but don't forget to @synthesize your `newMediaAvailable` in your implementation. Let's start with the Camera button, using the code in Listing 10–4.

Listing 10–4. Implementing the `useCamera` Method Attached to the Camera Button

```
- (void) useCamera
{
    if ([UIImagePickerController isSourceTypeAvailable:
         UIImagePickerControllerSourceTypeCamera])
    {
        UIImagePickerController *imagePicker = [[UIImagePickerController alloc] init];
        imagePicker.delegate = self;
        imagePicker.sourceType = UIImagePickerControllerSourceTypeCamera;
        imagePicker.mediaTypes = [NSArray arrayWithObjects:
                                            (NSString *)kUTTypeImage, nil];
        imagePicker.allowsEditing = NO;
        [self presentModalViewController:imagePicker animated:YES];
        [imagePicker release];
        newMediaAvailable = YES;
    }
}
```

Its implementation is pretty straightforward. The useCamera method checks that the device on which the application is running has a camera. On the simulator this isn't the case, so you need to run this application on a real device to test it thoroughly. It creates a UIImagePickerController instance, assigns the cameraViewController as the delegate for the object, and defines the media source as the camera. The property that specifies supported media types is set to images only. Finally, the camera interface is displayed and the UIImagePickerController object is released. You set the newMediaAvailable flag to YES to indicate that the image is new; this is used to differentiate a dirty camera roll.

You next need to provide an implementation for the camera roll functionality, accessed from the Roll button. See Listing 10–5.

Listing 10–5. *Implementing the Camera Roll Code Attached to the Roll Button*

```
- (void) useCameraRoll
{
    if ([UIImagePickerController isSourceTypeAvailable:
        UIImagePickerControllerSourceTypeSavedPhotosAlbum])
    {
        UIImagePickerController *imagePicker = [[UIImagePickerController alloc] init];
        imagePicker.delegate = self;
        imagePicker.sourceType = UIImagePickerControllerSourceTypePhotoLibrary;
        imagePicker.mediaTypes =
                [NSArray arrayWithObjects:(NSString *) kUTTypeImage,nil];
        imagePicker.allowsEditing = NO;
        [self presentModalViewController:imagePicker animated:YES];
        [imagePicker release];
        newMediaAvailable = NO;
    }
}
```

Again the functionality is pretty straightforward and very similar to the userCamera method, with the exceptions that the source of the image is declared to be UIImagePickerControllerSourceTypePhotoLibrary and the newMediaAvailable flag is set to NO, because it has already been saved.

You now need to implement a couple of important delegates. The first is the didFinishPickingMediaWithInfo method that is called when the user has finished selecting images. Its implementation is shown in Listing 10–6.

Listing 10–6. *Saving an Image with a Delegate*

```
-(void)imagePickerController:(UIImagePickerController *)picker
didFinishPickingMediaWithInfo:(NSDictionary *)info
{
    NSString *mediaType = [info objectForKey:UIImagePickerControllerMediaType];

    [self dismissModalViewControllerAnimated:YES];

    if ([mediaType isEqualToString:(NSString *)kUTTypeImage])
    {
        UIImage *image = [info objectForKey:UIImagePickerControllerOriginalImage];
        imageView.image = image;

        if (newMediaAvailable)
            UIImageWriteToSavedPhotosAlbum(image, self,
@selector(image:finishedSavingWithError:contextInfo:), nil);
    }
}
```

Extract the mediaType, dismiss any open image-picker dialog boxes, and check that you are dealing with images (as opposed to video). Then, save the image to the image roll, providing it's a new image. When the save operation is complete, you call another method that displays an error if the save fails. This method is shown in Listing 10–7, along with the image-picker-cancel delegate that dismisses the open dialog box.

Listing 10–7. *Trapping Errors and Dismissing the Picker Window*

```
-(void)image:(UIImage *)image
finishedSavingWithError:(NSError *)error contextInfo:(void *)contextInfo
{
    if (error) {
        UIAlertView *alert = [
                [UIAlertView alloc]
                initWithTitle: @"Image save failed"
                message: @"Failed to save image"
            delegate: nil
                cancelButtonTitle:@"OK" otherButtonTitles:nil];
        [alert show];
        [alert release];
    }
}
-(void)imagePickerControllerDidCancel:(UIImagePickerController *)picker
{
    [self dismissModalViewControllerAnimated:YES];
}
```

Finally, you need to tidy up. When you initialize the form, you set your image to nil; and when you deallocate memory, you release any memory the image may be taking up. These actions are achieved with the methods in Listing 10–8.

Listing 10–8. *Tidying Up*

```
- (void)dealloc
{
    [imageView release];
    [super dealloc];
}
// Implement viewDidLoad to do additional setup after loading
// the view, typically from a nib.
- (void)viewDidLoad
{
    [super viewDidLoad];
    self.imageView = nil;
}
```

If you try debugging the application using the simulator, then as mentioned, nothing happens, because the camera isn't supported. The camera roll is supported but in this case is empty; so if you choose this option the screen in Figure 10–3 is shown and the Cancel button should dismiss the dialog box as expected.

Figure 10–3. *Viewing the camera roll in the iOS simulator*

Using the Accelerometer

The iPhone and the iPad are capable of measuring both gravity and device acceleration by detecting the inertial force on a device in a given direction. In layman's terms, this means you can tell the orientation of the device, the speed of change, and whether the force of change is greater on one axis than the other, and therefore direction.

This three-axis detection capability means the device can detect these movements in all directions. Thus if you have your device facing you, moving it left/right is the x axis, moving it up and down is the y axis, and tipping it forward or backward is the z axis. You can see how this affects the x, y, and z axis values in Figure 10–4. (Note that the arrow points to the top of the device.) Zero represents no movement, and a positive or negative value represents force in a given direction. The trouble with diagrams is that representing z is a little difficult, so I describe it as the amount of acceleration your device is exhibiting. At a standstill, it represents gravity; and when you're lifting the device up or down, it's a positive or negative value proportionate to the acceleration.

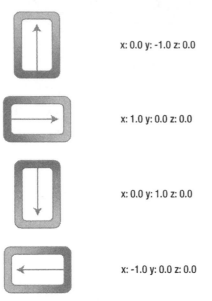

x: 0.0 y: -1.0 z: 0.0

x: 1.0 y: 0.0 z: 0.0

x: 0.0 y: 1.0 z: 0.0

x: -1.0 y: 0.0 z: 0.0

Figure 10–4. *Axis values with rotation*

The SDK provides access to the accelerometer feature using the Quartz 2D framework, although you have the option of using the OpenGL ES API that provides a finer level of control. The simulator doesn't support accelerometer functionality, so rather than take you through an example, I leave you to explore its capabilities using the example code provided and a real device.

With the default SDK implementation, you can implement a UIAccelerometer class instance as a singleton (only one instance). To retrieve this class, you use code like this:

```
UIAccelerometer *accelerometer = [UIAccelerometer sharedAccelerometer];
```

To then receive events that reflect a change in orientation, you use a pattern similar to that for the GPS. You set the delegate for the class to point to a class that conforms to the UIAccelerometerDelegate protocol. A difference, however, is that you have the ability to control the frequency of the updates by using the updateInterval property, which defines how many times per second the device is polled and so fires events, although it's not precise and isn't guaranteed. This lack of precision is a byproduct of the hardware engineering and the device's ability to raise events with a sufficient latency for you to capture and interpret. But in most circumstances, including complex GPS-based applications such as road navigation, it's perfectly appropriate. There is a solution, but it's not simple and involves capturing the events and using algorithmic functions to sample the data and predict the location with higher fidelity. You can find more information about such filters at http://en.wikipedia.org/wiki/Low-pass_filter#Algorithmic_implementation.

Let's look at this in code, first you implement the class that uses the required protocol; this could be your viewController. It looks like this:

```
@interface MainViewController : UIViewController <UIAccelerometerDelegate>
{
        // Header declaration here
}
```

You then provide its implementation, specifically the didAccelerate method to capture the events, as follows:

```
-   (void)accelerometer:(UIAccelerometer *)accelerometer
didAccelerate:(UIAcceleration *)acceleration
{
        // Implementation to deal with the events goes here
        NSLog(@"%@%f", @"X: ", acceleration.x);
        NSLog(@"%@%f", @"Y: ", acceleration.y);
        NSLog(@"%@%f", @"Z: ", acceleration.z);
}
```

You've looked at instantiating your accelerometer class and seen how to define the delegate to capture the events, but you need to enable the accelerometer to do so. Choose a suitable location within your code to initialize the delegate and the update frequency—for example, in the application's view controller's DidLoad event. When you have a reference to the singleton class as shown earlier, you can use the following code to set the delegate and the update interval:

```
accelerometer.delegate = self;           // imps. UIAccelerometerDelegate
accelerometer.updateInterval = 1.0f/60.0f;       // every 60 seconds
```

There's not much more too it, other than to interpret the data as required in your code. Clearly, trying to bridge this code against a .NET counterpart is going to be difficult for two reasons: it is device dependent, and therefore the SDK will change. However, Windows Mobile devices have joined the iPhone and iPad in offering capabilities that let developers do everything from determining how often someone drops their phone to allowing users to control applications and games. If you were using an HTC-based device and managed code such as C#, you might access the API in the appropriate dynamic link library directly, which isn't nice; or if you were using Windows Mobile 7, you could use Microsoft.Devices.Sensors and the Accelerometer class, which is much better. Its implementation is very similar to that in iOS and is exposed through the Microsoft.Devices.Sensors namespace. As with the iOS accelerometer framework, the .NET implementation uses the Accelerometer class, which provides to its internal compass and gyroscope sensors through the Compass and Gyroscope properties, respectively. The Motion class is then used to capture data from the sensors, with different structures holding the data for the accelerometer, compass, gyroscope, and motion.

Overview of Gesture Detection

One of the most innovative features of the iPod Touch, iPhone, and iPad is the user interface's ability to detect gestures. This has given the device appeal to users of all ages and has brought one step closer the virtual-reality interface seen in movies. Cocoa Touch provides the UIKit framework that allows you to take advantage of this capability through features such as the UIGestureRecognizer class and the events it enables. Let's take a look.

Detecting Touch Events

The starting point is to capture the touch events sent by the user interface as you touch the screen. Using a standard view controller (UIViewController) or view (UIView), start by implementing the touchesBegan method:

```
-(void)touchesBegan:(NSSet *)touches withEvent:(UIEvent *)event
{
UITouch *touch = [touches anyObject];
NSUInteger      notouches = [tounches count];
gestureStartPoint = [touch locationInView:self.view];
}
```

All of the touch-related methods, including this one, are passed an NSSet instance called touches and an instance of UIEvent. The number of fingers currently pressed against the screen can be determined by getting a count of the objects in touches. Every object in touches is a UITouch event that represents one finger touching the screen.

The touch-event mechanism chains the touch events from different controls: this means you may receive a set of touches among which not all belong to your view. In this instance, you can retrieve a subset of touches that are relevant to your view by using a command similar to the following:

```
NSSet*         touches = [event touchesForView:self.view];
```

When the fingers are removed from the screen, the reverse event is fired: touchesEnded:withEvent. Or if an event occurs that distracts the gesture, such as the phone ringing, then the touchesCancelled:withEvent is fired. The following code traps these touch events and writes some text to the debug console to suggest which one has taken place:

```
- (void)touchesBegan:(NSSet *)touches withEvent:(UIEvent *)event
{
    NSLog(@"Touches Began");
}

- (void)touchesCancelled:(NSSet *)touches withEvent:(UIEvent *)event
{
    NSLog(@"Touches Cancelled");
}

- (void)touchesEnded:(NSSet *)touches withEvent:(UIEvent *)event
{
```

```
    NSLog(@"Touches Ended");
}
```

When I first touch the screen, I see the following:

`2011-08-25 21:47:23.044 Gestures[350:207] Touches Began`

Then, when I let go, I see this event:

`2011-08-25 21:47:23.116 Gestures[350:207] Touches Ended`

Detecting Swipes

Detecting swipes is very similar to detecting touches. For a start, the code required is again included in the `UIViewController` or `UIView` class. In your view, implement the two events matched to swipes:

```
-(void)touchesBegan:(NSSet *)touches withEvent:(UIEvent *)event
{
        // Event processing to go here
}

-(void)touchesMoved:(NSSet *)touches withEvent:(UIEvent *)event
{
        // Event processing to go here
}
```

Once you have trapped the starting event, you can revert to the iOS SDK to capture the existing positions and then perform some calculations to determine the direction of the swipe. For example:

```
UITouch *touch = [touches anyObject];
CGPoint currentPosition = [touch locationInView:self.view];

CGFloat deltaX = fabsf(gestureStartPoint.x - currentPosition.x);
CGFloat deltaY = fabsf(gestureStartPoint.y - currentPosition.y);

if (deltaX >= kMinimumGestureLength && deltaY <= kMaximumVariance)
{
        NSLOG(@"Horizontal swipe detected");
}
else if (deltaY >= kMinimumGestureLength &&
         deltaX <= kMaximumVariance)
{
        label.text = @"Vertical swipe detected";
      NSLOG(@"Vertical swipe detected");
}
```

Upon execution, you can use this information to detect direction and react to it as you would any other application event. Give it a try!

Targeting Multiple Devices with Your Code

If you want to write a single application that targets both the iPhone and the iPad, it's certainly possible—especially given that they both use iOS and the SDK framework. You need to detect the device and adapt your application dynamically to some obvious differences such as screen size; otherwise, your application will look very strange. You can also target more specific capabilities such as the iPad's ability to use popover view controllers, but again you need to detect this in code in order for your application to adapt.

There are a number of options to achieve this. You can of course use iOS SDK to target multiple iOS devices such as the iPhone and iPad. Additionally, if you want to target non–iOS-based devices, you can use one of the multiplatform third-party solutions discussed in Chapter 3—these even target non-Apple devices, but, as discussed, have their limitations. Another option is to write a web application, which is delivered to the device through the browser; but this limits the functionality available to you and doesn't work if you don't have connectivity to the web server hosting the application, unless you use some of the more advanced offline features of HTML 5.

Throughout the book, you've touched on a variety of mechanisms used for targeting different devices. Let's recap them:

- *Orientation:* Typically, all iPad applications support different orientations, and you should cater to this in your code. However, on the iPhone, it's not essential but advisable for your application to support different orientations.

- *Layout:* The large screen of the iPad provides more real estate for your application to use, and it should.

- *Split views:* An iPad-specific view controller allows you to split your application into two views, each of which is configurable.

- *Popovers:* In the same vein as split views, a popover is a unique way of presenting data on the iPad.

- *Device features:* Both devices have different hardware characteristics, and you should remember these when designing your application.

Here is a summary of considerations and techniques to keep in mind when you're writing code that is universal for both the iPhone and the iPad:

- *Device:* The iPad is the odd one out compared to other iOS devices, at least at the moment, because its screen is much larger than the iPhone or iPod Touch. Always consider how best to use this real estate.

- *User interface:* To create a user interface in your code that can target both devices, it's often easier to create an Interface Builder file (.nib) for each device type and dynamically load the appropriate file for each device.

- *Classes:* You should check to see whether a particular class exists for the device you are targeting before going ahead and using it. You can use the `NSClassFromString()` method to see if a class exists in your device's library. It returns `nil` if the class doesn't exist.

- *API capabilities:* In some cases, classes exist on both devices but their capabilities differ. For example, `UIGraphics` on an iPad has support for Portable Document Format (PDF), whereas the iPhone does not.

- *Publishing multidevice-capable apps:* It's important to highlight to your customer base that your application is multidevice capable. You can do this when you submit your application. A plus sign (+) is shown in the App Store next to such applications.

- *Images:* The iPhone 4, the latest iPod Touch, and future iOS generations have the Retina display built in, which has increased resolution. This means apps look much sharper. iOS does everything it can to use the higher resolution; for example, text is automatically upscaled properly, as are all built-in UI components (buttons, sliders, navigation bars, toolbars, and so on). But it can't upscale images and graphics that you provide without help. Either use specific graphics for both devices and add the `@2x` suffix to graphics for Retina displays (for example, `MyGraphic.png` for non-Retina and `MyGraphic@2x.png` for Retina), or in your code use manual upscaling based on points.

What's New and on the Horizon?

So what's next? It's a million-dollar question, and Apple fans are always keen to find out. Even if Steve Jobs has decided to step down as CEO, you can bet that as Chairman he will still be involved in the future direction of the company.

This section considers what might be on the horizon for Apple and for general development on both the iPhone and iPad. There are no guarantees, of course, but I hope you find it an interesting insight into what may come next. Other sources for such information include Apple's World Wide Developer Conference (WWDC) 2011 and the industry press.

The iCloud

As is the case in most of the industry, the *cloud* is playing far more of a part in Apple solutions today. No longer are the capabilities of the device the only thing your application can use—if you're connected to a network of some description, including the Internet, then you can consume and use capabilities provided via the network on your device. For example, this might be storage, or a network-based service that streams video content. Your application can use the cloud to extend its reach beyond the local device's capabilities to embrace such technologies and, for example, bring a catalogue of thousands of films onto your device.

Apple's iCloud contains a suite of applications that represents Apple's functionality in the cloud. iTunes in the cloud is one such application, allowing you to stream content. It can store all your content and push it to all your devices, all from the cloud.

One way of using the iCloud is to enable your code to take advantage of the user's iCloud account (they need to be logged in) to synchronize data from the local device to the storage provided by iCloud, allowing your application to carry state between devices. For example, the Safari Reader stores articles you've saved for offline reading in the iCloud, making them available to both the iPhone and iPad you may be lucky enough to own.

iOS 5

It's not like iOS 4 is a slouch—it's still a very good mobile operating system. However, as is true for the entire industry, there is always somebody trying to do better. In the case of mobile devices, that is Microsoft and Google—especially Microsoft, with the release of its new Windows Phone 7 platform. Apple hasn't sat back and relaxed; it's been working on iOS 5, which despite an increase in features can still run on all the same devices as iOS 4.3.

A major change is in the space of notifications, which instead of interrupting the flow of your application are now captured centrally on the device's Notification Center. Here you can view all your notifications at your convenience with a downward swipe of the screen, clearing them when you're finished.

Another cool feature is the Newsstand, an application that is very similar to iBook but allows you to manage digital publications such as magazines and newspapers.

Social networking is certainly nothing new, but native integration into iOS 5 of features such as Twitter has been introduced. A single application supports all the features you'd expect, such as uploading photos and videos, tweeting, and so on, and integrates them into other iOS applications such as your contacts. Yes, Twitter existed as an app on previous versions of iOS, but not with such tight integration.

Other applications have been upgraded to better compete with Apple's competitors and to allow better use of the device's capabilities. The Camera app is one such example, with more editing features, and the Mail application has been enhanced.

Some of the other device-wide features introduced include an OS-wide dictionary, wireless syncing with iTunes, and split keyboards for ease of use.

Let's take a look at some of the new additions to the iOS family in a little more detail.

Notification Center

Both a unique feature and an irritation for many is the fact your iOS device raises notifications for all kinds of events and against all kinds of applications. Whether it's a new e-mail, an SMS message, or a Facebook update, notifications are the way of the world on your iOS device. The Notification Center doesn't remove this functionality—far from it. It simply allows you to keep track of your notifications in one convenient location. You can still configure which ones you are interested in, but they present themselves subtly on your screen, much like the iAds in applications of today; and they fade if you do nothing with them—or you can swipe to interact with them.

iMessage

This new messaging service, built into the existing Messaging App, lets you hold single or group-based conversations and exchange text, photos, and video as part of those conversations. You can see when someone is typing at the other end of your conversation, recover delivery and read receipts, and even hold conversations that span devices—for example, starting on an iPhone and picking up on an iPad.

Newsstand

The use of the iPhone, and especially the iPad, for reading magazines and newspapers has grown significantly, and it's no surprise that Apple has released an app that helps you manage these different subscriptions. Your subscriptions are updated automatically in the background, so the Newsstand looks just like a shelf in a magazine store with each subscription showing the cover of the latest issue. Very neat!

Reminders

This simple little app enables you to manage your to-do list, allowing you to set reminders and due dates. It even works with iCloud and Outlook, meaning you can ensure that updates are reflected on any other devices you may have.

Twitter

The growth of social media has taken many by surprise, and Twitter's popularity has been recognized by Apple via its inclusion in iOS 5. It's no longer just an app, but an integrated capability. Once you've logged on, you can tweet from many of the default iOS apps including Safari, Photos, the Camera, and more.

Other Updated Features

The updates just mentioned are a taster of the features introduced in iOS 5. Many other improvements are included, such as the following:

- *Camera:* This is now available from the Lock Screen, allowing you to capture moments you might previously have missed while unlocking the device. You can also synchronize your photos with the iCloud if you have Photo Stream enabled; it's a cloud-based photo storage capability in iCloud.

■ *Photos:* You can now frame, crop, and rotate your photos, allowing you greater on-device control of the photos you've taken. A red-eye reduction feature has been included as well, as well as integration with iCloud, so you can synchronize your photos in the iCloud.

■ *Safari:* The browser has been upgraded with features that allow you to focus on web surfing and not be distracted. Safari Reader lets you read articles offline and even keep them in the iCloud for storage, so you can access this information from any of your devices that have access.

Summary

In this chapter, you looked at some of the more advanced features found in iOS and the SDK. You took a tour of how to use the GPS on your device to create location-aware applications. You saw how to use the accelerometer to detect movement and orientation of the device. You also looked at the camera and what support has been included in the SDK for you to embrace its capabilities for taking photos and video.

The ability to target multiple devices without writing two different applications may be important to you, and you looked at the ways you can do this and the considerations involved when undertaking this task. Finally, you examined what Apple may have in store in the future.

At the beginning of the book, I took you from understanding the capabilities of iOS-based devices such as the iPhone and iPad to the features available through Apple's own native toolset, such as the iOS SDK and Xcode. You also looked at third-party tool options and even built simple "Hello World" apps with some of them. You then stepped through an Objective-C primer, drawing parallels with the .NET C# language; and over a series of chapters, you walked through numerous iOS SDK frameworks that implement functionality similar to that found in the .NET Framework. Examples in the chapters got you started building a Lunar Lander example application, and you looked at means of extending that application's features through libraries. You finished with overviews of testing, deploying, and publishing iOS applications, and considered several advanced features in this chapter.

Now that you've completed the main body of the book, please take a look at Appendix A for suggestions for completing the Lunar Lander example app on your own. I look forward to seeing the App Store full of Lunar Lander variants built on the back of this book. Good luck!

Completing the Lunar Lander Application

As you've gone through the book, I've slowly been contributing toward your Lunar Lander game where it has made sense. I haven't completed it, though, and this is deliberate. Where would be the fun in providing you with the finished game?! The knowledge you've gained through the book in iOS, its SDK, and Xcode will allow you to complete the game and publish it—or you may want to start a completely different game.

However, it wouldn't be fair to leave you hanging, so in this appendix I discuss some of the elements you may want to consider adding to the game. The source code associated with the book includes code fragments that complement this chapter to help you complete your game.

Implementing the Game Physics

To ensure that your lander observes the laws of physics, you need to implement a simple physics engine for it. You can find a reference describing the physics required at www.physicsclassroom.com/class/newtlaws/u2l4a.cfm. Don't worry; I take you through the basics next.

Gravity

This simulation is quite simple. First the forces of gravity are applied:

`Y = Y + Gravity * TotalSecondsOfThrust;`

Here the Y value that controls the lander's height is adjusted by multiplying the Gravity figure (a double value of 9.8) by the number of seconds that thrust is applied, calculated by detecting the timestamp when the thrust key is held down, and the seconds elapsed from when it is released. You can use the NSTimeInterval() method to achieve this.

Thrust

You then need to apply the force of the thrust according to thrust and rotation. You need to use the Math.h include for this, but you have to implement your own angle-normalization macro, because the equivalent of NormalizeAngle() in .NET doesn't exist in Objective-C. No matter, it's easily done. First define this macro:

```
#define NormalizeAngle(x) ((return x % 360)+(x < 0 ? 360 : 0))
```

Then adjust your x and x axis according to the force of thrust:

```
Y = Y - Math.sin(NormalizeAngle(rotation + M_PI / 2)) * totalseconds * thrustspeed;
X = X - Math.cos(NormalizeAngle(rotation + M_PI / 2)) * totalseconds * thrustspeed;
```

The variable rotation obviously represents the angle of rotation for the lander, as affected by the user pressing the left and right keys and the totalseconds values (the number of seconds the thrust key is held down). The thrustspeed value is a constant value of 20 indicating how powerful the thrust is.

Finally, don't forget to reduce your fuel figure as the engine is thrusting.

Rotation

You won't cover rotating both left and right because they mirror each other. Let's look at what you need to do to rotate left. This method does of course assume the existence of a fuel tank, initialized with an initial value (here the value 1000) and that you pass the total number of seconds the rotation key was held down. Your method looks as follows:

```
// rotateLeft - rotate the lander left
- (void)rotateLeft:(float) totalseconds
{
    // You can't thrust if you've no fuel
    if (fuel <0)
        return;

    // Rotate left
    rotationMomentum -= M_PI / 2.0f * totalseconds;

    // Burn fuel
    fuel -= 0.5 // fuel burn evey time you thrust
}
```

The obvious difference for rotating right is that you increase the rototationMomentum value rather than decrease it.

Enabling User Interaction

The user is obviously required to interact with the game, although how you do this is up to you. Some options are to detect keypresses, or use onscreen images to detect a tap, or even use the accelerometer to detect the device being tipped left or right. In any case, you need to interpret the actions, and the following keys are used to interact with the lander. Doing nothing simply lets the lander drop to the ground as gravity is applied. For your lander, you do the following.

- If the up arrow is pressed, onscreen or on the keyboard, the thruster is being fired.

- If the left arrow is pressed, onscreen or on the keyboard, the lander is rotating left.

- If the right arrow is pressed, onscreen or on the keyboard, the lander is rotating right.

Catching Game Events

You need to monitor some additional game events: for example, detecting when you hit the ground and the speed at which you hit. This is fairly straightforward using a combination of lunar lander y position and ground height and using the speed of the lander as an indicator of whether you're moving too fast.

The method only works when the ground is flat. If you decide to implement a Moon surface that has different gradients, you need to detect this in your game—maybe looking at the pixel values surrounding the lander.

Handling the Graphics

Your Lunar Lander implementation has already made provision to draw the graphics for the game by implementing the drawRect method, although the default implementation simply draws the same graphic (the nonthrusting lander) at the x and y location.

You need to adjust this code to be representative of the other states, including when the game is running, looking for when it should be thrusting or just dropping, and drawing at the angle appropriate for the lander. The angle is obviously in relation to the rotate-left or -right keypresses.

To rotate your image, you could use the rotateAt() method in Microsoft .NET, but such a method doesn't exist in Objective-C. Instead, you can use a simple macro to convert between degrees and radians, the measure used by the UImage rotate equivalent called transform. First define a macro something like the following:

```
#define degreesToRadians(x) (M_PI * (x) / 180.0)
```

Then add the following line, assuming the deg variable represents the degrees you wish to rotate by:

```
myView.transform = CGAffineTransformMakeRotation(degreesToRadians(deg) );
```

If you're interested in knowing more, the post at www.platinumball.net/blog/2010/01/31/iphone-uiimage-rotation-and-scaling/ has a lot of detail about how to do image rotation and scaling.

Displaying a High Score

This should be straightforward because you covered how to create high-score code in Chapter 8, and you also looked at different mechanisms for displaying a dynamic user interface in Chapter 6. Combining these with the high-score mechanics of your game allows you to create a high-score chart that can be displayed when the game is at the main menu.

Resources

In addition to the information provided in this appendix to help you complete the Lunar Lander game, and the additional code supplied with the book, the following resources may help you complete and/or customize your game:

- *PhET Lunar Lander:* A number of resources including an online version of the game, provided as part of a teaching aid. `http://phet.colorado.edu/en/simulation/lunar-lander`.

- *LunarView.java:* A Java-based implementation of the Lunar Lander game for the Android mobile device. `http://developer.android.com/resources/samples/LunarLander/src/com/example/android/lunarlander/LunarView.html`.

- *Code Project:* A .NET-based implementation of the Lunar Lander game, written in C#. `http://www.codeproject.com/KB/game/lunarlander.aspx`.

- *History of Lunar Lander:* Wikipedia's history of the Lunar Lander game. `http://en.wikipedia.org/wiki/Lunar_Lander_(video_game)`.

Index

CPSIA information can be obtained at www.ICGtesting.com
Printed in the USA
LVOW050138171111

255379LV00005B/1/P